VICTORIAN LIFE

AND

VICTORIAN FICTION

"AFTERNOON IN THE PARK" (Gustave Doré)

Doré's explorations of the more fashionable part of London include this view of Hyde Park. A morning ride was a necessity for such privileged young ladies as Trollope's Adelaide Palliser or Meredith's Carola Grandison.

VICTORIAN LIFE AND VICTORIAN FICTION

A Companion for the American Reader

Jo McMurtry

1979

ARCHON BOOKS / HAMDEN • CONNECTICUT

Library of Congress Cataloging in Publication Data

McMurtry, Jo, 1937-
Victorian life and Victorian fiction.

Bibliography: p.
Includes index.
1. English fiction—19th century—History and
criticism.   2. Great Britain—Civilization—19th
century.   I. Title.
PR872.M2   823'.03   78-17049
ISBN 0-208-01744-5

©Jo McMurtry 1979
First published 1979 as an Archon Book,
an imprint of The Shoe String Press, Inc.
Hamden, Connecticut 06514
Printed in the United States of America

This book is dedicated to my students at the University of Richmond whose lively and sometimes disconcerting questions have given the book its impetus—in particular, to Judy Thornhill, Barbara Vann, Tim Evans, Shelley Bowman, Susan Brock, Charlotte Corelle, Nancy Landshof, Guy Ross, Ellie Watts, Kathy Boeple, and Becky Stout.

Contents

ILLUSTRATIONS

11

Acknowledgments

I am indebted to the University of Richmond for much aid and comfort during the preparation of this book, in particular for a Sabbatical leave and a travel grant enabling me to work in England. Some years earlier, Ronald Paulson and the late Alan McKillop at separate times left their customary eighteenth-century pursuits to lead Rice University seminars on the nineteenth-century novel, from which I profited greatly. I have received encouragement and advice from my colleagues at the University of Richmond, in particular Elaine Penninger, Charlotte Oberg, and Barbara Griffin. Edward Cutler of Mercy College and James Thorpe III, editor of The Shoe String Press, have given me valuable help with the manuscript.

I have been cheered along the way by the interested and efficient staffs of Boatwright Library of the University of Richmond; Alderman Library of the University of Virginia; the British Library, the National Army Museum, and the Victoria and Albert Museum in London; the Castle Museum in York; and the Museum of Costume in Bath. Finally, in preparing the manuscript and the illustrations, I am grateful for the expertise of Rhoney Snider, secretary extraordinary, and of Herbert Rudlin of the Adams Camera Shop, Richmond.

Introduction

This book is not a guide to all aspects of the Victorian
period nor is it a critical survey of all aspects of the Victorian
novel. It deals with a fairly simple category of information:
facts the authors of Victorian fiction naturally expected their
readers to know and consequently did not bother to explain
but that are not familiar to present-day American readers,
living as we do in a different culture and at a different time.

THE MIDDLE CLASS

A distortion this book may seem to produce, from the
standpoint of historians and others who wish to view the
Victorian age in its entirety, is its focus on middle-class life.
This limitation results from the fact that those works of
Victorian fiction that have endured to become part of literary
history were written for, about, and by members of the middle
class. The aristocracy might serve as subjects of wish-fulfillment fantasy, the poor, as objects of curiosity; but for the
most part readers of the realistic novel liked their fictional
worlds to reflect their own.

The product, however, is far from sociologically dull. The
middle class was a varied and fast-changing entity and in fact
may be more accurately referred to in the plural. The middle
classes included virtually anyone beneath the peerage ("Lord"
this or that) and anyone above what was called the working
class—those who lived by physical labor, factory hands, say,
or domestic servants—and the poor. (The working class and

the poor were essentially the same body, since if a worker lost his job he became poor; and sometimes he was poor even if he had a job.)

Within these middle classes one can find, in approximate order of status, the land-owning gentry, often baronets or knights, squires of their country estates; people who did not have to work but lived on the income of their inherited wealth, even though there may have been comparatively little of it; clergymen in the Church of England, who did work, but in a respectable way, and whose income might vary from that of a bishop to that of a country curate; lawyers, of whom some types had more status than others; bankers, industrialists, and tradespeople, often newcomers to prosperity; army officers; medical doctors, whose social standing was lower than it is today; and shopkeepers, clerks, and others scrambling to stay within what sometimes became the lower fringes of respectability. Added to all these as potential fictional characters are the wives, children, widows, and maiden aunts who belong to the middle-class panorama by virtue of the husband, father, or brother who heads their household and whose exertions or inheritances provide the status of his dependents. In short, the middle classes provided the novelist with challenge not only in the variety of its members but in its subtle, constantly shifting boundaries and subboundaries. There are few Victorian writers who do not portray the sport of social climbing—often with delicious humor, perceptible once the reader knows the ground rules.

A BRIEF LOOK AT THE BACKGROUND

Strictly speaking, Victorian fiction is that written during the lengthy reign of Queen Victoria (1837-1901). The queen's temperament—self-confident, domestic, deeply religious—is akin to that of her novel-reading subjects, so that the label "Victorian" is particularly apt for our purposes. Yet the period is allied to the decades that preceded it, and in discussing the Victorian novel one can easily include the works of Jane

Austen, for example; the conditions of her characters' lives continued without major change into the Victorian age.

In imagining the world of the Victorian novel, today's reader needs to follow something of the reverse of the procedure he might use in reading science fiction: Instead of adding technological advances to the world he is familiar with, he must, in a sense, look around the room and subtract them. The Victorians did not have electricity, automobiles, or telephones; medicine was in a comparative dark age, lacking for most of the century anesthesia and antiseptics; no one knew about vitamins. Yet the Victorians did not perceive their own setting as a barren one. The times seemed, on the contrary, bursting with excitement and opportunity—or, on the other side of the emotional coin, terrifyingly unstable and unpredictable.

The Industrial Revolution of the late eighteenth century had covered the north of England with coal mines and textile mills; steam engines not only ran power looms but turned themselves into railway locomotives and altered forever the relationship in everyday life between space and time; moral issues arising from these changes were vigorously debated and reform measures came into being. These concerns and many others make an essential contribution to the resonance of Victorian fiction.

SCOPE OF THE BOOK
AND SOME SUGGESTIONS

This book deals with the background of those nineteenth-century British novels that have become a permanent part of our literary heritage and that reflect, in a realistic way, life in nineteenth-century England. It is in this group that the present-day American reader finds the greatest gap between what he knows about Victorian culture and what the original author and his readers not only knew but took for granted. Thus fantasy (such as Kingsley's *Water Babies*) is excluded, since the terms upon which a fantasy is based are usually made clear within the work itself. Historical novels, such as those of Sir Walter Scott, do not come into question here because the settings are in what to the Victorians was the past and the author makes the necessary explanations. Finally, fiction set in the nineteenth century but in exotic places, as is true of much of the work of Kipling, was prepared by the authors for home consumption and is consequently self-sufficient enough to need no elaborate clarification here.

A category of fictional setting that is included although perhaps a stricter interpretation of the term "Victorian" would leave it out, are those novels written during the reign of Victoria but set earlier in the century, in what to the original readers was the domain of nostalgia. Here the present-day reader is often fortunate in finding explanations of objects or customs that had disappeared from the fast-changing Victorian scene. But at other times the clues are tantalizingly incomplete and help from outside is useful.

The reader interested in a particular novel is referred to the index, where specific references are listed. (Look under the author's name, then the title of the novel.) Browsing in chapters that seem to have a general or specific relevance to whatever Victorian fiction the reader has in hand is highly recommended; it has been impossible to list all the examples of every point discussed, and, even if it were possible, the resulting text would be too cumbersome for any reader's patience.

The annotated bibliography at the end of the book is intended to serve as a cluster of signposts, not as a complete repository of Victorian lore. Almost all the works listed contain bibliographies of their own, directing the student further into the intricacies of the period.

As the reader continues his quest for an understanding of Victorian times, he may begin to see, beneath the surface of a culture seemingly so different from the one we know, a substructure that is often similar to our own. For on both sides of the Atlantic we are, in many ways, still in the Victorian age. This statement might in fact hold more true for Americans than for the British, since the American economy still lifts us to a level analogous with the palmier days of the British empire. Our problems are similar—urbanization, industrialism, population shifts, demands for justice from hitherto trammeled classes. Our positive qualities stem from energy, optimism, and eagerness to explore the untried. Like the Victorians, we now seek to temper our ability to exploit our resources with a more humane respect for the individual citizen and a longer-range view of the need for sound planning. Thus, paradoxically, the more clearly we come to see the Victorian world's differences from our own, the more we find ourselves at home in it.

I

Titles and Social Rank

As most of us realize, the American claim to possess a "classless" society is a wobbly one. What we have is a startingly flexible society, fast moving and open ended; classes do exist, however, even though the elucidation of their boundaries may be difficult. Money usually counts in America, but not always and not necessarily in proportion to its mass. A person who ranks high in one social grouping may have no status at all in another; beauty, intelligence, youth, ethical principles, or solid achievements may be cashed in at high value in one status market and refused as worthless in the next. Although the result is in many ways an exciting mixture, a basic uncertainty thrives at the bottom of the dish and reveals itself in our typically American anxieties, particularly in our search for the unblemished personal happiness that our culture teaches us is within everyone's easy reach.

By contrast, the world of the Victorian novel offered its inhabitants a more secure pattern of social status even though most individuals found their personal ceilings, as a consequence, somewhat lower than our own. From our perspective, Victorian society appears less hectic, less fragmented, and often, once certain rules are understood, more comprehensible. (To the Victorians, of course, society frequently appeared, by constrast to their own expectations, in a wild state of flux.)

Since we are dealing with life as seen in the novels, this chapter will recognize only three very general levels of Victorian society: the peerage, the gentry, and the middle classes.

The lower orders will have to remain for the moment an unanalyzed body. Realistic fiction was written about the lower classes (see chapters 9 and 11) but seldom for them or by them, and the Victorian novels' predominantly middle-class-and-up perspective requires a limited emphasis at this point.

THE PEERAGE

We shall omit the royal family, since royalty seldom appears in the novels and remains at a distance when it does. (See chapter 4 for a description of the sovereign's role in politics.)

Next below the royal family and overlapping it to some extent (many of the sovereign's relatives hold one or more hereditary titles) comes the peerage, the "aristocracy" or "nobility" in the strict sense of the word. The peerage consists of the following five ranks:

> Duke (wife a duchess)
> Marquis or marquess (wife a marchioness)
> Earl (wife a countess)
> Viscount (wife a viscountess)
> Baron (wife a baroness)

A hostess who found herself entertaining any of this assortment would need to keep her guests' respective ranks very carefully in mind in determining who might sit where at the table and in juggling other questions of precedence.

Any member of the peerage may sit in the House of Lords, the upper house of the British Parliament, with the exception of holders of courtesy titles (explained below) and with the exception also of peers' wives, whose rank is dependent on that of their husbands. Baronets and knights, who are titled but who are not members of the peerage and do not sit in the House of Lords, will be discussed later in this chapter.

In reading novels set in the upper echelons of society, one should keep in mind the difference between the name of a title, whatever that may be, and the family name of the person who happens to hold that title. Confusion on this point can muddle considerably a reader's ability to keep track of characters and their family relationships. Many peerages originated during the feudal period, when land was held in fealty under the king; and the name of a title often denotes a geographical area. The dukedom of York, for example, was originally associated with the territory of Yorkshire. In later times titles were bestowed by the sovereign without reference to the holding in fealty of a piece of land. In any case, the holder of a title may (and usually does) belong to a family with a quite different name of its own. The Marquis of Steyne in Thackeray's *Vanity Fair* holds a hereditary title—"Steyne"—but belongs to and is head of the Gaunt family. (See the fuller discussion of *Vanity Fair* titles later in this chapter.) In a few cases the name of a family and the title of the head of the family coincide. Trollope's Earl De Courcy in the Barsetshire novels is an example; the family name is also De Courcy.

Hereditary titles (all ranks of the peerage plus the baronetcy) are passed from one generation to the next, from the holder to his nearest male heir. Unless a title has become defunct because of a lack of heirs, there is someone alive who bears it. (In Shakespeare's history plays, to the confusion of some students, titles are used instead of given or family names, and the same characters seem to persist for centuries.) The heir to the title almost always is the titled person's eldest son.

ADDRESSING PEERS

A duke is directly addressed as "Your Grace" or sometimes, although it sounds odd, as "Duke"; he is spoken about as "His Grace the Duke of Blankshire." He is not called "Lord Blankshire," this style belonging to other and lower ranks of the peerage. His wife is the duchess of Blankshire (or, in direct address, "Your Grace"), not "Lady Blankshire."

The other four ranks of the peerage do use the "Lord" and

"Lady"; a "Lord Blankington" may be a marquis, earl, viscount, or baron. His wife would be "Lady Blankington."

Because the form of address is the same, the reader of Victorian fiction who wishes to know whether a character addressed as "Lord So-and-so" is a marquis, earl, viscount, or baron needs to keep a careful ear out for any specific mention of the earl of So-and-So or Viscount So-and-So. If the rank seems never to be mentioned, chances are that the peer is a baron. One would speak, for example, of the early nineteenth-century poet as "Lord Byron" but not as "the Baron Byron," not only because of the uneuphonious result in this particular instance but because of the dictates of custom. Only in the most formal documents is an English baron referred to as "Baron" So-and-So. However, a man who holds a foreign barony may be spoken of as "Baron"; Baron Alfred de Rothschild of Naples is a real-life nineteenth-century example.

Another non-English title is that of "count," a rank that corresponds to an English earldom. (The kinship is easily remembered because the wife of an English earl is not an earless or any other feminine form of earl but a countess.) A count appearing in a novel, such as Wilkie Collins's Count Fosco in *The Woman in White,* can be assumed to be a foreigner.

A peerage is not necessarily of ancient date. New peerages are created by the sovereign for persons considered deserving of honor. The British peerage also includes Scottish and Irish peers, and with these the reader of Victorian fiction should keep in mind that a Scottish or Irish peer did not necessarily have a right to sit in the House of Lords, as did an English peer. A representative number of Scottish and Irish peers were elected by their fellow peers to the House of Lords.

PEERS' RELATIVES:
WIVES, SONS AND DAUGHTERS

Wives of marquises, earls, viscounts, and barons are all addressed as "Lady Blankington," the name of the title, not the name of whatever family the title holder may belong to. (Wives of baronets and knights, in the rank below the peerage with which we shall deal in a moment, are also "Lady," plus the family name, not the name of a title, since in this case there is no separate title as such.) In all these cases the wife has taken the rank of her husband. There is an exception, however, in which a woman's style of address derives from her father: If "Lady" is prefixed to a given name ("Lady Mary"), the holder is the daughter of a duke, marquis, or earl and has married, if she has married at all, a man whose rank is not as high as that of her father. This matter will be gone into in more detail below.

The eldest son of a duke, marquis, or earl holds by tradition a "courtesy title," one of the titles to which his father has a hereditary right but which he does not use. (At this level, as the reader can ascertain by a glance at any edition of Burke's *Peerage,* titles tend to stack up. The father would naturally use the highest one himself.) When Trollope's Plantagenet Palliser, nephew and heir of the duke of Omnium, succeeds to the title, his own eldest son is called the earl of Silverbridge, even though his father actually holds the earldom of Silverbridge. Mr. Palliser himself had not held any courtesy title before the old duke died, simply because he was the duke's nephew and not his son.

A younger son of a duke or marquis does not receive a courtesy title, even if his father has several to spare, but he does have the prefix "Lord" to his given name: "Lord Henry Smith" or, more familiarly, "Lord Henry" may be a younger son of the earl of Blankington, whose family name is Smith. Younger sons of earls, to continue this delicate shading-off, bear the prefix "the honourable" to their given names; they are not "Lord" anything.

At the bottom of the peerage ladder the forms of address for offspring are somewhat jumbled together: All children of viscounts and barons, whether eldest sons, younger sons, or daughters in any order of birth, bear the prefix "the honourable" before their given names.

Starting at the top again with daughters we find, as

mentioned earlier, that daughters of dukes, marquises, and earls bear the prefix "Lady" to their given names; "Lady Jane Smith." A "Lady Jane" will keep her prefix all her life if she remains unmarried or if she marries a man whose rank is lower than her father's. Should Lady Jane marry a man whose rank is equal or superior to her father's, she would take his rank and be called "Lady Blankington," the name of her husband's title. (Unless he is a duke: Trollope's Lady Glencora M'Cluskie, on marrying the then-untitled Plantagenet Palliser, is called "Lady Glencora Palliser." When her husband succeeds to his uncle's dukedom, Lady Glencora becomes "Her Grace, the Duchess of Omnium.")

The wife of a younger son of a duke or marquess would be styled "Lady Henry Smith" (a letter to her would begin, "Dear Lady Henry"); the wife of an "Honourable John Jones" is "the Honourable Mrs. John Jones."

Members of the peerage are addressed by acquaintances and social inferiors as "my lord" or "my lady"; titled husbands and wives may address each other in the same way. In Dickens's *Bleak House,* the third-person narrator takes a somewhat humble stance—with an edge of irony—as he describes the doings of "my Lady Dedlock."

BARONETS AND KNIGHTS

A baronet or a knight is technically a commoner, not a peer. He does not sit in the House of Lords; if he wants to enter Parliament, he must get himself elected to the House of Commons.

Both baronets and knights are addressed as "Sir" prefixed to the given name; the family name is added to both, so that one would say "Sir William Brown" or "Sir William," but never "Sir Brown."

A baronet's title is hereditary, passed from the holder to his nearest male heir, as is the title of a peer. By contrast, a knighthood cannot be inherited but must be earned, awarded by the sovereign for some reason. Knights originally won their honors on the battlefield; today's knights, and those of the nineteenth century as well, are more likely to be civil servants, artists, or successful businessmen.

The wife of a Sir William Brown, be he baronet or be he knight, would be spoken of and directly addressed as "Lady Brown." Sons and daughters of knights or baronets do not bear any indication of this fact in their names.

TITLES IN THE POPULATION

In very approximate figures, nineteenth-century Britain usually had on hand twenty dukes, thirty marquises, two hundred earls, a hundred viscounts, and six hundred barons, as well as a thousand baronets and three thousand knights. From these figures, one can get an idea of the relative likelihood of a titled person's becoming part of a middle-class reader's life—whether as a personal acquaintance, a neighbor or landlord, or a subject of newspaper accounts.

Dukes and marquises are obviously fairly remote as far as the personal experience of a middle-class reader is concerned. With a few exceptions (Thackeray, Trollope, Disraeli), authors whose characters inhabited the upper reaches of the peerage were producing popular romance based fairly directly on wish-fulfillment fantasy rather than the more realistic fiction that has remained a living part of the literary continuum. Another problem in writing about peers of whom so few real-life examples existed was that readers would tend to associate an author's characters with actual people. Of course, some authors made these associations deliberately; Thackeray's marquis of Steyne, for example, is supposedly based upon the third marquis of Hertford (1777_1842), and the same nobleman is said to have been the model for yet another fictional marquis, Lord Monmouth in Disraeli's Coningsby.

On the more populous level of earls, viscounts, and barons, the novelists had a freer rein. Not only were their characters less likely to be identified with specific persons, but for a novelist to place members of the middle class in some sort of proximity to a peer was not at this level unrealistic. Trollope's Countess De Courcy in *Barchester Towers* is a plausible guest at old Mrs. Thorne's entertainment; Jane Austen's Lady Catherine de Bourgh, daughter of an earl, condescendingly entertains the rector of "her" parish, Mr. Collins, in *Pride and Prejudice;* Elizabeth Gaskell's novel, *Wives and Daughters,* though focused on the middle-class inhabitants of the village of Hollingford, realistically includes as occasional visitors from another sphere the family of the earl of Cumnor, whose country place is nearby and who in fact owns much of the village.

Baronets—titled, hereditary, "Sir" but not part of the peerage—were even more familiar to the novel-reading population. To a considerable degree, the baronetage overlapped with the class of country gentry. In George Eliot's *Middlemarch,* the Brooke family, models of the country gentry, take quite for granted their social interaction with and Celia Brooke's eventual marriage to the neighboring baronet, Sir James Chettam. It is a mark of the social distance between the Brookes and the considerably lower ranking Vincy family that Rosamond Vincy is filled with awe at her new husband's uncle, a baronet, and schemes incessantly, though unsuccessfully, to cultivate the acquaintance.

Knights, lowest on the ladder of titles, are a different kettle of fish, at least in regard to their social status as reflected in Victorian fiction. Although knighthood was an individually earned honor, the fact that a knight's title was not passed on to his eldest son made his standing in an inheritance-conscious society a comparatively temporary one. Furthermore, the self-made quality of many knights (businessmen, for example) diminished their radiance. Novelists tended to regard knights from a satiric stance; Jane Austen's Sir William Lucas in *Pride and Prejudice* is a comfortably pompous gentleman whose knighthood had resulted from his having been mayor of Meryton at the time the sovereign paid a visit there. The father of William Dobbin in Thackeray's *Vanity Fair* is regarded by the other characters with some scorn because his civic honors and his knighthood are closely related to the fortune he has made dealing in soap and candles.

Since knights and baronets are addressed in the same way, a reader often cannot tell the rank to which a character belongs until another character or a helpful narrator happens to mention it. Picking up clues that would have been obvious to the original readers, such as an eagerness on the part of young lady characters to marry the eldest son of or form social connections with the family of a "Sir Somebody" who turns out to be a baronet, can be helpful. In written rather than spoken language, one could make this distinction simply by adding "Baronet" (or the abbreviation "Bart." or "Bt.") to the name: "Sir William Jones, Bt." This usage did not belong to spoken address. Dickens's Inspector Bucket in *Bleak House* addresses "Sir Leicester Dedlock, Baronet" to his face in these words (chap. 53), but the mannerism indicates Bucket's eccentricity and independence of the traditional ways of doing things and was not usual.

Forms of address:
A REVIEW

The reader of Victorian fiction should remain reasonably alert for clues to the precise rank of titled characters, since these technicalities may be important to the plot, to the ironic patterns with which the author is playing, or to other aspects of the book quite apparent to the original readers. But there are instances in which a vague reference to aristocratic connections is all an author means to give; one need not feel inept if one cannot deduce a nobleman's exact step on the peerage ladder.

A character spoken about or addressed as "Lord Blackstone" may be a baron, viscount, earl, or marquis, in which case "Blackstone" is the highest title he possesses, or may be the eldest son of an earl, marquis, or duke, in which case "Blackstone" is not really his own title but one of his father's, given him by courtesy until his succession (on his father's death) to his father's titles. In either case, "Blackstone" is probably not the name of the family to which the character belongs.

A "Lord Alfred Jones," perhaps spoken of casually as "Lord Alfred," would be the younger son of a duke or marquis if "Jones" were a family name and not a title. Lord Alfred's father would hold one title and his oldest brother still another; remembering the family connections might well be left to the reader.

A "Lady Stoneleigh" might be anything from the wife of a knight to the wife of a marquis; we cannot tell in this instance whether "Stoneleigh" is a family name or the name of a title. The mist clears in one direction if her husand is addressed as "Sir Humphrey," in another if he is addressed as "Lord Stoneleigh."

A "Lady Mary" is the daughter of a duke, marquis, or earl who has not married or has married a man whose rank is beneath that of her father. Lady Arabella Gresham in Trollope's Barsetshire novels is the daughter of an earl—Lord De Courcy—who has married a country squire.

"The Honourable Leigh White" may be any son or daughter of a viscount or a baron or the younger son of an earl. (Daughters of earls are "Lady" with the given name.) I have used a sexually ambiguous given name for syntactical ease, but usually the given name will denote the character's sex.

Women take their rank from their husbands or their fathers. (There were a few exceptions to this rule in the nineteenth century and there are considerably more today, but we are concerned here with the conditions reflected in the Victorian novel.) These titles are not affected by the deaths of the husbands or fathers; an earl's daughter need not give up her "Lady" if her father dies and somebody else becomes Lord Greenbay, ladying all his daughters. The earl's widow also retains her "Lady" (prefixed, remember, to the name of the title and not to her given name, as is the case with the daughters) but she may be spoken of as "the Dowager Countess of Greenbay" to distinguish her from the wife of the present holder of the title. The widow of a baronet, formerly called "Lady Brown," may be called "Anne, Lady Brown" to make a similar distinction. A knight's widow need make no alteration in the style of her address, since a knighthood is not hereditary.

TWO MISCONCEPTIONS

Before we leave our array of titled personages and go on to other Victorian social strata, we might take a look at two erroneous assumptions American readers are likely to make.

First, as the preceding descriptions may have made clear, the peerage is not a hierarchy in the sense that one is expected to start at the bottom and work one's way to the top. The use of courtesy titles and the fact that new peerages can be created for highly prominent heroes do give this rough impression, but the fact is that a character in realistic fiction would have very little if any hope of acquiring anything higher than a knighthood by his own efforts: Inheritance or perhaps some form of skullduggery are the only feasible routes.

Second, the "aristocracy" or the "nobility", as the terms were understood by Victorian readers, were a quite exclusive body composed essentially of the five ranks of the peerage. Many families of wealth and power were outside this group and, even though they might have wanted in their hearts to get into it, were able to live in fashionable pomp nevertheless. Thus to think of a group of characters as "the aristocracy" because they live in large houses with numerous servants is to risk blurring some of the distinctions the author may wish to present to us.

COATS OF ARMS

Coats of arms are not limited to the aristocracy but may be borne by anyone authorized by the College of Heralds, a royal corporation that grants and registers English coats of arms, to do so. To be eligible, one must be descended through the male line from a person entitled to bear such arms. The fact that the arms had to be granted for the first time at some point is lost in the mists of antiquity in which coats of arms, as a means of recognizing one's commander in battle, came into being. In the nineteenth century most families of the landed gentry (see below) were entitled to bear coats of arms. And, despite the theoretical difficulties, many newly-rich families who found themselves in need of a coat of arms were able (often with professional help) to trace an ancestral right to one.

These heraldic devices are so complicated that a disproportionate amount of space would be needed to give the significance of their markings, colors, curious beasts, and so on. Fortunately, the Victorians found them complicated, too. A present-day reader, unless he wants to go into the matter for its own sake, need remember only a few things about coats of arms.

Coats of arms were customarily painted on the outside of their owners' private carriages. Having a private carriage at all was an expensive and high-status thing to do (one spoke of "setting up" a carriage); and, since a coat of arms was also a status item, the need to acquire a coat of arms often coincided with the ability to set up a carriage. Once painted on, the coat of arms was an aid to identification by the socially knowledgeable; fictional characters who recognize their friends' carriages in the thick of traffic are probably simply spotting the arms. Such emblazoned carriages, as representatives of the families whose arms they bore, became an important part of funeral processions; and if the carriages were closed and the blinds drawn, the family members might actually occupy them or not, as they chose.

When a marriage took place between two persons each of whose families was entitled to bear arms, the couple might "quarter" the arms, that is, combine devices from the two shields by arranging them on a single shield that had been divided into four equal areas. For the novel reader, "quartered arms" simply signifies a marriage between two families of fairly high to very high social status.

Two other technical terms are sometimes used without explanation. A "hatchment," displayed outside houses in which there had been a death in the family, was a wooden panel on which was painted the coat of arms of the deceased. A "lozenge" was the diamond-shaped marking inside which was painted the family coat of arms of an unmarried woman. Had she been a man, she would have borne the arms (or had them painted on the doors of her carriage, rather) upon a shield; had she married, she would have borne her husband's arms, her arms and her husband's quartered, or, if her husband had no arms, none at all. A widow might bear her husband's arms inside a lozenge as well. (A "lozenge" was also a medicinal tablet to be dissolved in the mouth. The context of a fictional passage will help a reader decide which meaning is appropriate.)

THE GENTRY AND THE MIDDLE CLASSES

Since Victorian society was based upon land-holding patterns that had developed in feudal times, the "landed gentry" formed an ancient and respectable class. *Burke's Landed Gentry,* a directory to be found in most American college libraries, has since 1837 listed the members of the landed gentry and reproduced drawings of their family coats of arms. The publisher's requirement of land ownership (at least three hundred acres) has been dropped in modern times but was in force for the Victorians. A number of landed but untitled families are of great antiquity. Squire Thorne of Trollope's *Barchester Towers* and Squire Hamley of Elizabeth Gaskell's *Wives and Daughters,* both of whom consider their own blood superior to that of neighboring earls and baronets, were typical of many of their class.

The rural squire lived in his "manor house," a term going back to feudal times, and leased land to tenant farmers, who usually lived in comfortable farmhouses, hired their own laborers, and ran their own operations generally. (See chapter 8 below.) The squire often owned the village in which or near which he lived, collecting rent from the tenants of houses and shops; the "living" or benefice of the parish church might be in his gift. Despite his typically old-fashioned ways, a rural squire's social status was often considerable. Families of the landed gentry often intermarried with the families of baronets and with the daughters and younger sons of peers.

This picture becomes increasingly complex in the nineteenth century when the traditional land-oriented system had to share its facilities, so to speak, with the rising urban middle classes—people with no land and no family in the sense of ancient pedigree but with money from various strange sources, with some education (especially after a generation or so), and often with a considerable quickness in acquiring delicate sensibilities, fashionable taste, and other psychological accoutrements of success. And, of course, as soon as they could they bought some land. It is this constantly shifting pattern, the struggle of the new to get in (or, if repulsed by the current in-group, to form an in-group of their own), the equally energetic if often baffled and indignant determination of the incumbents to retain their position, and the fact that yesterday's new people tend to become today's established people, that gives resonance to the social comedy portrayed by the Victorian novel. The old-versus-new theme is met, in fact met often, in modes other than comedy; but it is in comedy especially that today's reader, unless he picks out the thematic references, is apt to miss the joke.

FORMS OF MIDDLE-CLASS ADDRESS

The style "Esquire" following the family name—"William Jones, Esq."—was originally given only to landed proprietors. As time passed, the distinctions blurred, until "Esquire" was taken up by anyone who felt he could get away with calling himself a "gentleman." (This last term had itself changed, in earlier centuries designating a person entitled to bear a coat of arms but broadening by the Victorian period to include persons of education, refinement, or respectability. The boundaries were vague; and the word "gentleman," like "lady," came to carry a great deal of emotional weight.) "Esquire" or its abbreviation was used as part of the written address but was not spoken.

The word "squire" (originally a form of "esquire") retained its rural connotations and was used in speaking to or about a landed proprietor, particularly the principal landowner of a rural district. A "Squire Jones" was so called by custom; no special ceremony or legal process was required. Usually the form of address descended by custom to his son, who during his father's lifetime might be spoken of as "the young squire." However, this form of address was a matter of custom only; unlike a baronetcy, for example, the condition of being a squire was not a formal hereditary honor.

"Mr." was the usual form of address for a member of the middle class, as it is today, and was used in both writing and in speaking to or about the person. If one were writing an address, however, and wanted to use "Esq." at the end of the person's name, one had to remember to omit the "Mr." at the beginning.

Usage for "Mrs." and "Miss" was essentially as it is today or, rather, as it was before the recent invention of "Ms." to denote any woman, married or unmarried. The Victorians observed several exceptions; for example, an upper servant, such as a cook or housekeeper, might be called "Mrs." even if she were unmarried—as she usually was. The distribution of "Miss"es in a family with several daughters observed a kind of feminine primogeniture: The eldest daughter was spoken of as "Miss Jones," her younger sisters, as "Miss Mary Jones," "Miss Jane Jones," and so on. Upon the marriage of the eldest, the next sister in age became "Miss Jones."

The present-day reader might keep in mind the much greater degree of formality in Victorian custom with regard to the use of first or given names. Normally, servants were addressed by their given names, with the exception of upper servants (butlers, housekeepers, cooks, and often ladies' maids). To call an acquaintance or even a fairly good friend by his or her first name was a familiarity that might well have been resented; such a privilege was reserved for family members and very close friends. An American reader accustomed to first-naming anyone to whom he is introduced (assuming the two are approximate social equals) might think a Victorian fictional character is showing coolness or displeasure by addressing a friend as "Mr.," while the author may have intended the friendship to be self-evidently a very warm one.

Between friends of different sexes these proprieties were observed with special prudence. Often in the novels a scene in which a young man abruptly calls a young woman by her given name shifts at once into a proposal of marriage, and to Victorian readers the sequence seemed perfectly natural.

SOCIAL CLASSES IN FICTION

It is worth repeating that the realistic Victorian novel was centered in the middle-class reading public and that the novel's view of the classes above and below this center was, consequently, less than sociologically objective. The working classes, and below them the poor, enter fiction as if they were natives of a foreign land. In fact, the unfamiliarity with which the Victorian reading public regarded working-class life has become something of an advantage to the present-day reader in that many puzzling details are explained on the spot; the author does not take for granted that his readers know all about the scenes he describes. On the other hand, those parts of the working class and the poor that went into domestic service were familiar to the middle-class reading public, but in a warped perspective. Readers tended to see servants as they wanted to see them: cheerful, respectful, industrious, grateful to their employers, and so on. The novels reflect this fairly one-sided view.

At the upper end of the social scale, the aristocracy was often viewed negatively in the middle-class novel. A certain amount of ambivalence is present here. Members of the nobility are often portrayed as decadent, sometimes as evil, often as callous and selfish. Yet the tone is not one of social revolution, and novelists do not advocate any sort of general overthrow. Middle-class virtues—duty, decency, comfort without ostentation—consistently triumph by the end of the story, but the idea of aristocracy is not so much exiled as tamed and absorbed. Often, in fact, the title in question is given into the hands of Providence for bestowal, along with other good things, upon the deserving middle-class protagonists.

THE PEERAGE IN *Vanity Fair*

One of the rare fictional appearances of an actual sovereign occurs in Thackeray's *Vanity Fair:* Becky Sharp Crawley goes to court to be presented to "the First Gentleman in Europe," George IV (chap. 48). The monarch, though technically onstage, is seen only from the point of view of his subjects and is further distanced by time; the action of *Vanity Fair* takes place twenty-five and more years before the novel's publication in 1847, seventeen years after the death of George IV.

With this exception, the highest aristocracy in *Vanity Fair* is chiefly represented by the Gaunt family, headed by the marquis of Steyne, and the Sheepshanks family, headed by the earl of Southdown. The reader should keep in mind the difference between the name of a title and the name of the family that has a hereditary right to that title, since these differ in both cases.

In chapter 43, the Gaunt family is convened around the breakfast table for the reader's inspection. Here Lord Steyne joins his wife, the marchioness of Steyne, and his two daughters-in-law, Lady Gaunt and Lady George Gaunt. The marchioness was before her marriage Lady Mary Caerlyon, daughter of the earl of Camelot (chap. 47). Caerlyon is the family name, Camelot, the name of the title; Lady Mary has lost the "Lady" prefixed to her given name because she has married a man whose rank is equal to or (as in this case) greater than her father's and consequently takes the rank of her husband, being addressed as Lady Steyne, or, more usually by narrator and characters, as "my Lady Steyne."

The first of Lord Steyne's daughters-in-law, Lady Gaunt, is the wife of the eldest son of Lord and Lady Steyne, whose courtesy title happens to be the same as the family name. Lady Gaunt was formerly Lady Blanche Thistlewood, daughter of the earl of Bareacres, and, like her mother-in-law, has lost the "Lady" prefixed to her given name. Her husband, the present Lord Gaunt, will become marquis of Steyne upon the death of his father; but, as he and his lady have had no children, he will be unable to leave the title to a direct descendant and it will go instead to the son of Lord Gaunt's younger brother, Lord George Gaunt. Lord George has unfortunately gone mad and is off the scene; but he has produced offspring to save the title, and his wife, Lady George Gaunt, is present at the breakfast table. Unlike her sister-in-law, Lady George does not come of the traditional aristocracy but rather of the newly wealthy class pressing to acquire new peerages and marry into old families. She had been the Honourable Joan Johnes, daughter of John Johnes, first Baron Helvellyn.

Vanity Fair's most central character from the Sheepshanks family is Lady Jane Sheepshanks, daughter of the earl of Southdown, a docile and highly ethical young lady who marries Pitt Crawley, son of the old baronet (see discussion below). Lady Jane is so called throughout the novel, even after her father-in-law dies and her husband becomes Sir Pitt, because an earl outranks a baronet. Lady Jane's mother, the dowager countess of Southdown, a formidable old lady who doses everybody in sight with strong medicine, is referred to as "the dowager countess" to indicate that she is not the wife of the present holder of the title. This peer is Lady Jane's brother, whom the narrator often calls "little Lord Southdown"; the "little" is not a traditional appendage of any sort but describes the young man's harmless, benevolent personality.

"Fancy Sale on the Grounds of Chelsea Hospital" (Illustrated London News)

Thackeray's *Vanity Fair* takes its title in part from the custom of raising money for worthy causes with "fancy fairs"; prominent society ladies kept the booths, and crowds came to see and be seen. This particular fair, held in 1848, benefitted impoverished former governesses—a deserving group.

Vanity Fair:
THE CRAWLEY BARONETCY

When Becky Sharp enters the Crawley family as a governess, she mentally pictures the baronet, old Sir Pitt Crawley, wearing a traditional court suit with decorations and ruffles, his hair correctly powdered. But she receives a shock: Sir Pitt in person is so shabbily dressed and so rude of manner that Becky takes him for a servant.

Once properly identified, the family takes a fairly simple shape with regard to the title. Old Sir Pitt has two sons, his namesake, Pitt Crawley, and his younger son, Rawdon. During the course of the action, Pitt Crawley marries Lady Jane Sheepshanks and they have a son, so that the baronetcy seems likely to descend in a straight line. Old Sir Pitt does die and the younger Pitt Crawley inherits the title (occasioning a remarkable announcement to the new Sir Pitt about his predecessor—"If you please, Sir Pitt, Sir Pitt died this morning, Sir Pitt"—in chapter 40); but a series of unexpected deaths complicate the succession. Sir Pitt's and Lady Jane's son dies, followed by Sir Pitt's brother Rawdon, followed by Sir Pitt himself. The estate and title finally go to what was then the nearest male heir, Rawdon's young son.

In the meantime, another pattern of hope and greed prevails among the have-nots of the Crawley family: Two younger brothers, of different generations, compete for the affection and the money of a wealthy maiden aunt, old Sir Pitt's half-sister, Miss Crawley. Old Sir Pitt has a younger brother, Bute Crawley, rector of the parish of Queen's Crawley and father of a large and threadbare family. His rival in the attempt to win Miss Crawley's favor is his younger nephew, Sir Pitt's son, Rawdon Crawley. Both competitors are fairly far removed from any hope of inheriting the title and estate, although Bute's chances are slimmer than Rawdon's, and neither has any expectation of gain from other sources. As the plot progresses, Rawdon loses his initial advantage with Miss Crawley by his marriage to the adventuress Becky Sharp; Bute loses his by the smothering nature of his wife's attentions to Miss Crawley; and some shrewd maneuvering by the elder brother Pitt eventually results in his inheritance of Miss Crawley's fortune—in addition, of course, to the title and estate he inherits from his father.

ARISTOCRATS AND GENTRY IN TROLLOPE'S BARSETSHIRE

Like many Victorian authors, Trollope frequently portrayed members of the peerage almost as allegorical figures of pride and callousness; and with a few exceptions, this tendency holds true of the titled characters in the six Barsetshire novels (*The Warden, Barchester Towers, Dr. Thorne, Framley Parsonage, The Small House at Allington,* and *The Last Chronicle of Barset*).

The De Courcy family, headed by the earl De Courcy and domiciled at Courcy Castle, permeates Barsetshire with a decidedly negative aura. The Countess De Courcy arrives at Miss Thorne's party hours late and complaining ungraciously of the roads (*Barchester Towers,* chap. 37); one of the daughters, Lady Amelia, advises her cousin against marrying a wealthy solicitor (a type of lawyer; see chapter 6 below) on the grounds that his family is not good enough for a De Courcy connection and then marries the gentleman in question herself (*Dr. Thorne*); another daughter, Lady Alexandrina, commits the more reprehensible deed of taking Adolphus Crosbie away from his fiancee, the charming Lily Dale (*The Small House at Allington*). Crosbie is a weak-willed man and the reader can hardly help feeling Lily is well rid of him, but the moral blame falls strongly on the De Courcy family for their failure to give a modestly circumstanced young girl the simple courtesy of respecting her engagement. The fact is that, to a De Courcy, other people do not really exist.

Perhaps because the name of the De Courcy family happens to be the same as the title of the head of it, keeping the relatives straight is fairly simple. All the daughters are "Lady"—Lady Amelia, Lady Rosina, Lady Margaretta, Lady

Alexandrina. The eldest son, Lord Porlock, bears by courtesy a title to which his father has a hereditary right and is referred to by his family simply as "Porlock." The remaining sons, George and John, bear the prefix "the Honourable" before their given and family names: "the Honourable George De Courcy."

Lord Lufton in *Framley Parsonage* has inherited his title early in life and, as a sought-after and carelessly cheerful bachelor, displays little of the pride that so often accompanies fictional peers. His mother, however, makes up for the lack and energetically blocks her son's marriage to the untitled and penniless Lucy Robarts. Nomenclature is easy to follow, with the possible exception of the fact that Lord Lufton's mother is called "Lady Lufton" during most of the novel's action, since her son is unmarried; when Lord Lufton does marry Lucy, his mother is referred to as "the dowager."

An unusually pleasant, unpretentious Barsetshire peer is the old earl De Guest, who also bears a title that is the same as his family name. Lord De Guest's sisters, Lady Julia and Lady Fanny, have a "Lady" to their names not because they are the sisters of an earl but because they are the daughters of an earl, the late bearer of the title. Lady Julia has not married, and Lady Fanny has married a commoner, a brother of a nearby country squire.

Since Trollope's six political "Palliser" novels include Barsetshire in their geographical scope, there is naturally some overlapping of characters, titled and untitled. One aristocratic group, the duke of Omnium and his family, are discussed below, since it is in the Palliser novels that the family connections become most complex. Another peer who takes a minor role in both sets of novels is the earl of Dumbello, who bears a courtesy title belonging to his father, the marquis of Hartletop, when he marries Griselda Grantly, daughter of Archdeacon Grantly *(Framley Parsonage)*. The couple become Lord and Lady Hartletop upon the death of the old marquis. Trollope's continuing moral pattern associating titles with pride here comes through in the personality of the former Griselda Grantly, who, as her family agrees, seems born to become the wife of a peer; she snubs her maternal grandfather, old Mr. Harding, hero of *The Warden*, and to the original as well as to present-day readers she thus puts herself outside the pale of warmhearted humanity.

Barsetshire shows a deficiency in the proportion of baronets usually to be found in a fictional English county. The most visible one, Sir Roger Scatcherd, is a newly created baronet who acquired wealth as a building contractor for canals and railways—a thoroughly nontraditional path to power. Not only Sir Roger but his son and heir, Sir Louis Scatcherd, successively drink themselves to death; and the baronetcy becomes extinct.

Barsetshire's country gentry fulfill the Victorian reader's expectations. Untitled but with extensive property and ancient pedigree, these men—Squire Thorne of Ullathorne (*Barchester Towers*), the three generations of Squire Greshams the reader meets in the opening chapters of *Dr. Thorne*, and Squire Dale in *The Small House at Allington*—are of unquestioned social position within their rural sphere. They may be over-stern with their families, extravagant, eccentric, and politically stiff jointed, but the novels leave no doubt that, unlike the cold and mercenary aristocracy, they have warm and ultimately loving blood in their veins.

TROLLOPE'S PALLISER NOVELS

Dominating the titled personages in the six Palliser novels (*Can You Forgive Her?, Phineas Finn, The Eustace Diamonds, Phineas Redux, The Prime Minister,* and *The Duke's Children*) is the duke of Omnium—first the old one, then his successor.

The old duke has no immediate family; his heir is Mr. Plantagenet Palliser, who as a nephew and not a son has no courtesy title and must remain a plain "Mr." until his uncle dies. The old duke of Omnium does manage to cause a flutter when, at an advanced age, he threatens to marry Madame Max Goesler and perhaps to have a son who would oust Mr.

Palliser from his succession (*Phineas Finn*). The danger passes, however.

Mr. Palliser's wife is the former Lady Glencora M'Cluskie, an heiress and daughter of a peer; she of course retains her "Lady" upon her marriage to a commoner. When her husband does become duke of Omnium (*Phineas Redux*), Lady Glencora drops this style of address to be known simply as the duchess of Omnium (or "Her Grace" or "the Duchess"), as her husband's rank now surpasses that of her father. The new duke's children also take new styles of address upon their father's succession: The eldest son receives the courtesy title of Lord Silverbridge; the younger son is Lord Gerald Palliser; and the daughter, named for her mother, is now Lady Glencora Palliser. (A problem arises in that *The Duke's Children*, two novels later, does not include this Lady Glencora among its characters but substitutes a Lady Mary Palliser. The elder daughter may have died or Trollope may simply have dropped a thread in his complex tapestry.)

Another family the connections between whose members may not be immediately apparent is made up of the earl of Brentford, Lord Chiltern, and Lady Laura Standish (*Phineas Finn*). This trio consists of a father and his two children, a son and a daughter: "Standish" is the family name, "Brentford," the title of the head of the family, and "Chiltern," the courtesy title given the eldest son. Lady Laura marries a commoner named Kennedy and retains her "Lady." Lord Chiltern marries Violet Effingham, who simply becomes Lady Chiltern; upon the death of Lord Chiltern's father the pair will be the earl and countess of Brentford.

The baronetcy of Sir Florian Eustace, whom Lizzie Greystock marries shortly before his death (*The Eustace Diamonds*) descends to the infant son of the marriage; he will of course keep it, no matter what his mother does or whom she marries next.

II

Money

Victorian money differs from that of present-day America and also, as of the 1970s, from that of present-day England: In 1971 the United Kingdom switched to a decimal system of currency in which the penny is worth one-hundredth of a pound and other traditional coins are arranged conveniently within that scale. The transition has gone more smoothly than many people expected. The time may come when even English readers of Victorian novels will require an explanation of nineteenth-century currency.

GLOSSARY OF TERMS

The relative values of the sums of money given here are, of course, pre-1971 and apply to the world of Victorian fiction.

Pound: worth 20 shillings or 240 pence
Crown: worth 5 shillings
Half crown: worth 2 shillings and sixpence
Shilling: worth 12 pence
Sixpence
Penny
Halfpenny
Farthing: worth one-fourth of a penny

The actual coins in use varied somewhat during the nineteenth century. Many coins mentioned in Victorian novels are self-explanatory— a threepenny piece (pronounced "thrup-ny"), for example. The florin was a silver coin worth two shillings, first minted in 1849; the sovereign, a gold coin worth one pound, was first minted in 1817. The sovereign was in wide use and is the coin most often meant by a novelist's reference to one or more "gold pieces." The guinea was a coin no longer in circulation during most of the century, as its minting stopped in 1813; but the word remained in use to denote the value of the coin, twenty-one shillings (or one pound and one shilling).

Slang terms for sums of money are often explained when they occur in the novels or are made clear in context, but terms for which middle-class readers seemed to need no explanation include the following:

Pony: twenty-five pounds; the word is often used among fashionable young men who might place a bet of that amount

Quid: one pound

Bob: one shilling

Tanner: sixpence

WRITTEN SYMBOLS AND ARITHMETIC

The symbol for the pound, a form of the letter L (£), is derived from the Latin *libra* (scale), used in the sense of a specific amount of silver measured by weight. The symbol for shilling was s., not hard to remember; but the symbol for "penny" was in Victorian times not p., but d., from the Latin *denarius*, a coin of small value.

One can see the arithmetical difficulties of the system. Recording a number of purchases, for example, would involve adding one column that carried over by twelves and another that carried over by twenties, all the while using numerals that do their best to be nothing but decimal. In fact, arithmetical problems involving sums of money were quite understandably a shadow over the life of the young. The insistence of Mr. Pumblechook in Dickens's *Great Expectations* that Pip tell him at once how many shillings could be got out of forty-three pence (chap. 9) was not as farfetched as a reader might think.

BANK NOTES AND CHEQUES

The paper currency appearing in Victorian novels consists of notes issued by individual banks and not, as is the case in present-day America, by a central government authority. In the nineteenth century virtually any bank, large or small, could issue its own notes representing a promise to pay, in gold, the stated amount to the bearer upon demand.

The large number of nineteenth-century banks issuing their own notes and the fact that many of these banks overextended themselves by issuing more notes than they could pay off if all the notes were presented for payment simultaneously resulted in an unstable situation. Essentially, the value of any bank note rested on the reputation for solvency of the bank that had issued it. A typical, though to American readers rather puzzling, situation appears in Elizabeth Gaskell's *Cranford* when a shopkeeper refuses to accept a note issued by a bank he knows to be in difficulties (chap. 13). Miss Matty Jenkins, by chance in the shop at the time and a shareholder in the bank, feels it her duty to cash the customer's note from her own purse. When the bank does fail, Miss Matty has, of course, lost the amount of that note as well as her own investment in the bank's shares.

Cheques first appeared in 1825. Despite their obvious usefulness—allowing a payer to transfer from his own account a specific amount to an individual payee—they were accepted rather slowly. People are suspicious of new systems, and it was easier for a criminal to forge a cheque than a bank note.

WHAT THINGS COST

As the reader is no doubt aware, the relative value of currency fluctuates from day to day and sometimes undergoes severe and sudden shifts. The rate of exchange during most of the nineteenth century, however, remained fairly stable and was much higher, equaling five American dollars to the pound. In addition, the buying power of both the pound and the dollar was in the nineteenth century something like five times what it is today.

A family living on four hundred pounds a year in 1850, consequently, would have an income similar to that of twelve thousand dollars today. This equation is, of course, a very rough one. Nevertheless, the American reader who forms the habit of multiplying any sum of nineteenth-century fictional pounds by twenty-five and calling the result dollars is taking a step toward approximating the original readers' impressions.

At the least, a gentleman's household—wife, children, servants— required for its support an income of four to five hundred pounds a year. Sixty-five pounds of this might well go to feed the pair of horses that pulled the family carriage; the cook's wages would be something like twenty-five pounds a year, the scullery maid's, perhaps ten. (Room and board were provided for servants, so these sums are not quite as scandalously low as they may seem.) Rent for the house might be forty pounds annually; most members of the Victorian middle class, unlike their counterparts in today's America, did not own the houses they lived in. Of course, all sorts of variations were possible. One could have more of a cook by having less of a carriage, for example, and one's rent would be greater or less, especially in London, according to one's neighborhood's degree of fashion.

A bachelor in furnished lodgings could live comfortably, even fashionably, for a great deal less. In fact, the expense of a domestic establishment at even the lower edges of respectability largely accounts for the late age at which many middle-class men married and for the considerable number of middle-class women who never managed to marry at all, the pool of available husbands being reduced by those men who preferred bachelorhood or who simply could not afford to set up a household. The obstacle that so frequently blocks the lovers' path to happiness in Victorian novels—lack of enough money to marry—was a very real one.

PROMISSORY NOTES

A form of personal debt frequently encountered in the Victorian novel, particularly as a means by which young men get themselves into financial difficulties, was the promissory note. (The terms "note" and "bill" in this sense meant the same thing.) This transaction represented a loan of money upon the debtor's promise to pay the amount plus the interest, which was usually quite steep, by the end of a specified period. The loan might be extended or a new loan made at the end of this period, a process called "renewing." Promissory notes had to be drawn up in a prescribed form, bearing an official stamp; the stamp itself was sometimes used a a reference to such loans. Rawdon Crawley, boasting of his reformed ways, claims that "since I'm married, except renewing, of course, I give you my honour I've not touched a bit of stamped paper" (Thackeray, *Vanity Fair*, chap. 30).

The original moneylender, the holder of the note, might sell the bill to someone else if he chose for a price less than the total amount of the loan plus the interest when the note became due. The seller would make some profit, in other words, but not as much as he would make if he held the note for the full term. Such negotiations were called "discounting" bills, and a series of discounting transactions might take place before the bill actually fell due; the demand for payment might be made by a person whom neither the debtor nor the original creditor had ever seen before. Normally, a bill would be accepted for discount purchase only if it had been drawn upon a person who could be depended upon to pay; Trollope's George Vavasor, having villainously obtained his fiancée's

signature on notes for two thousand pounds, finds on attempting to sell them that "bills with ladies' names on them—
ladies who are no way connected with business—ain't just the
paper that people like" (*Can You Forgive Her?*, chap. 60).

To "accept" a note for a friend is to countersign it, indicat-
ing that one accepts the responsibility of repaying the note
should the original debtor, one's friend, fail to do so. Among
the numerous characters in Victorian fiction whom this practice plunges into difficulties are Fred Vincy of George Eliot's
Middlemarch, who upsets the domestic happiness of his
sweetheart's family, and Mark Robarts of Trollope's *Framley
Parsonage*, who endangers his own. Both learn their lesson.

DEBT AND BANKRUPTCY

Until 1868, a debtor could be arrested and imprisoned at
the suit of any one (or more) of his creditors; if he then found
the money to pay these creditors, he would be released, no
matter how many other debts he might have contracted. In
other words, one did not go to prison automatically because
one could not pay one's debts; somebody had to bring suit.
Arrests for debt were made by sheriff's officers called bailiffs,
and the more imprudent characters in pre-1868 Victorian
fiction—Mr. Micawber, Dick Swiveller, Rawdon Crawley—
habitually keep an eye cocked for the bailiff.

Once imprisoned, debtors were not treated like criminals
in that they were not thought of as undergoing punishment.
They might entertain visitors in their rooms or even have
their families move into the prison with them. Mr. Micawber
(*David Copperfield*) and Mr. Dorrit (*Little Dorrit*) among
Dickens's characters do this, while Mr. Pickwick (*Pickwick
Papers*) is accompanied in his imprisonment by his valet. In
Thackeray's *Pendennis*, Captain Shandon quite competently
edits a fashionable magazine from the confines of a debtors'
prison.

A debtor is a private individual; a bankrupt, by contrast,
is the head of a firm, a trader, or a merchant who comes to

financial grief through his business or occupation. A bankrupt was not imprisoned as an ordinary debtor might be, but his effects could be seized and sold for the benefit of his creditors. A bankrupt's creditors normally received only a percentage of the amounts due to them; and for a bankrupt eventually to pay his creditors in full, even though he did not have to, was considered an honorable act. Tom Tulliver in George Eliot's *The Mill on the Floss* keeps the promise he has made to his father to repay his creditors and buy back, in a sense, the family respectability.

TYPES OF INVESTMENTS

Perhaps it should be emphasized that all this money needed to run the middle-class Victorian household, to provide cooks and carriages and flowered carpets, did not necessarily come in large part or even in any part from the head of the family's paycheck. It is true that middle-class men often were in business, and if they prospered their paycheck could be large enough to swallow up whatever financial arrangements the household had depended on in earlier years. However, the foundation of a family's finances was traditionally expected to derive not from someone's day-by-day exertions but from landed property that brought in rent or from capital put out in some dependable investment.

As reflected in the novels, there were respectable investments and less respectable investments. Rent-producing property was always respectable, no matter what the edifices themselves might be: The Dragon of Wantley Inn, scene of low political doings in Trollope's Barsetshire, belongs to Mrs. Arabin (formerly Eleanor Harding Bold), wife of the dean of Barchester Cathedral (*The Last Chronicle of Barset*). On the other hand, investment in railways, especially in the early decades of development (the 1830s and 1840s), was of questionable respectability: The whole concept was startlingly new and in fact railway companies did fail. Defying tradition in this respect works out well for Ernest Pontifex in Samuel

Butler's *The Way of All Flesh* and for Tom Redworth in Meredith's *Diana of the Crossways*; both become comfortably wealthy as a result of what their respective novels portray as faith in the future.

An eminently respectable form of investment was the Consolidated Annuities, the government securities, often referred to as the "Consols." Throughout most of the nineteenth century the Consols paid three percent interest and were thus unattractive to the overly greedy. Consols investment created, in fact, a high-status image of not needing the extra cash a riskier investment might bring. In *The Way of All Flesh,* Butler tells of a widow whose children needed more money than the Consols would pay; she bought railway stock "with shame and grief, as of one doing an unclean thing," gave her children their start in life, then shifted her capital back into the Consols and "died in the full blessedness of fund-holding" (chap. 80).

PROPERTY:
ENTAILS AND SETTLEMENTS

Land and houses were not bought and sold among the Victorians as briskly as they are in our society. British economic history is quite different from our own, going a great deal farther back and including a period in the Middle Ages when it was illegal to alienate from one's self or from one's heirs any estate granted to one by a feudal lord. Owning the house one lived in, consequently, had not become a near-necessity of Victorian middle-class status, as is the case in the United States today; most of the characters in middle-class novels, like most of the readers of those novels, live in rented houses as a matter of course.

Most of the landed property in nineteenth-century England was in the hands of a comparatively small group who had held their land (farms, houses, entire city blocks) for generations and who had no intention of letting it go if they could help it. (See chapter 8 for details of the various kinds of landholding.) Some property, in fact, could not legally be sold or willed to anyone other than a specific heir, usually the possessor's eldest son or nearest male heir. Such property was said to be "entailed," its succession settled upon a designated person or series of persons. In fiction (Jane Austen's *Pride and Prejudice*, for example), an entail often seems a quite negative thing, and in fact it is difficult for the present-day reader to see why anyone would want to restrict one's family's future negotiations to such an extent. British tradition took a longer view, however. Through the centuries, the uncertainties of a family's year-to-year fortunes and the considerable advantages in power to be gained from a unified estate had made regularized succession a matter of family self-interest. But the increasing flexibility of nineteenth-century economy made the disadvantages of entails increasingly obvious, and, beginning in the 1830s, a series of acts made the barring of entails progressively easier.

Another type of restriction on property was known as a "settlement" and is particularly related to the question of women's property rights. (See chapter 13.) A marriage settlement consisted of a property deed drawn up by lawyers upon the occasion of a woman's marriage. The property—land, a sum of money, whatever it might be—might have come from the bride's family, perhaps from her mother's estate, or from her prospective husband; a wealthy man marrying a woman from a poorer family might agree to settle a part of his estate upon his bride. Usually the woman could not spend or sell the capital, though she might have the income from it. This arrangement allowed a woman to make some provision for her daughters and her younger sons, who under the system of primogeniture would be cut off from inheriting the bulk of the family estate.

The custom of settling property upon a woman about to be married was virtually limited to the upper and upper-middle classes, since the property to be settled would have to be large enough to justify the lawyers' fees. Most middle-class women did not have a formal marriage settlement, and everything they inherited or earned belonged by right to their husbands until the last quarter of the century, when a series of Married Woman's Property Acts effected a change.

The sum of money settled upon an upper or upper-middle-class bride, or that people assumed would be settled upon her whenever she did marry, was spoken of as the woman's "fortune"; the word when used in this context did not have a connotation of enormous wealth and might in fact refer to a comparatively modest sum.

MONEY IN THE NOVELS

The Victorian realistic novel is usually fairly accurate about details of shillings and pence: When Mrs. Fitchett in George Eliot's *Middlemarch* offers to sell chickens to Mrs. Cadwallader at half a crown for two, the present-day reader safely assumes (and the original readers may have known) that this is not a wildly unreasonable price for two chickens. What is not statistically accurate in fictional portraits of Victorian life is the frequency with which the happy ending bestows a sudden mass of wealth upon the protagonist or his bride. Here the sturdy roots of wish-fulfillment fantasy onto which the novel's realistic branches are grafted make their presence felt. However, the reader needs to follow the fantasy, and translating the protagonist's final blessings from Providence into an approximate present-day sum can give us the kind of emotional participation the author wished to create.

Smaller financial transactions can be well worth watching. In George Eliot's *The Mill on the Floss,* for example, the gypsy who returns the runaway Maggie to her father hopes for a reward of half a crown, apparently the usual tip for this sort of thing. When Mr. Tulliver gives the gypsy five shillings (chap. 11), it is useful to realize that this sum equals twice the gypsy's expectations. Here Mr. Tulliver demonstrates both his special fondness for Maggie and his expansive, generous disposition—traits that will be of importance as the story develops. Lady Dedlock in Dickens's *Bleak House* gives the crossing-sweeper Jo a golden sovereign for guiding her to the cemetery where her lover is buried, but the sovereign (one pound) represents so much wealth to Jo, who might ordinarily receive three or four pennies during a day's sweeping, that he cannot deal with it effectively. Jo is unable to get the sovereign changed for full value (chap. 19), and his neighbors steal much of the money when he does get it changed. The incident is one of a sequence of Lady Dedlock's attempts to do good that turn out badly.

A reader's ability to visualize and to add up actual coins can increase the drama of numerous scenes in Victorian fiction. In Hardy's *The Mayor of Casterbridge,* for example, the sailor who has bid five guineas for Henchard's wife must pay the amount in some combination of other coins or notes and coins since the actual guinea was no longer minted. The sailor "unfolded five crisp pieces of paper, and threw them down upon the table-cloth. They were Bank-of-England notes for five pounds. Upon the face of this he clinked down the shillings severally—one, two, three, four, five" (chap. 1). Years later, on his wife's reappearance, Henchard welcomes her with a letter and a sum of money, "taking from his pocket-book a five-pound note, which he put in the envelope with the letter, adding to it, as by an afterthought, five shillings. . . . The amount was significant; it may tacitly have said to her that he bought her back again" (chap. 10).

Actual guineas appear in a more remote territory of Hardy's imaginary County Wessex. Mrs. Yeobright of *The Return of the Native* owns a bag of "spade guineas," coined in the late eighteenth century and so called from the escutcheon on the reverse side, which she plans to give her children although, as she observes, the guineas must be exchanged for sovereigns before they can be spent. These are the coins for which Christian Cantle and Wildeve and Diggory Venn gamble by the light of glowworms on the heath (chap. 26/3.7); the coins' antiquity makes them a fitting part of so strange a scene.

ENOUGH TO LIVE ON

David Copperfield's friend Tommy Traddles persuades his fiancée's father to permit the couple to marry when Traddles' income reaches the sum of two hundred fifty pounds a year; the couple then sets up housekeeping in Traddles's barrister chambers and lives merrily if unorthodoxly (chap. 59) until Traddles makes his way into the more prosperous reaches of the middle class. Two hundred fifty pounds is pretty much the bottom line, if not below the bottom line, and Dickens's picture was understood by the original readers to be something of a caricature. Dorothea Brooke Casaubon in George Eliot's *Middlemarch* supplies the necessities for her second marriege with the more substantial income of seven hundred pounds a year, although in Brooke circles seven hundred was considered a very small sum. This income, incidentally, Dorothea has inherited from her mother. The provision left her by her first husband is stopped, by the terms of his will, when she marries Will Ladislaw; but her mother's money has been legally settled upon her and cannot be affected (chap. 83).

Often an individual novel or sequence of novels will set up within itself a relative scale of incomes by which the comfortably-off can be distinguished from the threadbare on the one hand or the wealthy on the other. In Trollope's *The Warden*, for example, Mr. Harding's annual income of eight hundred pounds, in addition to his clerical benefice of Crabtree Parva worth eighty pounds a year, provides Mr. Harding with what seems to him the moderate and reasonable comforts of life. In the meantime Mr. Quiverful, rector of Puddingdale, attempts to raise twelve children on an income of four hundred pounds annually. The desperation this state of affairs evokes in Mrs. Quiverful appears when, in *The Warden*'s sequel, *Barchester Towers*, she attempts to make certain of Mr. Quiverful's appointment as successor to Mr. Harding's wardenship of Hiram's Hospital—a change that would literally double the family income.

III

Religion

For the present-day American reader, the basic things to keep in mind about the Victorian religious picture might be grouped very broadly under two main principles.

First, religion in its traditional forms had a much greater importance in the daily lives and in the social structure of the Victorians than it has in our own. The salvation of one's own and other people's souls was a matter of public concern, often a major point in debate upon national issues, and this emphasis caused no embarrassment but was simply taken for granted. The pattern was strengthened by centuries of tradition and by a national church that had been built into the government since Henry VIII broke away from the Roman Catholic Church in the sixteenth century—a situation Americans would find literally unconstitutional. There were, in fact, Victorians who sincerely felt that any effort to weaken the power of the Church of England was an act of treason.

The second thing to keep in mind is the distinction between the national Church of England and all other denominations and faiths, grouped collectively under the label of Dissenters (or Nonconformists). In previous centuries Dissenters had been perceived as a danger to the government and rigidly excluded from the power structure. Many of these restrictions were relaxed before or during the nineteenth century (see fuller explanations later in this chapter), but a social stigma remained. In the novels, consequently, one may find members of such solid and conservative denominations—from an American standpoint—as Methodists, Presbyterians, and Baptists regarded by the other characters, and often by the author as well, with hostility or derision.

HIGH AND LOW CHURCH IN THE NINETEENTH CENTURY

In the nineteenth century groups of opposing trends within the Church of England had been categorized as "Low," "High," and "Broad." Readers of novels recognized these terms at once and could add, on their own, the associations the authors meant to evoke when they used them.

"Low church" tendencies are associated in the Victorian age with the evangelical revival of the previous century, which stressed a return to bibical simplicity of worship and taught that faith alone, without the help either of good works or of the sacraments, was enough to ensure salvation. The beliefs of a low churchman in fact might differ from those of a Dissenter only in that the low churchman continued to function within the episcopal and parochial structure of the Church of England. In their fictional appearances, low churchmen are frequently typified by the number of things they are against: To a low churchman, ornamentation and elaborate music in the churches, for example, were superficial and even idolatrous manifestations of worldly pride, all too likely to distract the mind from true worship. In daily life a low churchman could be expected to disapprove of dancing and card games at any time of the week, of travel or other frivolous amusements on Sunday. But low church preoccupations were not entirely negative. Like the Dissenters, low churchmen were often especially aware of the pressing need for education among the poor, and the setting up of Sunday Schools that added basic reading and writing to their religious instruction was a favorite low church project.

The "high church" movement in the nineteenth century originated at Oxford University in the late 1820s and 1830s, when John Henry Newman, later Cardinal Newman, and his companions worked their spiritual way back to what in their minds represented the principles of the pre-Reformation church—of the English church before its separation from Rome. In many cases, including, obviously, that of Cardinal Newman, this quest led to conversion to Roman Catholicism. High churchmen who stopped short of this solution retained the Anglican nonacceptance of the authority of the Pope and stressed the importance of the sacraments, the traditional parts of the worship service, and the authority of the bishops.

Members of the so-called "broad" movement within the Church of England believed, as the term implies, in a tolerant, comprehensive view of church doctrine. The term "broad church" is not associated in the novels with types of ritual or ornament; its connotations belong more to the political sphere. Trollope's Bishop Proudie owes his advancement to the fact that he has "become known as a tolerating divine," connected with the political aspects of church reform (*Barchester Towers*, chap. 3).

ARCHBISHOPS AND BISHOPS

The Church of England in the nineteenth century had two archbishops, the archbishop of Canterbury and the archbishop of York. The archbishop of Canterbury had, and still has, precedence. The number of bishops rose slightly during the century, but in 1901, at the end of Queen Victoria's reign, there were thirty-seven. By tradition, both archbishops sit in the House of Lords, as do the bishops of London, Winchester, and Durham; another twenty-odd seats are filled according to seniority of consecration. In other words, a newly consecrated bishop would expect to wait until enough bishops already in the House of Lords had died for him to move up in line.

In heraldic theory, archbishops rank as dukes and bishops rank as barons; the church does not provide ranks for the three levels of the peerage in between, so the alignment is not very neat. Nevertheless, an archbishop is addressed as "your grace," a bishop, as "my lord." The residence provided by the church for either is officially called a "palace." No title or form of address is given to the wife of an archbishop or bishop, since usages of this kind were established before the Reformation, when clerical dignitaries did not marry.

The appointment of archbishops and bishops was originally in the hands of the sovereign, but by the nineteenth century a shift of political power had placed this choice actually with the prime minister: An appointment was then made by the sovereign upon the recommendation of the prime minister.

PARISH CLERGY:
RECTORS AND CURATES

Each bishop of the Church of England heads a specific district, called a diocese; each diocese is divided into parishes. The parish is the basic unit of the Church of England, and, since the church is entwined in many ways with the national government, the parish has been responsible for such secular business as the upkeep of roads or the administration of the Poor Laws (welfare code). Parishes vary considerably in size, rural and scantily populated ones often being quite large. Each parish has its church, and each parish church, its parson.

The parson of a parish church is called a "rector" if most of the parish revenues—the parishioners' tithes or offerings, theoretically a tenth of their tithable income—go directly to him. If the tithes go to some other part of the ecclesiastical hierarchy and the parson receives a stipend, he is called a "vicar." There is no difference in authority.

A parish benefice—the "parson-ship" of a parish church—is often called a "living"; nineteenth-century appointments to livings were in the gift variously of bishops, cathedral chapters, university colleges, and private individuals. Any of these might, in other words, appoint a parson to a parish church, provided, of course, that the parson were duly ordained. For the most part, the private individuals with this power were peers or large landowners or both.

Such appointments were regarded by law as salable property and could be bought outright; the term "gift" is in this sense perhaps a misnomer. The price paid took into account the amount of the parishioners' annual tithes as well as the value of the parsonage itself—the house provided for the parson and his family—and the "glebe" or parcel of farmland. One could also buy the "reversion" of a living, the next appointment to it after the death or retirement of the incumbent; one then simply waited for the living to "fall in," as the grisly saying went.

Since the number of parishes within the Church of England was fairly permanently fixed, give or take some alterations that rather belatedly followed population shifts, and since the church was a favored vocation for the sons of middle- and upper-middle-class families, it was quite possible for a young man to finish college, be ordained, and then find himself unable to obtain a living. He might stay on at his college on a fellowship; he might get an appointment as chaplain to a bishop or to a nobleman who lived in grand enough style to hold services in his family chapel; but the most frequent recourse was to accept a job as a curate and hope for something better by and by.

A curate was employed directly by the parson whom he assisted and the pay was very low: Fifty to eighty pounds a year is representative. (One could do better as a coachman or butler, but this option was, of course, not open to the respectable middle class.) A curate's duties consisted in conducting parts of the church services, visiting the sick, assisting in any schools connected with the church, and generally greasing the wheels of pastoral care. A curate might also officiate at a "chapel of ease," a sort of auxiliary church found in large parishes in which it was difficult for all the people to get to the official parish church.

Curates were usually ordained as deacons, the lowest of the three orders of clergymen. The others are priest's orders, in which one would usually find the parson, and bishop's orders, for both bishops and archbishops.

CATHEDRAL CLERGY

The word "cathedral" has in many people's minds the connotation of a very large gothic church full of monuments. This picture is accurate in many cases, but the essential meaning of the word is "bishop's seat"; without a bishop one cannot have a cathedral, no matter how large the building.

Cathedral clergy are separate from the parish organization and show more clearly their pre-Reformation monastic origins. The dean of a cathedral is head of the chapter, or body of canons, attached to the cathedral. During much of the nineteenth century the office of canon (also called "prebendary" or "prebend") could be considered a sinecure, although canons sometimes took part in cathedral services. Minor canons, who unlike canons are not required to take holy orders although they may have done so, assist in the cathedral services. The precentor, who leads the singing of the choir or congregation and who may chant the responses during a service, is a minor canon, as is the sacristan, who has charge of the sacred vessels, vestments, and so forth.

The archdeacon of a diocese is appointed by the bishop to assist in the ecclesiastical administration of the diocese. This use of the term has nothing to do with deacon's orders in the Church of England or, for that matter, with the office of deacon in a Protestant church such as the Presbyterian.

PARISH LAY OFFICERS

Returning from the cathedral to the parish church, we find, besides the rector and curate, who are in holy orders, the following officials who are not.

A churchwarden is a lay assistant to the rector in administrative duties; he may authorize repairs to the church building, for example. Usually there are two of them, elected annually from members of the congregation. The office is considered an honor and does not usually carry a stipend; thus churchwardens are drawn from the upper classes, relatively speaking, of a congregation. Most of the remaining parish lay officials are from the lower social strata and frequently appear in Victorian fiction as quaint, humorous characters, people to whom the middle-class readers might safely feel superior.

The beadle, almost always a comic character in fiction, is

employed by the parish to keep order during church services and to perform other constabulary chores. The beadle had duties connected with the administration of the Poor Laws until the mid-1830s, when a new Poor Law Act transferred his authority; Dickens's *Oliver Twist*, which deals in part with the effect of these laws, shows the beadle Mr. Bumble rather anachronistically carrying out his old functions. This overlap of old and new was probably realistic, since every parish in England could hardly change its traditional structure overnight. Mr. Bumble wears the traditional garb by which beadles can usually be recognized in Victorian fiction; three-cornered hat, wide-skirted coat with elaborate gold braid, knee breeches, and gold-headed cane. The cane originally played a part in the beadle's order-keeping duties: He was empowered to thump on the head worshippers who talked or were otherwise unruly during services.

The parish clerk, also a paid functionary, has as a major qualification for his job the ability to read, write, and keep clear records. The clerk often assists the parson during a service by reading the lesson or portion of the scriptures appointed for that service and by leading the congregation in responses. He is in charge of keeping the parish records of marriages, baptisms, and burial and usually attends these events in an official capacity.

The sexton rings the bell and digs the graves. In fiction he is often an old man, cantankerous and hard of hearing.

The verger is responsible for the inside of the church and often acts as a guide to visitors.

The pew-opener, who conducts churchgoers to a pew or seat, was often a woman in the nineteenth century, generally a woman of advanced years. If the pew were the old-fashioned enclosed kind, the pew-opener would literally open the door to it. The usual tip from the churchgoer was sixpence or a shilling.

The parish choir in the early part of the century often included not only singers but players of such instruments as clarinets, oboes, "serpents"—bass wind instruments—violins, and cellos. Members received a small stipend.

REFORM IN THE ESTABLISHED CHURCH:
PLURALISM AND NONRESIDENCY

Centuries of unquestioned political dominance had allowed room in the Church of England for the growth of numerous abuses, two of the most prevalent of which were pluralism, or the holding of more than one benefice (living), and nonresidency, or living elsewhere than in one's parish—a natural consequence, of course, of pluralism. A clergyman who had acquired several livings might reside in one of them, conducting services and generally taking care of the parishioners, and employ curates for the others. Since curates' wages were low and the parishioners' tithes might be considerable, most of the money would thus accumulate in the hands of the pluralist and the parishioners might or might not have their spiritual needs adequately attended to. Some isolated parishes had not even a whole curate to themselves and could attend services only every few weeks, when their turn came.

A series of parliamentary acts eventually set about making the needed changes in this area and remedying other abuses as well. The income of bishops, which had been widely varied and in some cases disproportionately large, was regularized in the 1830s; the number of canons allowed each cathedral chapter was limited a few years later, with the understanding that the church funds saved in this way were to be used to aid the poorer clergymen. A series of acts limiting pluralism were passed from the 1830s through the 1880s, and the abuse was corrected to a large extent.

TITHES

Traditionally, a tithe is one-tenth of the yearly increase of the earth. "Increase" is not the same as "whole amount"; a tithe of one's timber, for instance, would be a tenth of the amount of wood actually cut, not of the amount of wood one owned. A tithe of sheep would be a tenth of the new lambs, not of the entire herd.

Every parishioner whose holdings bore a tithable increase owed tithes to the parish is which he lived; if he failed
to pay his tithes, the parson could bring an action in an
ecclesiastical court to recover them. Originally, payment was
literally in kind—the tithe of a parishioner's hay, for instance,
would be sent to the parson's "tithe barn"—but an act passed
in the 1830s allowed the tithes to be commuted to money
payments.

Tithing as a requirement enforceable by law has been
gradually abolished throughout the United Kingdom, and
today all gifts to the church are voluntary. It is useful to keep
the system in mind as part of the background of nineteenth-
century fiction, however, for it was to a considerable extent
the flow of tithe income that enabled the church to play its
prominent part in the nation's political and economic scenes.
And the parish churches dotting the countryside, the bishops
sitting in the House of Lords, the young curates taking tea, in
fiction and in life, with respectable matrons who wonder as
they pour if the young man's prospects of a comfortable living
are bright enough to make him a favored suitor for one of her
daughters, were backed up by a solid system of dollars and
cents, or pounds and shillings rather.

TYPES OF DISSENTERS

So far, the established Church of England has received
what might seem a disproportionate amount of attention. The
obvious reason is that I am dealing, since the novels do, with
middle-class life, of which the Church of England was a
standard component. Nevertheless, the large and varied category of Dissenters deserves notice because middle-class Victorians, however strong their allegiance to the established
church, knew something about the dissenting world and picked up references to it in fiction and because there were after all
exceptions to this rule of Church of England solidity: Many
middle-class readers were Dissenters of one kind or another,
and many authors treated Dissenters sympathetically.

Although the term "Dissenter" can technically refer to anyone who is not a member of the Church of England and thus can include Roman Catholics, Jews, and Moslems, among many others, the term is most often applied to Protestants who dissent from the Church of England. The variety to be found here is considerable; at the end of the nineteenth century, for example, almost three hundred dissenting denominations were in existence. Many of these denominations were so small that membership was limited to one congregation. Others were much larger and might be possessed of a complex organization and a history going back to the English Reformation. The Methodists, relative newcomers as they had separated from the Church of England only in the eighteenth century, were most numerous; others of importance were the Congregationalists, Independents, Presbyterians, Baptists, and Unitarians. The Quakers, whose religion comprised an entire way of life, were usually included in the dissenting category.

The beliefs of the various bodies of Dissenters are difficult to generalize. Usually the emphasis was upon a personal relationship between the individual and his deity; any intervening hierarchies of human ministers or fixed ceremonies of worship were in most denominations very simple. Music was usually uncomplicated; some sects forbade instrumental accompaniment to congregational singing. The sermon was usually the major part of the service, and preaching styles favored the extemporaneous, in which the preacher appeared to be speaking from the inspiration of the moment rather than from previous preparation.

Some dissenting sects adhered to a doctrine of the elect, that is, to the belief that one was saved or one was not, and that there was nothing one could do in the way of faith, prayer, sacraments, or good works to alter the outcome. The protagonist's mother in Kingsley's *Alton Locke,* who could not even pray that her children might be included among the elect because to do so would be to demonstrate her lack of submission to divine will, is an extreme example of the unbending spiritual severity often associated with Dissenters. Other groups were more optimistic and held that God's grace was available to latecomers.

The Victorian stereotype of the dissenting congregation, a stereotype often transferred into fiction, shows a ragged rabble trembling in terror as an uneducated itinerant preacher depicts for them the torments of the damned. This picture was accurate with regard to a limited though perhaps highly visible proportion of the Dissenters. Many denominations, particularly the older ones, valued education and required it of their ministers; many individual Dissenters were wealthy, and many took an active part in philanthropy and government.

DISSENTERS:
CIVIL DISABILITIES

In the late seventeenth century, following the English Civil War and "Glorious Revolution", the newly victorious adherents of King and Church attempted to ensure the safe-keeping of political power in their own hands through a number of acts intended to keep Dissenters out of the running. There was even an attempt, fortunately for the cause of religious freedom short lived, to prevent any of the nation's Dissenters—Catholics as well as Puritans—from gathering publicly to worship. The "Test Acts" of this period prevented Dissenters from holding any public office, national or municipal; from attending the only universities then existing in England, Oxford and Cambridge; from holding any church benefice or university fellowship; and from entering military service. The "test" in question was that of taking the Anglican communion and subscribing to or swearing agreement with the thirty-nine articles expressive of Anglican beliefs. These prohibitions were not officially done away with until the late 1820s, although they had been evaded since the early eighteenth century when Parliament began the practice of annually passing a law exempting from the prescribed punishment any Dissenter who did hold municipal office, sit in Parliament, or join the army. (Catholics, incidentally, although barred from the power structure along with the Protestant Dissenters, sometimes found themselves on a different timetable when it came to getting back into it.)

The nineteenth century saw the relief of Dissenters from a number of other disabilities. In the 1850s, Dissenters were allowed to enter and to take degrees at Oxford and Cambridge; the right to receive a fellowship was given to Dissenters at both universities in the early 1870s. In the meantime, a number of other colleges and universities were opened to or founded by Dissenters during the century.

CHAPELS AND PREACHERS

In Victorian and in present-day British usage, the word "chapel" specifically denotes a dissenting place of worship. (The "chapel of ease" described above as part of the Church of England parish tradition is an exception.) Dissenting chapels were not usually named for saints, as Anglican churches were, but employed biblical names for places of worship: Zion, Bethel, Ebenezer. The word "conventicle" was sometimes used for a dissenting meetinghouse or as a metonym for nonconformity in general.

The minister of a dissenting church was often spoken of as its "preacher," a term that has become standard for the shepherd of any flock in America; in the Victorian novel one sometimes finds the word "preacher" used with the derogatory connotation common to many references to Dissenters in general.

RELIGION AND THE NOVELS

As the preceding pages have emphasized, the conservative middle-class orientation of the Victorian realistic novel makes understandable the novel's bias toward the established church. The heroine is married at the parish church as a matter of course; one of the cousins falls in love with the curate; a maiden aunt's preference for high church ritual brings a satirical comment from the narrator. Even rebellion—Caroline Helstone, for instance, in Charlotte Bronte's *Shirley*, hates doing needlework for parish projects—is usually an individual and temporary matter, unlikely to disturb the church's sheltering presence.

Dissenters, with some exceptions, usually appear as caricatures: Dickens's Mr. Stiggens in *Pickwick Papers* and Mr. Chadband in *Bleak House* are charlatans and hypocrites, preaching the simple life but enjoying a wide range of luxuries at the expense of their hoodwinked flocks. The joyless severity of Mrs. Clenham in Dickens's *Little Dorrit* is also part of a familiar stereotype. Thackeray's slighting reference to the dissenting chapel of the village Clavering St. Mary in *Pendennis* (chap. 15) is tangential to the conflict between high and low Church of England congregations with which the passage is concerned, but its simple assumption of the Dissenters' lack of claim to social prestige is typical of many such references throughout the middle-class novel. Thackeray considers another aspect of dissent in the opening chapters of *The Newcomes:* The wealthy but hardworking mercantile family would have been familiar to many readers. However, it is noticable that the "Quaker connexion" has only a step-relationship to Colonel Newcome and his son Clive, the central figures of the book, and that the industrious virtues of their forefathers are absent from the later generations of dissenting Newcomes.

For the most part, religion in the Victorian novel appears as a social rather than a spiritual phenomenon. Thus the novels may give a misleading picture in this respect; the Victorians found in their lives and surroundings cause for energetic and often anguished soul searchings. New scientific discoveries, the theory of evolution, the seamy sides of industrialism and social mobility, diverse and conflicting political theories, and numerous other challenges to the traditional status quo had made religious belief increasingly hard to reconcile with the rational mental processes that appeared so rewarding in the everyday walks of life.

There are some exceptions to the Victorian novel's apparent failure to deal with the more serious crises of religion and contemporary life; in fact, a whole category of nineteenth-century "religious novels" can be labeled as such in literary history. The most popular of these, Mrs. Humphry Ward's *Robert Elsmere*, covers a wide range of intellectual topics while telling the story of a young rector's loss of faith in the traditional tenets of the Church of England, his resignation of his living, and his making of a new life in a broader interpretation of Christian service. Again, a rector's loss of faith, the subsequent necessity of his leaving the ministry, and the new life he and his family create make up the backbone of the plot of Elizabeth Gaskell's *North and South*—a novel not centrally focused on religious questions but that accommodates them nevertheless.

HIGH AND LOW CHURCH
IN CHARLOTTE BRONTË'S *Jane Eyre*

Eliza Reed, one of the cousins with whom Jane Eyre spends her unhappy childhood, grows up into an unpleasantly rigid young woman whose life is focused on an almost obsessive devotion to high church practices. Eliza's day, portioned into a scrupulous routine, allots time for studying the rubrics (directions for conducting the services, administering the sacraments, and so forth) in the prayer book and for stitching an ornate red and gold altar cloth. In addition, Eliza attends three worship services on Sunday and any midweek saint's day service that comes along (chap. 21). To the average Victorian, this preference for elaborate ceremonial has negative connotations; and these suspicions are confirmed when Eliza goes to France, is converted to Roman Catholicism, and enters a convent.

A contrast to Eliza's high church rigidity appears in St. John Rivers, one of the other set of cousins whose existence Jane is surprised to discover in the middle of the book. St. John, a clergyman, has a typically low church zeal for education—he opens the village school of which Jane becomes mistress—and for evangelism—he wishes to become a missionary to foreign lands. In the final chapter he, like Eliza Reed, has left England to pursue his religious goals and is literally working himself to death in India.

St. John is less a caricature than Eliza, and he is a considerably more important character in the book, representing values of which Jane sincerely approves—from a distance. She has declined St. John's proposal of marriage and missionary work in intemperate climes. The contrasting cousins, nevertheless, demonstrate on a religious plane a central fact of Jane's personality: that Jane's actions and self-image are not to be influenced by anyone else's expectations of her, however heavily authorized these expectations may be.

TROLLOPE'S BARSETSHIRE CLERGY

Much of the description of Church of England organization that appears earlier in this chapter might be taken as a guide to Trollope's imaginary Barsetshire County where, especially in the cathedral town of Barchester, a full range of clerical specimens encounter concerns of timely interest to the church.

In *The Warden*, the point at issue is a type of corruption that has come about not through anyone's direct schemes but through the church's tendency to leave the status quo undisturbed. A charitable office set up in the fourteenth century has by the nineteenth, because of the increasing value of the land given to finance the charity, become in effect a sinecure: The holder of the position is paid much more than his efforts really deserve. To the American reader, with his shorter historical perspective, the centuries-long duration of Hiram's Hospital (a charitable, not a medical, institution) is the only large-scale difference between this novel and his own world. *The Warden's* main elements of conflict—the tendency of all the characters except Mr. Harding to see the situation for what can be got out of it and to oversimplify both the problem and their own projected solutions—are very much present in our own world.

Barchester Towers touches on several aspects of Victorian clerical life that Trollope assumes his readers will know but that the present-day American often does not, among them the procedure for choosing new bishops and the conflict between "high" and "low" sympathies within the Church of England.

The bishop question seems simple enough, for new bishops were appointed by the prime minister, but in this case there is a complication. The old bishop of Barchester is dying; his son, Archdeacon Grantly, hopes to be appointed to the position thus vacated; but the bishop dies just as one prime minister is going out of office and another is coming in. Since the archdeacon has some influence with the outgoing conservative prime minister but none with the incoming liberal one, he finds himself accruing the subtle guilt—for, as Trollope makes clear, the archdeacon is fundamentally a good man—of wishing his father would hurry up and die before the political situation should irrevocably shift. But the timing is wrong and the archdeacon misses the prize.

The war between high and low church factions begins with the appointment of Bishop Proudie, the choice of the prime minister who takes office as old Bishop Grantly dies, and continues through the rest of the novel. The low church side can be identified by its opposition to elaborate music and intoning (the chanting or singing of passages more usually read in speaking tones) and its advocacy of Sunday Schools and of a ban on Sunday traveling. In fact, determined low churchmen favored the cancellation of all trains on the Sabbath. Champions of low church principles in Barchester are Mrs. Proudie, wife of the bishop, and the bishop's personal chaplain, Mr. Slope. These two are jealous of each other, since each wishes to dominate the bishop and thus rule the diocese; but they are able to cooperate against a common foe. On the high church side—favoring forms and ceremonies, candles on the altar, intoning, crossing oneself, and elaborate clerical garments—are Archdeacon Grantly, who is fact shows his opposition to Mr. Slope and Mrs. Proudie by taking up some high church practices he had hitherto neglected, and his old friend Mr. Arabin, imported from Oxford as a special reinforcement. (Mr. Arabin is so authentically high church that he was tempted, at an earlier stage of his life, to follow his mentor Newman into Roman Catholicism.) At the center of the developing conflict is the young widow, Eleanor Bold, who numbers among her suitors both Mr. Slope and Mr. Arabin. Eventually the high church party wins Barchester and Mr. Slope departs; Mr. Arabin wins Eleanor, and the final chapter shows her indulging in "a few high church vagaries" of ritual and ornamentation, to the amusement of her sister, Mrs. Grantly.

A minor group of characters in *Barchester Towers*, the Reverend Vesey Stanhope and his family, touch upon another matter of interest to the Victorian readers, that of pluralism and nonresidence. Dr. Stanhope, one of the canons of Barchester Cathedral, also holds two livings near Barchester; for both of these he employs curates while he himself, something of an archetypal pluralist, lives far from the scene of his supposed labors, collecting butterflies on the shores of Lake Como in northern Italy. Trollope's treatment of this state of affairs is comparatively gentle; Dr. Stanhope is not portrayed as a deliberate villain, and he does not come to grief. Nevertheless, the original readers would have seen the author's implied criticism as part of a larger pattern in their society.

Doctor Thorne, third in the Barsetshire group, abandons as its main setting the cathedral town of Barchester for the environs of Greshambury, a village several miles away, and abandons as well the clerical callings with which the earlier characters have occupied themselves. The Dr. Thorne of the title is a medical rather than a clerical gentleman. Perhaps the only religious episodes that may not appear self-explanatory to today's American readers concern the husband-hunting adventures of one Miss Gushing. In pursuit of the high church vicar of Greshambury, Mr. Oriel, Miss Gushing participates in every new observance with which Mr. Oriel surprises his flock: She fasts on Fridays, works an ornamental cover for the credence table, and even attends Mr. Oriel's daily services at six o'clock in the morning—the only member of the congregation to do so. Mr. Oriel, however, becomes engaged to someone else. From the moment she hears this news, Miss Gushing betakes herself, spiritually, to the opposite extreme and beyond; she leaves the Church of England, not even pausing at a low church way station, and becomes a Dissenter—specifically, a Methodist. Here her enthusiasm is appreciated and she marries the preacher. While Miss Gushing's quest is not hard to follow in itself, the distance from high Anglicanism to Methodism seemed farther to Trollope's original readers than it does to us today; reminding ourselves of these differences can clarify Trollope's satirical point.

Framley Parsonage centers, as its title suggests, on a clerical household. A major problem in the book concerns the efforts of the young rector, Mark Robarts, to rise in the world—to move in fashionable circles, cultivate important friends, and receive political preferments. Mr. Robarts does succeed in being made a canon (or "appointed to a prebendal stall") at Barchester Cathedral, a sinecure worth six hundred pounds a year. However, in his eagerness to win friends Robarts "accepts" (countersigns) a bill for a young member of Parliament who is unable to repay the loan and disaster threatens. The present-day reader should keep in mind the fact that Mr. Robarts's ambitions were quite plausible, not as far fetched as they might seem to us. Since the Church of England as the national religion was a political as well as an ecclesiastical hierarchy, it was possible to make one's way upward as Mr. Robarts attempted to do—but, obviously, one should make a better choice of friends and observe greater prudence all round.

The Small House at Allington has the least to do with the clerical world of any of the Barsetshire novels. The book is connected with its predecessors through the De Courcy family, a worldly crew, who figure prominently in *Dr. Thorne.*

The Last Chronicle of Barset returns to the world of Barchester Cathedral and its environs. Mr. Crawley, perpetual curate of Hogglestock, a few miles from Barchester, is wrongly accused of having stolen a check for twenty pounds; the pattern of complexities revolves around the stern, proud personality of Mr. Crawley. Mr. Crawley's position as "perpetual curate" requires some explanation, since an ordinary curate in the pay of an individual parson could be dismissed quite simply, on suspicion of any wrongdoing or none at all, without any of the complex judicial investigation that Mr. Crawley's case requires. Lawrence Lerner observes in an editor's note appended to the Penguin edition of the novel that a perpetual curate held an office derived from monastic times and similar to that of a vicar; he could be removed only through the ecclesiastical courts.

Tess of the d'Urbervilles:
BAPTISM AND BANNS

In *Tess of the d'Urbervilles,* as in much of his fiction, Hardy uses religious motifs on several levels. Many of the characters' traditional Church of England beliefs are mixed with pagan superstitions and form part of the novel's folk background. In more intellectual conflicts, such as those between the low church rector, Mr. Clare, and his sons (two of whom become new-fashionedly high in their beliefs, the third of whom, Angel, repudiates formal Christianity), Hardy shows the impingement of modern thought upon traditional English life. These patterns of belief and disbelief are reasonably self-explanatory, taken in context, in *Tess*. A few factual details of the novel's religious setting may puzzle the present-day reader, among them Tess's baptism of her dying baby and the references to the crying of banns for the wedding of Tess and Angel Clare.

Tess's baptism of her baby, whom she names Sorrow, is actually a quite orthodox undertaking. The Church of England teaches that a layman (a person not in holy orders) may baptize in case of need as long as the layman uses water, invokes the name of the Trinity, and has a sincere intent to baptize. Tess more than fulfills these conditions as she and her awed congregation of siblings follow the baptismal service in the prayer book (2.14). However, Tess is not sure she has done the right thing and consults the village parson, who grudgingly tells her that little Sorrow's salvation is as secure as it would have been had he performed the baptism himself. To the parson, this answer is technically untrue. He had called at the Durbeyfield house on the evening the baby died, ready to baptize it, and had been roughly turned away by Tess's father; consequently, since he assumed that Tess had known about or been party to this refusal, in the parson's mind the "plea of necessity" needed to validate the irregular baptism could not be made. Tess, however, did not know that the parson had been there or that her father had turned him away. She had in fact asked her father to send for the parson and had been refused; and the parson did not know that Tess did not know of his attempt. Through this fog of misunderstandings, the parson compromises his conscience (needlessly, as the original readers would have realized, since to Tess the necessity was genuine) in order to give Tess the comfort of feeling that she has saved her child from eternal torment.

Although the crying of banns, the "publication" or verbal announcement by a clergyman to a congregation of a forthcoming marriage, was a familiar ritual to Victorian readers, Hardy uses a dialect phrase he felt called on to explain in a note: "Called home" is the way Tess's friend Izz Huett refers to the custom (4.32). Tess and Angel Clare have planned to be married on New Year's Eve; since the banns must be cried on three successive Sundays before the marriage, Tess is disturbed to learn that the first of the series has not taken place. She then finds that Angel has decided, without consulting her, to be married by license instead. (This alternative represented an ecclesiastical dispensation from the requirement that banns be cried; a marriage license was not granted by a civil authority apart from the church, as is the case in the United States.) Angel's preference for this less public type of preliminary—as he tells Tess, the license is "quieter"—indicates rather ominously his ambivalence about marrying her. Despite his protestations, he is in some ways ashamed of her.

Tess's relief at Angel's explanation stems partly from the realization that he does mean to marry her after all and partly from a fear she has had that when the coming marriage was announced in church someone would "stand up and forbid the banns on the ground of her history" (her having given birth to an illegitimate child). This eventuality was quite unlikely, as Hardy's original readers would have known. Banns could be forbidden only by a parent or guardian of the prospective bride or groom and then only if the bride or groom were a minor—a circumstance that did not obtain in the case of Tess or Angel. No teaching of the church forbade the marriage of a woman who had borne a child out of wedlock, and one's personal life, however scandalous, could not constitute a valid impediment to marriage unless it in some way violated a canon law concerning marriage. Tess's fears in this regard would seem to imply that she did not know the finer points of the ecclesiastical rules within which she lived or that her anxieties about her coming marriage had caused her to imagine dangers that would not have troubled her at other times. Either or both these possibilities would fit Tess's character and her situation.

RELIGION AND THE GOOD OLD DAYS: CHURCH MUSIC

Within the Church of England, one of the most obvious gaps between old and new in the nineteenth century was the shift of taste in church music. This development is a complex one, having to do with (among other things) the low church—high church controversies and the preference for spirited evangelistic songs on the one hand and for traditionally authentic hymns and chants on the other. The distinctions were not always clear-cut; in fact, some of the most popular hymn books appealed to congregations in both camps. The trends in church music to which one most often finds references in the novels are the decline of the old form of church choir and the use of newly written hymns instead of the older scripture-based ones.

This musical nostalgia usually appears as a passing reference in a fictional work more directly concerned with something else, but Hardy's *Under the Greenwood Tree* is an exception. Much of the novel concerns the last months in the official existence of an old-fashioned parish choir that the vicar has decided to replace with a new organ and a young lady organist. The Mellstock choir, as mustered for Christmas caroling, consists of four men and seven boys as singers, accompanied by stringed instruments: a bass fiddle, a cello, and three violins. In a still earlier period the choir had included clarinets and "serpents," old-fashioned wooden wind instruments. Within its context, and especially with Hardy's prefatory comments, the Mellstock choir as a symbol of changing times is self-explanatory to the present-day reader and in fact serves to illumine the passing references of other novelists.

SYMPATHETIC VIEWS OF DISSENTERS:
ELIOT

George Eliot's Dinah Morris in *Adam Bede* represents an unusual combination of characteristics for a sympathetic figure—one of whom the reader is expected to approve—for Dinah is not only a Dissenter, specifically a Methodist, but a woman preacher. The Church of England, as represented by Parson Irwine, and Dinah's Methodism coexist quite comfortably, each having a separate sphere and neither impinging on the other—a state of affairs that might not have lasted long in real life. Parson Irwine gets the green pastures of his traditional rural village; Dinah gets the slums of the new industrial towns. The notion of a woman preaching, startling and perhaps threatening to the middle-class Victorian reader, was softened by two aspects of *Adam Bede*: The story was set fifty years or so in the past, at the turn of the nineteenth century, so that oddities of all sorts could be accepted, and Dinah at the end of the novel gives up her pulpit. Conference (the annual assembly of Wesleyan Methodists), as Adam explains, has ruled against women preachers and Dinah accepts the ruling.

In George Eliot's *Felix Holt, the Radical,* the conflict between the Church of England and the Dissenters is sharper and thus more realistic. The setting, Treby Magna, was originally a market town in the midst of prosperous farms and has grown in size and shifted in economy with the development of mines and factories. The dissenting congregation is drawn from these new working classes—"eager men and women, to whom the exceptional possession of religious truth was the condition which reconciled them to a meagre existence" (chap. 3). Meanwhile, the upper-class members of the Church of England parish church felt uneasy; the rector even thinks that action should be taken to prevent the Dissenters from getting any land to build more chapels. The reader, as the novel progresses, comes to know and admire the dissenting preacher, Mr. Lyon; but the image of Dissenters is never substantially improved in Treby Magna, and the townspeople continue to see them as an uneducated, overemotional and somehow spiritually irresponsible body.

CATHOLICS IN FICTION

By the nineteenth century, England's fear of her ancient foe, the Roman Catholic Church, was sufficiently reduced for fictional Catholics to appear in roles other than that of automatic villain. In fact, many Catholic characters are sympathetic: The Catholic heroine of Disraeli's *Sybil* becomes an embodiment of Christian charity. Trollope's Phineas Finn, a member of Parliament who is also an Irish Catholic, is the protagonist of two of the "Palliser" novels (*Phineas Finn, Phineas Redux*) and appears in several others, welcomed by the other characters and, or so Trollope seems to expect, by the reader as well. An association between the Catholic faith and a kind of long suffering sweetness—martyrdom, perhaps—adds to the poignancy of such put-upon characters as Lucy Desborough in Meredith's *The Ordeal of Richard Feverel* and Lady Steyne in Thackeray's *Vanity Fair.*

When a character's Catholicism was not an established

fact but a possibility on that character's horizon, a matter for decision, the traditional English response seemed to revive and the author would expect the reader to regard the character, or at least the danger of a decision for Catholicism, in a negative light. Eliza Reed in Charlotte Bronte's *Jane Eyre*'(see above) and Mr. Arabin in Trollope's *Barchester Towers* provide examples. Eliza Reed accepts Catholicism enthusiastically, and this acceptance is portrayed as another unfortunate aspect of her generally unappealing character. In the second case, the reader is expected to regard Mr. Arabin's repudiation of the papal tendency in which his Oxford studies were leading him as a lucky and perhaps providential escape.

JEWS IN FICTION:
FAGIN versus DANIEL DERONDA

The fictional stereotype of the Jew, like that of the Catholic, had at least two sides. The negative side was a powerful one. Because of the banishment of Jews from England from the thirteenth century to the seventeenth, an absence that encouraged the English mind to regard Jewish culture as mysterious and threatening, and because of the sanction for the persecution of Jews that could be extracted from the New Testament, a literary tradition had been established in which Jews played the role of bogeyman or worse. Dickens's Fagin, for example, in *Oliver Twist*, retains an almost medieval diabolism—stealing children, hoarding wealth, cold bloodedly sending men to their deaths. It is noticeable that Fagin's villainy extends to his ignoring even Jewish standards of right behavior: He gleefully cooks sausages, forbidden by Jewish dietary laws, and on the eve of his execution he sends away the "venerable men of his own persuasion" who have come to pray with him in his cell.

A figure similar to Fagin is Svengali, the Jew in Du Maurier's *Trilby* who turns a tone-deaf artist's model into a world-famous singer by means of hypnotism and who eventually calls her to him from beyond the grave through the

"ARCHERY" (*Illustrated London News.*)

Archery was a sufficiently decorous sport for young ladies—and it showed off the figure. Gwendolyn Harleth, in George Eliot's *Daniel Deronda*, attracts her future husband at an archery meeting.

agency of a photograph. Mr. Melmotte in Trollope's *The Way We Live Now* lacks Svengali's supernatural power but wields considerable financial power—and turns out to be a swindler.

Smaller scale, more everyday, but still negative images of Jews appear frequently in the novels of Thackeray and Trollope. These figures, seldom individually named but referred to generically as "Ikey" or "Moses", have their hands full of their middle-class betters' financial dirty work, buying up the furniture of families who have been ruined in the stock market or lending money on promissory notes at high interest to young men with heavy fox hunting expenses.

During the later part of the nineteenth century, a reaction set in to the more flamboyantly exaggerated Jewish stereotype, a reaction that owed something perhaps to the success of many Jews in public life and something to the sincere urge toward reform of all kinds that characterizes the period. Dickens created Riah in *Our Mutual Friend* as one of his benevolent paternal figures, a sort of Jewish version of Mr. Brownlow in *Oliver Twist*. Disraeli's Sidonia in *Coningsby* and *Tancred* becomes something of an embodiment of the mysterious wisdom of the East. (Disraeli was himself of Jewish descent.) Trollope's *The Way We Live Now* contains not only the swindler Mr. Melmotte but the admirable Mr. Brehgert, whose dignity and integrity perhaps appear the greater in contrast to the decadence of his surroundings.

In one of the most energetic attempts to change the stereotype of the Jew as perceived by the British reading public, George Eliot created in *Daniel Deronda* a protagonist who, caught in a familiar fictional problem with a bit of a twist, sets out to discover his unknown parentage and finds, to his satisfaction, that it is Jewish. Present-day readers need to keep in mind the fact that the emotional mood of the book was relatively new to the original reading public; the degree of moral and intellectual purity ascribed to young Deronda, which may seem to us so exaggerated as to undermine our interest in him, was more functional in a society that had felt licensed for generations to look upon Jews as nonpersons.

IV

Politics

In its basic pattern of representative government, the American political structure is fairly close to the British, even though we lack royal panoply at the top. References to politics in Victorian novels, consequently, usually make a general kind of sense to American readers. But, as always, we will be able to pick up a larger proportion of what the author is sending out if we have sharper receiving equipment.

The political aspects of the changing nineteenth-century scene are closely related to shifts in power and in concepts of the individual brought about by the Industrial Revolution. England's power structure had been based largely on land, and the need throughout the century to adjust the political system to include new and unfamiliar sources of wealth caused a great deal of upheaval. In addition, England underwent a process of moral readjustment in which the individual human being, threatened with transformation into a cog in the industrial machine, instead won greatly increased rights and responsibilities. The fiction of the period reflects these changes, although, because of the authors' and the readers' predilection for the good old days, references to current political reforms were not always approving.

SOME GROUND RULES
OF BRITISH POLITICS

Despite the splendor of his or her way of life, the sovereign of Great Britain has little direct political power. This has not, of course, always been the case, and in a sense the history of British government is that of the gradual shifting of power from an absolute monarch to a body of noble peers to, finally, the elected representatives of the people.

There are two Houses of Parliament. The upper, the House of Lords, consists of peers of the realm and a number of bishops (see chapter 3). A courtesy title accorded the eldest son of a duke, marquis, or earl does not admit the bearer to the House of Lords; and, consequently, one cannot assume that all fictional characters called "Lord" Something-or-Other sit in the House of Lords.

A member of the lower house, the House of Commons, is elected by a constituency and is referred to as a member of Parliament, "M.P." for short, initials appended to the member's name in formal written address. A difference between the British and the American representative systems is that a member of parliament does not have to live in the district he represents.

The House of Commons, despite its designation as the "lower" house, is the site of the real power in Parliament. Bills originate here; the prime minister and the cabinet must have the confidence of the House of Commons and must resign if they lose it. This resignation, incidentally, is referred to as the "fall" of a "government" and is a fairly matter-of-fact and orderly part of the political scene, although to Americans accustomed to more predictable political cycles the idea of a government's "falling" carries overtones of anarchy and chaos.

Major decisions are made by the cabinet of ministers— the "government" in this sense. The prime minister is at the head; the fourteen to twenty other members, all high officials, are appointed to their posts by the prime minister and are drawn from both Houses of Parliament, although all belong to the same political party. (An exception is the "coalition" ministry, made up of members of more than one party; such a government occurs rarely, although it figures in Trollope's *The Prime Minister*.) Thus one might speak in the nineteenth century of a "Tory" or a "Whig" government and refer not to the entire machinery of regulating the country's affairs but simply to the cabinet.

A new prime minister is chosen or is "asked to form a government" by the sovereign. This choice is seldom a surprise, since the incoming prime minister is normally the leader of the party that has gained a majority of seats in the House of Commons.

ELECTIONS

Elections are not held at regular intervals only, as they are for the most part in the United States, although any House of Commons is automatically dissolved after five years in session. (This tradition may be ignored during a grave national crisis such as a war.) At any time during this period, the cabinet may call for a general election or the resignation of a prime minister who has lost the support of the House of Commons may precipitate one. All members of the House of Commons must then take their chances at the polls. A "bye election" is held to replace a member of Parliament who has died or resigned; the proceedings, of course, are limited to the constituency involved.

Thus the tides of political life are in many ways less predictable than those to which Americans are accustomed. The comparative ease with which a British government may fall has the advantage of making the ruling powers more immediately responsive to public opinion and of allowing less opportunity for long-range, self-sustaining corruption. A disadvantage is that a member may no sooner find himself in Parliament than the government falls and he has his whole campaign to do over again. Trollope's George Vavasor and Phineas Finn are at different times victims of this perfectly plausible set of circumstances (*Can You Forgive Her?*, *Phineas Finn*).

The Constitution

The British Constitution is not a single document like that of the United States but is a noncorporeal, somewhat mystical entity. It depends highly upon precedent and has been developed through centuries of lawmaking and interpretation. The constitution is, however, "unwritten" in the sense that its components cannot be listed. A bill or action described as "unconstitutional" is, in the opinion of the person doing the describing, at odds with the preexisting body of customs and legislation. To literal-minded Americans, accustomed to a constitution that may be cited by article and section, this state of things is disconcerting. The British find it natural; a reference in a novel to, say, a reform that threatens to "undermine the constitution" is not necessarily intended as part of a legal argument but may simply emphasize the opinion of the speaker that such a project is not in harmony with tradition or with the customary British self-image.

Nineteenth-century Elections and the Secret Ballot

British election campaigns today are rational, orderly, and inexpensive by American standards. It was not always so: As late as the 1880s an act of Parliament listed penalties for such actions as providing voters with free beer and free transportation to the polls. And bribery and violence had been even more widespread at earlier points in the century, before the Reform Bills of 1832 and 1867 enlarged the electorate. The election at Dickens's imaginary borough of Eatanswill (*Pickwick Papers*, chap. 13) and that at George Eliot's Treby Magna (*Felix Holt, the Radical*, chap. 31-33) are based on actual conditions.

Corruption was abetted by the fact that the secret ballot did not come into existence in England until 1872. Until then a voter announced his choice orally at the polling booth and a clerk wrote it down. No effort was made to keep the process confidential; representatives of the rival candidates might in fact sit within hearing distance, keeping their own tallies as the election proceeded. Under such circumstances, it would take a great deal of courage for an ordinary voter to deny the candidate favored by his landlord, employer, and wealthiest customer—three influential personages often rolled into one as the local squire. This point seems obvious in present-day perspective. Many Victorians, however, did not see the oral ballot as a restraint but felt, with what may seem a typical injection of unbending morality, that a man who deserved the ballot at all should not be afraid to speak his political preference aloud.

A PARLIAMENTARY GLOSSARY

Readers of Victorian political novels will find it useful to keep in mind the following terms:

Address: the formal reply of Parliament to the speech with which the sovereign has opened the session

Borough: a municipal district that elects one or sometimes two members of Parliament. These representatives are not required to live in the borough for which they stand. A "rotten" borough was one the population of which was too small to justify its representation; the Reform Bill of 1832 attempted to eliminate these. A "pocket" borough was one in which all the votes were controlled by one person, usually the landlord, and the landlord could then give or even sell the representation of his borough simply by telling his tenants whom to vote for.

Chiltern Hundreds: a piece of ground in Oxfordshire and Buckinghamshire the stewardship of which is now an obsolete office. However, as members of Parliament cannot legally resign directly, a member who wishes to leave office may apply for the stewardship of the Chiltern Hundreds and then resign from that.

County: a rural district, one of the "shires" (Oxfordshire,

Kent, and so forth) into which England is divided and which sends its own representatives (usually two) to the House of Commons. The boroughs are, of course, located inside counties, but an individual voter belongs either to a borough or a county, not to both.

Division: a vote taking. Members of either House rise from their seats and pass into two separate lobbies, designated for those supporting and those opposing the measure in question, where their numbers are counted by tellers.

"On his legs": members of Parliament speak in their place, standing up. To be "on one's legs" is to be making a speech.

Scrutiny: an official investigation of an election, to eliminate invalid votes

"Standing for a seat": what Americans would call "running" for public office

Treasury Board: not concerned with national finances, as is the Exchequer, but a group of purely political offices. The first lord of the treasury is usually the prime minister; the junior lords of the treasury (five or so in number) act as assistant whips in the House of Commons. Trollope's young members of Parliament often aspire to seats on the treasury board.

Whip (or Whipper-In): a member of Parliament whose duty is to be sure all the representatives of his political party are present during an important vote. The party in power had during most of the nineteenth century four whips, paid from public funds; the opposition party or parties had to make do with unpaid whips. One of the whip's duties is to arrange to "pair" a member of his party who wishes to be absent from a debate with a member of the opposition who does not plan to attend, either; the missing votes will then hurt neither party.

Woolsack: The seat of the lord chancellor, Speaker of the House of Lords, is made from a bag of wool. The woolsack is often used as an allusion to the lord chancellor or to his office.

PARLIAMENT:
PHYSICAL DETAILS

During the nineteenth century Parliament usually met from February of each year until July or August, although this schedule could be extended or otherwise altered. Members of Parliament customarily occupied houses (or, especially in the case of bachelors, lodgings) in the West End of London—perhaps in Westminster itself, quite close to the scene of their parliamentary labors, or in the nearby and highly fashionable district of Mayfair.

Parliamentary debates were held at night, allowing those members who had to make a living (and who could do so in London) to practice law, for example, during the day. Most nineteenth-century members of Parliament were unsalaried.

Both Houses of Parliament were in Victorian times and still are housed in the gothic Westminster Palace, erected beside the Thames in 1840 to replace the buildings that burned in 1834. Present-day visitors taking an escorted tour of the buildings (a simple matter to arrange) or attending a debate in either chamber (a more difficult one) will find that today's facilities do not differ greatly from those mentioned in Victorian fiction. The most extensive changes occurred during the rebuilding of the House of Commons chamber after a German bomb fell on it in 1941, and even in this case the original proportions and atmosphere of the room have been retained.

The complex of parliamentary buildings includes the meeting chambers for both Houses as well as committee rooms, libraries, courtyards, and Westminster Hall, part of the ancient Palace of Westminster to which the present buildings have been attached. The meeting chambers for the House of Lords and the House of Commons are, by American standards, surprisingly small; neither, in fact, can comfortably hold all the members who are entitled to sit there and an important debate takes place in an atmosphere of crowded excitement. "Strangers," or visitors to the chambers, occupy special sections in the galleries (balconies), as do reporters for

the official parliamentary publication and for the newspapers. In Victorian times, shorthand reporters (male ones)
were already a familiar sight; when Dickens's David Copperfield briefly takes up this pursuit, the original readers could
easily visualize it.

Ladies visiting the House of Commons in Victorian times
sat in a special section of the gallery, protected from view by
an iron grating. Thus Trollope's Lady Glencora Palliser describes her husband's political doings: "Plantagenet was on
his legs last night for three hours and three-quarters, and I sat
through it all. As far as I could observe through the bars I was
the only person in the House who listened to him . . . " (The
Eustace Diamonds, chap. 54). The suffragettes, at the end of
the century, made a less modest use of these iron bars: After
gaining access to the ladies' gallery they chained themselves
to the grille in order to make their forced removal more
difficult and thus to add to the time in which they might
address the House on the subject of votes for women. The
ladies' gallery was a part of the old (pre-1941) House of
Commons chamber that was not incorporated into the design
of the present one.

WHIGS AND TORIES

These names or nicknames for the major political parties
at the beginning of the Victorian age originated in the late
seventeenth century. Their connotations fluctuate with varying political issues, and there are many differences in the
opinions of individual members of both parties. In other
words, a party label should be taken as a very general indica-
tor of the attitudes and opinions of the person labeled.

Broadly, the term "Whig" is identified with the mercantile
and industrial interests. A typical Whig as perceived by the
middle-class reading public might be of urban rather than
rural background and aware of the needs of the urban working classes; he might be newly wealthy and even of a dissenting religion. His political tendencies were liberal, though

sometimes quite moderately so. Among the many exceptions to this picture is the young Queen Victoria, certainly no newly rich mill owner, who began her reign as an ardent Whig. Trollope includes two thoroughly aristocratic and thus atypical Whig families in his Barsetshire, the Pallisers and the De Courcys.

The term "Tory" has the connotation of the traditional landowning interests, rural, authoritarian, conservative, and Church of England. The "old Tory squire" is a recognizable stock figure in fiction and journalism. Novels that go beyond stereotypes in their political characterizations may show considerable variation in their Tories, as was the case in historical fact; it was the Tory government of Sir Robert Peel, for example, that abolished the high tariff on grain, thus lowering the price of bread and benefiting the poor, and that put through numerous other reforms. Disraeli's novels reflect their author's political convictions in showing the Tory party as the answer to the nation's troubles and in assigning to their aristocratic heroes a deep and almost mystical sympathy with the common people.

Very roughly, the Whigs may be seen as the ancestors— with many transmutations of opinion and many exceptions— of the modern Liberal party; the Tories correspond to today's Conservatives. The new terms came into use during the Victorian age, and sometimes they seem to be used interchangeably with the old ones. By the end of the century "Whig" had an old-fashioned ring; "Tory" seemed to remain in everyday use somewhat longer.

SECRETARIES AND UNDER SECRETARIES

Although the United States has only one Secretary of State, the British use the term more generally, so that one reads, for example, of a "Secretary of State for Home Affairs" (or "Home Secretary"). The number of secretaries of state varied during the nineteenth century, rising from three (Home Affairs, Foreign Affairs, and the Colonies) to five with the addition of a Secretary of State for War and a Secretary of State for India. These are cabinet positions, held by members of either House who have been appointed to their secretary-ships by the prime minister. Other cabinet posts include the lord high chancellor, the lord privy seal, the chancellor of the exchequer, and others. The number of cabinet members var-ied, and some important parliamentary posts did not in fact carry with them a seat in the cabinet.

An "under secretary," which sounds to Americans some-thing like a file clerk, is an official who works under a principal secretary of state and ranks just beneath him. Two under secretaries were the usual number of assistants per secretary in the nineteenth century. Under secretaries were members of Parliament who had been appointed to their posts by the prime minister, although they did not belong to the cabinet.

THE REFORM BILL OF 1832

At the beginning of the nineteenth century, the districts from which members were elected to the House of Commons had not been altered for more than a century, despite the shifts in population that had occurred in the meanwhile. The resulting situation was most unjust. The great industrial cities of Liverpool and Manchester in northern England had virtually no representation; at the other extreme, some rural boroughs had become almost entirely depopulated but con-tinued nevertheless to send duly elected representatives to Parliament.

Agitation for realigning the population and its represen-tatives and for enlarging the body of voters, which in the early part of the century was still a small and privileged segment of the population, had occurred frequently; but it was not until the death of George IV that conditions became favorable. The dissolution of Parliament that followed the death of the sov-ereign created an opportunity for reform to become an issue, and the cause was energetically taken up by the Whigs. A reform-minded House of Commons was elected; a bill was then passed by the Commons only to be rejected by the Lords, whose commitment to the maintenance of the status quo was naturally strong.

Considerable tension followed until the problem of getting the reform bill through the House of Lords was solved in an ingenious manner: The king, William IV, having been reluctantly convinced that the reform bill was a necessity, authorized the prime minister to create enough new Whig peers to flood the House of Lords and assure passage of the bill. The new peers, as it turned out, were not needed—to the disappointment of some prominent but untitled Whigs; the threat of creating them was enough. The opposition simply stayed home and the reform bill was voted through the House of Lords.

The effect on the political map was considerable. Eighty-some underpopulated boroughs were deprived of some or all of their representation; more than forty towns, previously without any representation at all, became boroughs and received one or more members. The number of county members (representing the large "shires" into which Britain is divided) was increased, and some of the larger counties were divided into two or more parts for representational purposes.

In addition, the Reform Bill of 1832 extended the franchise to a much larger proportion of the middle class. One could qualify to vote for a borough representative, for example, by owning a house (or other property) worth ten pounds or more in annual rental or (a more frequent case) by renting property from someone else for a minimum of that amount. Fictional references to this "ten pound householder" usually have the connotation of a newly arrived member of the middle class to whom possession of any sort of political power is something of a novelty.

As far as Victorian fiction is concerned, the Reform Bill of 1832 is the most crucial legislation of its kind, and this is the bill usually meant by references simply to the reform bill. However, in subsequent reform bills, the vote was given to a larger proportion of the working class in 1867 and to farm laborers in 1884. A reference to either of these bills can usually be clarified by the context of the reference, by the time setting of the novel in question, or by both.

CORN LAW REPEAL

"Corn" to the British means specifically wheat, or, more generally, the cereal grains of wheat, barley, and rye. Corn does not include maize or Indian corn, which is the word's main denotation in the United States. (Maize does not grow well in England; the nights are too cold.) The corn laws, in force in the first half of the nineteenth century and a major political issue, were protective tariffs that kept the price of homegrown wheat high. The situation was good for landowners, whose representatives in Parliament naturally voted to continue it; it was bad for the poor, who had to buy bread at high prices but whose voice in the government was small. During economic depressions, when the poor literally starved to death for want of bread, reformers sometimes pointed out that it was cheaper to buy opium in the quantities required to still a day's hunger.

In 1845, the Irish potato crop failed, a dire event because the Irish population had become almost entirely dependent upon this cheap and filling tuber. As all of Ireland was then under British rule, it was up to Parliament to provide some means of relief for a famine that took between two and three hundred thousand lives. Large supplies of imported grain became a clear necessity. In 1846, after the harvest had failed again, Sir Robert Peel, the Tory prime minister, successfully advocated "the removal of all impediments to the import of all kinds of human food—that is the total and absolute repeal forever on all articles of sustenance."

The Tories had supported the high tariffs, and after Peel's change of heart his colleagues considered the Tory party fragmented; landowners considered themselves ruined. (See chapter 8 for a closer look at the specifically agricultural aspects.) As years passed, however, and low wheat prices failed to undo the country, Peel's disloyalty to his party was seen in a kinder perspective.

POLITICS IN TROLLOPE'S PALLISER NOVELS

Although some knowledge of British politics is helpful in reading any of Trollope's novels, the six "Palliser" novels (*Can You Forgive Her?*, 1864; *Phineas Finn*, 1869; *The Eustace Diamonds*, 1873; *Phineas Redux*, 1873; *The Prime Minister*, 1876; *The Duke's Children*, 1880), so called after a family that figures prominently in them, frequently deal with politics in a close-up way, and today's American reader needs to be fairly alert.

Two broad qualifications might be made about the relationship of fiction to real life in Trollope. First, the political novels are not entirely about politics—an obvious fact on the face of it, as even a present-day American can distinguish a fox hunt from a debate in the House of Commons; but the proportionate mixture of politics to recreation, romance, murder, or whatever else is afoot in the plot should not be taken as typical of a politician's life. Second, even though Trollope has based some of his characters on real-life politicians, the reader should not try to match up, point by point, the figures and events in the novels with those of history. For those American readers who are making their first acquaintance with Victorian politics through Trollope's novels, this temptation will be easy to resist; but one should not assume that Trollope provides a kind of code by which the Victorian political scene, when one does get around to reading up on it, may be illuminated. Trollope creates a world analogous to that of his readers, but not predictably so.

In *Can You Forgive Her?*, the problems facing George Vavasor in trying to win a seat in the House of Commons are mainly financial and are quite in accordance with fact. A member of Parliament at that time received no salary (though holders of special positions within the Parliament might) and consequently had to have some income from another source.

His life-style, if he were ambitious to form useful friendships and to appear a gentleman of fashionably leisurely habits, had to permit at least membership in a good club, some loose money for card playing, and, if possible, horses for hunting. Campaign expenses were heavy as well, and here Trollope gives us a glimpse of the seamy side of election procedures. "Election agents," a sleazy crew, charged the candidates considerable funds for flags, placards, and the openly acknowledged though discreetly conducted bribery of voters. And the fact that a Parliament might be dissolved only months after it was formed, leaving any member who wanted to get back in with an entire campaign to fight over again, did nothing to improve George Vavasor's changes of success.

In the case of Vavasor, who is quite a villain, the reader does not decry any amount of ill fortune that comes his way and tends to assume that anyone who wants to go into so underhand a game deserves what he gets. However, it is useful for one's view of the entire picture to realize that the difficulties of entering public life for a young man of no fortune or strong social connections would apply to the just as well as the unjust.

Phineas Finn introduces us to a pleasanter young man for whom, it would seem, such difficulties pose less of a problem. Yet Trollope's original readers would have seen that Finn's way in the world was more hazardous than his apparent success in making it would imply. An Irishman and a Roman Catholic, Finn could expect to arouse prejudice for which he personally was not responsible. Roman Catholics had been permitted to sit in Parliament since the late 1820s, but hostility to the faith and its adherents was still alive in the population. As for Ireland, which had at that time no governing body of its own and sent representatives to the British Parliament, prejudice often took the form of regarding all Irishmen as irresponsible chatterers, prone to drink, incapable of following a sustained plan.

Like George Vavasor, Finn has a small income and many social temptations for spending it. Unlike Vavasor, however, Finn has a pleasing personality, and it is his social charm rather than his more solid abilities that allows him to rise. The power that controls the Irish borough for which Finn stands, one Lord Tulla, is willing to let him have the seat; and campaign expenses are consequently slight. When he anticipates losing his seat in a general election two years later, he is offered another, this time in England, by an elderly acquaintance in possession of a pocket borough—a borough the votes of which are controlled by one interest, usually that of the landlord. This acquaintance, the earl of Brentford, is quite open in describing the situation: His tenants at Loughton hold their property on short leases or none at all, and, as the earl says, "I do like the people round me to be of the same way of thinking as myself in politics" (1. 33). Lacking the secret ballot, at British voters did at that time, Lord Brentford's tenants would be unlikely to risk the nonrenewal of their leases by voting against their landlord's candidate.

As was obvious to Trollope's original readers from their familiarity with the scene, Finn's political opportunities—including another session in his Irish borough after the English one was dissolved by a fictional approximation of the Reform Bill of 1867—were extended to him on a trial basis. Should he cause his benefactors to regret their help, his political career would be over, for the system provided no way for him to succeed entirely or even by a large part on his own. Thus Finn's eventual decision to leave Parliament, following a disagreement with his supporters within his party, is an act the original readers would have seen as sensible and not as indicative of cowardice or low self-respect on Finn's part.

The Eustace Diamonds is the most tangential to politics of the Palliser series, although members of both Houses of Parliament figure as characters. Most of the political references make sense to today's readers in their context. One passage might be mentioned: The shrewd and opportunistic Lady Eustace displays her remarkable ignorance of the facts of political life by claiming, quite untruthfully, that her fiancé, Lord Fawn, is a member of the cabinet (1. 20)—assuming, since she apparently is not quite sure what the cabinet may be, that her listener will not catch her out. To the original readers such a lapse may have seemed on the verge of the incredible; nevertheless, women were educated haphazardly in the nineteenth century, and some of Lady Eustace's later actions become more understandable if one sees her as possessing large blocks of ignorance about the structure of the world she lives in.

Phineas Redux continues the adventures of Mr. Finn, who returns to the political scene with the renewed confidence of his associates and stands this time for the borough of Tankerville, a coal-mining town in the north of England. An important issue is corruption, specifically the bribing of voters, and the reader should be alert to the implications of "spending money" when this activity is ascribed to the opposition candidate. As the voters of Tankerville are greatly increased in number, the colliers (coal miners) having been enfranchised by the Reform Bill of 1867, such bribery would have to be on a larger scale than had previously been necessary. Nevertheless, Finn's opponent goes in for it, and Finn "has him out on petition," that is, challenges the result of the election, demands a "scrutiny" or official investigation, which reveals the invalidity of the bribed votes, and claims the seat. The reader is expected to realize that this has been the game plan from the beginning: A letter in the first chapter from Finn's colleague, Barrington Erle, outlines the situation in language the present-day reader is likely to find technical and oblique unless he is on his guard.

The Prime Minister concerns chiefly the duke of Omnium, who formerly figured in these and other of Trollope's novels as Plantagenet Palliser and who inherited his uncle's title upon the latter's death (Phineas Redux, 1.26). The duke, a Liberal, is asked to form a coalition ministry, does so, and keeps it together for three years. The coalition does not get much done, a fact that is not surprising in view of the difficulties under which ministers of widely differing principles might be expected to labor when attempting to act in harmony. The complexities of putting together a cabinet, filling secondary posts, and so on are fairly clear in context.

A conflict develops when the duchess of Omnium (formerly Lady Glencora Palliser) tries to set up her own candidate for member of Parliament for Silverbridge, a pocket borough of the duke's; although she refrains from threatening any nonrenewal of leases, she does imply to the tradesmen that further orders from her household would depend on the right result of the election (1.32). The duke's opposition to his wife's activity comes not from a wish to further another candidate—even though there is one he prefers—but from a determination to abandon the old custom, taken quite for granted by the previous duke, of telling one's tenants whom to vote for. The duchess's candidate loses and the new election ethics are vindicated. Readers might note that the secret ballot, an innovation that appeared in real life four years before *The Prime Minister* was published and that is referred to by the characters simply as "the ballot," seems to have some bearing on the Silverbridge voters' willingness to make their own choice.

In *The Duke's Children*, the plot focuses less on politics than on the generation gap, although at one point Lord Silverbridge, the duke's eldest son, dramatizes this gap by abandoning the family's traditional allegiance to the Liberal party and going into Parliament as a Conservative. But this and other political events, if taken in their context, are fairly self-explanatory to today's readers.

Vanity Fair:
QUEEN'S CRAWLEY AS A ROTTEN BOROUGH

Most of the action of Thackeray's *Vanity Fair* takes place well before the Reform Bill of 1832, and the old baronet, Sir Pitt Crawley, may be seen as occupying a niche in life typical of many that Thackeray's readers could remember, even though conditions had changed before the novel appeared in 1847. Queen's Crawley, the baronet's estate, comprising his house and grounds and a small village, has sent two members to Parliament since the sixteenth century; and the voters, depending for their well-being on the good humor of their landlord, are unlikely to vote against his preferred candidates. Thus Queen's Crawley is both a "rotten borough" (of insufficient population to merit its high degree of representation) and a "pocket borough" (in the control of its landlord).

Of the two seats, Sir Pitt fills one himself and sells the other (chap. 9) for fifteen hundred pounds a year—$10,500 by the rough calculation suggested in chapter 2 above for transforming nineteenth-century pounds into present-day dollars. Thackeray gives no details about this commercial transaction; presumably Sir Pitt simply takes the money from the aspiring candidate and then announces his choice to his voters. To the original readers, however, a rather audible clock was ticking: Queen's Crawley's seats in Parliament surely cannot survive the reform bill. They do not; and the younger Sir Pitt, "both out of pocket and out of spirits by that catastrophe, failed in his health" (chap. 67). On Sir Pitt's death, brought about in a sense by the end of the corruption that has sustained his family, the estate and title go to a worthier possessor, the upcoming generation as represented by young Rawdon Crawley.

DICKENS AND POLITICS

Dickens's deep dislike for politics, perhaps essentially a distrust of the idea of solving individual human problems through impersonal authority, makes itself seen in his novels as a gallery of negative caricatures. Today's reader, especially if he is operating in a vacuum, so to speak, having begun with Dickens and not having yet encountered Victorian authors of differing attitudes, might do well to keep in mind that Dickens's outlook is not necessarily representative of the Victorians in general, that it often irritated his original readers, and that Dickens may in some instances have been trying to correct by negative satire what he saw as a dangerously unquestioning approval of political institutions.

Corrupt election procedures are an object of attack in *Bleak House,* in which the political situation corresponds roughly to a curious real-life crisis of 1851: For almost two weeks after the resignation of Lord John Russell as prime minister, minister after prospective minister found himself without enough support to form a cabinet until at last Russell's government returned to office. In Dickens's version, "Lord Coodle would go out, Sir Thomas Doodle wouldn't come in, and there being nobody in Great Britain (to speak of) except Coodle and Doodle, there has been no Government" (chap. 40). (To "go out" or "come in" refers, of course, to a prime minister's resignation or his acceptance of the sovereign's request that he form a government. By "no government" Dickens did not mean that a state of anarchy prevailed but simply that the highest posts were unfilled.) *Bleak House* is not in any way a point-by-point transcript of events in 1851, and in fact the overall time setting of the novel, though vague, could hardly be later than the early 1830s, since the characters travel about by coach rather than by train. The governmental crisis of 1851, only a year or so before *Bleak House* appeared, probably seemed to Dickens a good example of the ponderous and, in his eyes, ridiculous machinery of British politics.

In *Little Dorrit*, Dickens uses the extended metaphor of the "Circumlocution Office" to satirize both government bureaucracy and, on a larger scale, the country as a whole. "Office" in this context means a government department, not a suite of rooms; real-life analogues would be the Foreign Office, the Home Office, and so forth. The Circumlocution Office is controlled by the Tite Barnacle family, who, whenever a vacancy occurs, propose one another for the position. Here Dickens refers to the actual state of things in the civil service: Appointments were made in essentially this way, by nomination followed by a quite perfunctory examination. Often the candidate was nominated by a friend or relative already in the department concerned—a Tite Barnacle. The matter was one of which Dickens's original readers were already aware, for it was while the early chapters of *Little Dorrit* were appearing in serial form that a more stringent civil service examination was instituted.

In other novels, Dickens glancingly attacks other aspects

of the political scene. The election at the borough of Eatanswill in *Pickwick Papers* (chap. 13) is self-explanatory as slapstick comedy, and American readers might in fact be startled by the fact that the violence and bribery were recognizably close to actuality. In *Nicholas Nickleby*, the hero has a brush with the evils of politics when he is interviewed by a member of Parliament in need of a secretary; it becomes apparent that the secretary's job is in effect to serve as his master's brains, to learn all about finance and foreign policy in order to "cram" his ignorant employer before his speeches. In *Oliver Twist*, handsome young Harry Maylie actually plans a career in Parliament at the urging of his ambitious mother, but events are more favorable and he is happy to settle down at the end of the book in a country parsonage.

Oliver Twist AND THE POOR LAW

In *Oliver Twist*, as his original readers would have recognized, Dickens has depicted a parish in which the new regulations of the Poor Law Amendment Act, passed by Parliament a few years before *Oliver Twist* appeared, in 1837 are broken or stretched in ways that seem quite plausible. Two of these violations of the spirit or even the letter of the law are represented by Mr. Bumble's power and by the children's diet.

Mr. Bumble, the parish beadle in charge of the workhouse and of the supervision of the parish's relief in general, does not occupy this post as part of a beadle's regular duties. Originally the beadle was a parish constable who kept order during church services and carried messages for higher-ups in the parish hierarchy; the custom of giving the beadle charge of the workhouse was an innovation, and Mr. Bumble has in a sense risen upward to occupy a power vacuum. The framers of the new law, hoping to see it intelligently administered and suspicious of beadles, had provided for a new set of paid officials for the workhouses; but many parishes kept the old ones or simply rehired them under the new labels. In fact, it is possible that even a conscientious parish if at a loss for funds, as virtually all of them were, might see Mr. Bumble and his kind as the best they could get for the money: Mr. Bumble is at least energetic, joying as he does in tyrannizing over the workhouse inmates. And there was, of course, no guarantee that any parish would conscientiously attempt to do its best, as the Poor Law rather idealistically assumed it would, for an influx of paupers that, in the parish's view, it had not deserved and could not pay for.

(The reason the administration of welfare and other programs fell to the parishes is, essentially, the close relationship between the Church of England and the national government; see chapter 3. The term "civil parish" might be used for a district constituted for the administration of some aspect of civil government, such as the Poor Law; the civil parish was often, but not always, coterminous with the ecclesiastical parish.)

Oliver Twist depicts a clear violation of the new law in the reduction of the children's diet, for to the members of Parliament who framed the legislation Oliver's request for more food would have been quite justifiable. Children were to be given a nutritious and sufficient diet; it was only the ablebodied paupers, who theoretically were in the workhouse in the first place only because they had refused to take a job outside it, who were to be kept on small bowls of thin gruel. Such careful distinctions were beyond the powers or the concern of the parish in *Oliver Twist* and perhaps of some in real life as well. Besides, as Dickens's board of governors perceived, a basic intention of the new law was to relieve the financial pressure on parishes by reducing the number of persons on relief; and to starve them indiscriminately out of the workhouse accomplished this goal as effectually as and perhaps more quickly than the more discriminating methods advocated by the law. Dickens's original readers might in fact have concluded from *Oliver Twist* that the Poor Law's attempt to cut expenses and simultaneously to deal humanely with the paupers represents an impossible combination, even a cruelly hypocritical one in view of the apparent predominance of the cost-cutting motive. Welfare, as the Victorians were beginning to learn, is a problem that can be solved neither by simple morality nor simple arithmetic.

An unrealistic detail in *Oliver Twist* is that the parish board of governors appears to be in continual session, available to make disparaging comments about Oliver every evening of the week. This circumstance was not usual, for the parish board was unpaid, consisting of rural squires and village tradesmen, and the members had many other things to do. However, since Dickens was using his board of governors as something of an allegorical body representing the attitudes of the dominant middle class, he had little choice but to place it constantly on the scene.

POLITICAL BACKGROUND
IN GEORGE ELIOT'S *Middlemarch*

The time setting of *Middlemarch* extends from the late 1820s to the summer of 1832, with the addition of a "Finale," the standard distribution of rewards and punishments to the characters, which brings the action to some point close to the date of the novel's publication (1871-72). Politics play a definite role in the environment of the characters, most of whom are pictured as alert, reasonably well informed, and concerned about the state of the country. In addition, politics form a standard of comparison between two of the three men upon whom the heroine, Dorothea Brooke, successively depends for her social identity.

The novel opens in the fall of 1829, when Dorothea's uncle, Mr. Brooke, worries about the implications of the bill allowing Catholics to be seated in Parliament (chap. 1). The next major political event is the death in 1830 of King George IV, whose illness is mentioned in a kind of counterpoint to the reading of the will of old Peter Featherstone (chap. 35). Also a subject of Middlemarch conversation is the successor to George IV, his brother, the duke of Clarence, who was to reign as William IV from 1830 until 1837, when upon his death he was succeeded by his niece, Queen Victoria. Upon the king's death in 1830, Parliament is dissolved and Middlemarch and its environs, along with the rest of the country, becomes fervently political. The community's reaction to the activities of Mr. Brooke in particular (chap. 37) are given in such detail that the picture becomes both vivid and self-explanatory, as does, for the most part, poor Mr. Brooke's attempt to stand for election as a reform-minded independent candidate. The mocking crowd that throws eggs on Mr. Brooke as he attempts to make a speech and then parades him about in effigy (chap. 51) is not an exaggerated danger of nineteenth-century elections; such events transpired in real life. At the end of the main action of the novel, the reform bill has just been rejected by the House of Lords in the early summer of 1831, and the ladies are gossiping cheerfully about the proposed Whig tactic of persuading the king to allow the creation of enough new peers, all pledged to vote for the bill, to carry the motion on its next trip through Parliament (chap. 84). The original readers knew, of course, as do today's, that the reform bill would be passed the next year, though without the need of creating new Whig peers.

It is the youthful and energetic Will Ladislaw who contributes to Mr. Brooke's campaign what bits of vision or common sense it possesses. Eventually, as the novel's "Finale" tells us, Ladislaw goes into politics himself, although he lacks the financial means customarily needed to do so, and is "returned to Parliament by a constituency who paid his expenses"—a high compliment to Ladislaw's abilities, as such payment was at that time neither required nor usual.

V

The Law

American law, not surprisingly, is similar in its basic principles to English law; during the colonial period our law was, of course, a direct importation and many of the American lawyers practicing before and after the Revolution had been educated in England. Consequently, American readers of Victorian novels are most likely to have difficulty not so much with the basic concept of justice as perceived by the Victorians as with details of procedure and terminology.

COMMON LAW AND EQUITY

Throughout most of the nineteenth century, the legal picture was greatly complicated by the fact that over the hundreds of years English law had been operating two separate court systems had grown up—the courts of common law and the courts of equity.

Common law in theory makes decisions based upon the precedent of previous cases and is concerned with abstract principles of justice; equity, again in theory, is concerned with the individual and attempts to relieve individuals from the too-strict application of other laws. An example might be that of a person bound by a contract into which he has entered through some mistake of identity; it is to an equity court that he would apply for relief. (Equity originated in the eleventh century as an ecclesiastical concept, an appropriately Christian urge to temper justice with mercy, and was administered by ecclesiastical courts.)

By the nineteenth century, the complexities of a double system of courts, each with its own judges, lawyers, and other officials and each with its private and sometimes mutually exclusive sets of precedents, had become too much for the country to bear. Plaintiffs often did not know into which of the systems they should take their case. Neither did their legal advisors, and a plaintiff might get far into an expensive action in one system only to be told that he had mistaken his system and must start over again somewhere else.

Reform finally came in the 1870s with the passage of the first of a series of Judicature Acts. The jurisdiction of common law and equity courts were merged into one system, the Supreme Court of Judicature, of which today's textbooks of British law present coherent diagrams; and a uniform procedure for pleading was established.

BARRISTERS

In England the term "lawyer" covers several quite distinct categories. A major distinction, that between a "barrister" and a "solicitor," is especially important to readers of Victorian fiction.

A barrister belongs to the bar and may plead cases in superior courts of law. (As in the United States, the term "bar" essentially means the body of lawyers qualified to practice. The word in this sense has an interesting history, deriving from the barriers separating various parts of a medieval courtroom.) A Victorian barrister would be "called to the bar" after satisfactorily completing his studies at one of the four Inns of Court, ancient law colleges in London—the Inner Temple, Middle Temple, Gray's Inn, and Lincoln's Inn.

The typical Victorian barrister had taken a degree at Oxford or Cambridge before entering one of the Inns of Court. No degree was actually required for entrance—Thackeray's Pendennis, "plucked" from his university for failing his final examinations, goes on to an Inn of Court regardless—but a candidate for admission had to be at least twenty-one years of age, and this requirement conveniently allowed a young gentleman to spend time at a university. Students must have kept twelve terms or quarters before they could be called to the bar; and, to prove they were really there, they had to eat a certain number of dinners in the halls of their respective Inn of Court. Thus "eating one's dinners" came to mean studying for the bar.

Barristers might aspire to rise to various levels of the legal hierarchy. A "serjeant" (when used in this sense always spelled with the "j") was a member of a superior order of barristers. The order was abolished in the early 1880s, but many serjeants appear in Victorian novels published before that time; the reader must be careful to visualize not a minor official, someone standing at the courtroom door with a mace perhaps, but a quite prestigious person in gown and wig. Serjeant Snubbin and Serjeant Buzfuz in Dickens's *Pickwick Papers* orchestrate the case of Bardell versus Pickwick from prominent positions in the courtroom. (Spelled with the "g," however, a "sergeant" might be a noncommissioned officer in the army or a police officer, as is the case in the United States.)

The rank of Queen's Counsel (or, if the sovereign is male, King's Counsel) is the highest to which a barrister may attain. Queen's Counsel barristers are distinguished by the silk gowns they wear in court (other barristers wear gowns of "stuff," or worsted fabric) and by the initials "Q.C." (or "K.C") appended to their names. The term "silk gown" or simply "silk" is used to refer to barristers of this rank.

At the height of many Victorian barristers' ambitions was that of becoming a judge. Tommy Traddles, David Copperfield's friend, goes through various phases of poverty as a law student and then as a "briefless barrister" (one who has no "brief" or summary of facts about a case upon which one is engaged—no business, in short), but by the end of Dickens's novel Traddles feels that his success is established and that a judgeship is in sight. Different kinds of judges were chosen from different ranks of barristers; common law judges, for example, must have reached the rank of serjeant.

SOLICITORS

The second kind of lawyer, besides the barrister, is the "solicitor," a label that for American readers may need some sorting out from other connotations. The word in this context has nothing to do with either door-to-door selling or prostitution. Rather, a solicitor is a lawyer but not a member of the bar; he may plead cases only in the lower courts. Most family lawyers in Victorian fiction are solicitors, guarding property, making wills, and drawing up marriage settlements. The word "attorney, when it occurs in Victorian fiction, is equivalent to the word "solicitor."

Unlike barristers, solicitors deal directly with the public, and, also unlike barristers, they may combine with other solicitors to form a law firm. Victorian novelists enjoyed inventing names for these: Affairs of property in Trollope's novels are conducted, interminably, of course, by the firm of Messrs. Slow and Bideawhile. Becky Sharpe in Thackeray's *Vanity Fair* retains for some of her dubious financial doings a firm called Burke, Thurtell and Hayes—an innocuous-sounding assemblage whose names Thackeray's original readers recognized as three of the country's most infamous murderers.

One became a solicitor essentially by being employed by a solicitor or a firm of solicitors as an "articled clerk" and by passing an examination. It was possible for a solicitor of at least five year's standing to become a barrister by passing an examination, but this course was not usual. The aspiring solicitor need not, and typically had not, attended a university; and in the view of the middle-class novel the solicitor occupied a slightly lower rung on the status ladder than did the barrister.

INNS OF COURT

Today's visitor to London should try to get at least a glimpse through the gateways of the Inns of Court. Much of the pleasant gardens and old gothic buildings are unchanged since Victorian times or much earlier times, and, if one can ignore the street traffic (a necessary step in trying to recapture nineteenth-century ambiance in any country), one can join the original readers of Victorian novels in envisioning the entrance of numerous youthful heroes into the legal profession.

In the nineteenth century the building not only housed the "chambers" or offices of barristers and other legal functionaries who went about their business in the various courts of London but provided the student with cheap and convenient, if not very elegant, places to live; "rooms in Gray's Inn," for example, is a fairly standard address for a bachelor in Victorian fiction. One did not have to be studying for the bar in order to live in one of the inns, and elderly gentlemen who had never bothered to move out formed part of the population. Mr. Overton, the narrator of Butler's *The Way of All Flesh,* is an example.

The four Inns of Court belonging to the legal societies that had the right to admit persons to the bar—the real Inns of Court—were loosely related to a number of Inns of Chancery, smaller operations for the most part rented out as barristers' or solicitors' chambers. Originally there were nine of them; those mentioned in fiction include Clements' Inn, Clifford's Inn, and Furnival's Inn, and here, too, in the same setting of courtyards and passages, elaborate gateways, narrow staircases, and many-paned windows, young Londoners-about-town might live.

DOCTORS' COMMONS

In the late 1850s, Parliament dissolved the ancient institution of Doctors' Commons, and the buildings they had occupied were taken down a decade later. Consequently, some Victorian novels allude to Doctors' Commons as an established fact of life while later ones are quite silent. Dickens's David Copperfield, in the earlier part of the century, becomes an articled clerk in Doctors' Commons; he first receives a quite good explanation of this body from his friend Steerforth (chap. 23) and then, as he comes to know the scene, gives the reader a vivid description of his activities (chap. 39).

The proctors (solicitors) of Doctors' Commons were concerned with the probate of wills, the issuing of marriage licenses (a dispensation from the necessity of having banns cried at church), and the earliest stages of the long, complex, and expensive proceedings required to obtain a divorce. In fiction, most allusions are to the marital doings. Thus a reference to "business at Doctors' Commons" naturally brings a blush to the cheek of the fictional bride-to-be. On the other side of the marital coin, for a husband to threaten "recourse to Doctors' Commons" is a dark hint at divorce.

THE ATTORNEY GENERAL
AND THE SOLICITOR GENERAL

The British attorney general is a high-ranking barrister, although, somewhat confusingly, the term "attorney" was by the nineteenth century used only for solicitors. The attorney general's function was (and still is) to manage all legal affairs in which the crown is a party. Both the attorney general and the solicitor general belong to the House of Commons; until the 1890s each was quite free to engage in private practice alongside his official duties. Sir Abraham Haphazard in Trollope's *The Warden* wears all three of these hats: He serves as attorney general, which to Archdeacon Grantly simply recommends him as the most impressive legal counsel available, the Harding case not involving the crown; he is active in the House of Commons, "on his legs, fighting eagerly for the hundred and seventh clause of the Convent Custody Bill" (chap. 16); and he takes on Mr. Harding as a private client, although, not surprisingly, he has difficulty finding time for an interview.

The British attorney general is not a cabinet member, although the official with the same title in the United States government is.

The solicitor general assists and ranks beneath the attorney general; he does not have any particular authority over the nation's solicitors.

MAGISTRATES

There are two sorts of Victorian magistrates. Those associated with the police courts, such as Dickens's Mr. Fang, who deals out a very rough sort of justice in *Oliver Twist* (chap. 11), were called "stipendiary" magistrates and were required to be barristers of considerable experience. As their name implied, they were paid for their work. The second type are sometimes called "justices of the peace" as well as "magistrates." In rural areas these were usually drawn from the landed gentry. The country squires and baronets encountered in Victorian fiction often serve as magistrates, receiving, like their real-life counterparts, no pay and sometimes having had no legal training at all. Their duties were to commit offenders to trial before a judge and jury or, in minor cases, to try and to sentence the offenders themselves. (A first poaching offense, for example, would usually be brought before the local magistrate or magistrates.)

British justices of the peace cannot perform marriages, as officials of the same name may in the United States.

LAWYERS IN FICTION

Especially in fiction, the law was one of the few things a middle-class Victorian gentleman could respectably do for a living. The other choices were to go into the church, to serve in the army (as an officer), and, just on the fringe, and only in the highest ranks of the medical hierarchy, to become a physician. (Best of all, of course, was the have no profession, simply to inherit a lot of land and live on it.) Trade, both wholesale and retail, banking, shipping, railroading, textile manufacturing—all the things hundreds of Victorians actually did and from which some of them became quite wealthy—made them nervous, especially at those moments when, ready for reassurance about the traditional values of the good old days, they sat down to read a novel.

The barrister-hero, then, was an eligible suitor for the hand of the young lady heroine. Like the curate-hero, whom he may resemble, he is often hindered from marrying the girl of his choice by lack of funds. And, again like the curate-hero, the barrister-hero is often well educated and of good family: an excellent catch if the financial problem can be solved by a lucky inheritance or simply an increase in practice. Trollope's Frank Greystock of The Eustace Diamonds is a typical figure. An atypical figure is Henry Lennox of Elizabeth Gaskell's North and South, who, though an eligible and fairly well off barrister, loses the girl to a northern industrialist. But Mrs. Gaskell is writing to prove several points, one of which is that northern industrialists have a claim to respectable middle-class roles.

In comparison to solicitors, the barristers who appear in fiction are understood to be socially superior. This distinction, in a subtle way, controls the friendship of Eugene Wrayburn and Mortimer Lightfoot, barrister and solicitor respectively, in Dickens's Our Mutual Friend. Victorian readers would know at once who is the prospective hero and who the sidekick, although the two seem to meet on equal terms at the beginning of the story. The familiar figure of the middle-aged solicitor, trusted guardian of the family funds but not quite a social equal, may be represented by Mr. Camperdown, also of The Eustace Diamonds and a good balance to Frank Greystock in the role of the young barrister. Trollope does, in another novel, show a young lady marrying a middle-aged solicitor, but the young lady is the snobbish Lady Amelia De Courcy, and the social discrepancy is part of a complex pattern of satire in which the reader feels that the solicitor, Mr. Gazebee, is the one to be pitied (The Small House at Allington). Again, Mr. Carlyle of Mrs. Henry Wood's East Lynn is a middle-aged solicitor who does turn out to be more or less the hero; the moral, though, is that his wife should have preferred her dependable, unexciting husband to the dashing army officer (another familiar stereotype) with whom she runs away.

LAWYERS IN DICKENS AND TROLLOPE

The outstanding fact about Dickens's lawyers is that most of them are villains. Jaggers of *Great Expectations* and Mr. Tulkinghorn and Mr. Vholes of *Bleck House* are pretty much of the deepest dye, morally obtuse, without human sympathies, dedicated to the maintenance of the status quo, which is for them so profitable: "The one great principle of English law is, to make business for itself" (*Bleak House*, chap. 39). Dickens's original readers saw his point but naturally put it into the context of their varied and complex surroundings and were unlikely to conclude, as a puzzled American reader might, that Dickens was advocating the overthrow of the legal system.

With his portrayals of lawyers' clerks, Dickens becomes more sympathetic—perhaps because the clerks themselves are in the grip of the lawyers. Dick Swiveller of *The Old Curiosity Shop* and William Guppy of *Bleak House*, with their impoverished but roistering friends, are incapable of manipulating their own lives, let alone anyone else's. Richard Carstone, who becomes an articled clerk while under the sway of Mr. Vholes, is a weak but sympathetic figure; and David Copperfield's short tenure as a clerk in Doctors' Commons comes across as a cheerful interval.

By contrast with Dickens, Trollope is kinder to lawyers of all degrees: Even the formidable Mr. Chaffanbrass, "than whom no barrister living or dead ever rescued more culprits from the fangs of the law" (*Phineas Redux*, chap. 57), becomes increasingly humane in his successive appearances in *The Three Clerks*, *Orley Farm*, and *Phineas Redux*. Trollope's main problem with his lawyers and legal episodes, as his original readers perceived it, was realism: Sometimes the drama of the courtroom was just not dramatic enough, and Trollope was accused of bending probability, or of not taking the trouble to find it out, for purposes of novelistic effect. In one instance Trollope circumvented criticism by obtaining from an actual solicitor the opinion concerning the disputed jewels ascribed to Mr. Dove in *The Eustace Diamonds* (chap. 25).

VI

The Army

To the present-day reader, the Victorian army as it appears in the fiction of the period has at least two odd characteristics. Its organization seems remarkably loose and informal, and it apparently consists entirely of officers.

The army's decentralized structure resulted from its historical origin as a collection of regiments, raised and sometimes maintained by individual commanding officers. Each regiment had its own uniforms, traditions, and reputation; its officers often had a sense of personal identification with their regiment and might, for example, at their own expense design and distribute regimental medals for bravery or good conduct. Most regiments were raised from single locations, so officers and men might have known one another from childhood. Characters in novels, consequently, quite realistically speak of "the regiment" as a present-day American might speak of "the army." The rest of the army, to the Victorian soldier, was simply all those other regiments.

The social difference between officers and what Americans would call enlisted men was roughly as large as that between a middle-class Victorian family and its servants. Very few enlisted men—with such exceptions as Dickens's Bagnet family in *Bleak House,* Sergeant Troy in Hardy's *Far from the Madding Crowd,* and Kipling's Sergeant Mulvaney and friends, these last near the turn of the century—appear as sympathetic or even rounded characters. Most are comic figures, suspected of seducing kitchen maids and consuming large amounts of food from the pantries of their sweethearts' unwitting employers. In real life, especially in the first half of

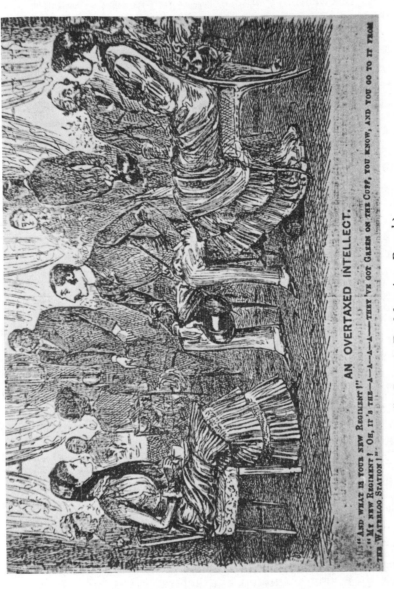

AN OVERTAXED INTELLECT.

"And what is your new Regiment?"
"My new Regiment! Oh, it's the —a—a— they've got Green on the Cuff, you know, and you go to it from the Waterloo Station!"

"An overtaxed intellect!" (George Du Maurier. Punch)

Officers' commissions were obtained by purchase, not by promotion, and while most officers would presumably have a clearer memory of the regiment they had just joined than does Du Maurier's rather inept specimen, the situation was close enough to real life to amuse the readers of Punch in 1882. The Army, however, increasingly felt that incompetent officers were no laughing matter, and the purchase system had been replaced by merit promotions by the end of the century.

the century, the ordinary soldier was an object not only of amusement but of fear on the part of the middle classes. The ranks were filled with desperadoes and vagabonds, forcibly captured by the army's "press gangs"; parish officials often cooperated with the press gang's raids by turning over to them men the parish wanted to get rid of. The duke of Wellington, commander of the British forces at the Battle of Waterloo, made a much-quoted remark to the effect that his men may or may not have frightened the enemy but they certainly frightened him.

THE PURCHASE SYSTEM

Until the 1870s, infantry and cavalry officers purchased their commissions from the government. One had to begin at the bottom, as an ensign (second lieutenant) in the infantry or as a cornet in the cavalry, and buy one's way up step by step as vacancies occurred and as one wished to make another step in one's investment. It was not necessary to stay in the same regiment while making these upwardly mobile purchases or "exchanges," as they were called since one had simultaneously to dispose of one's commission to the rank one was leaving behind. In time of war the situation was changed and officers might be promoted by merit. Another exception was made for students at the Royal Military College at Sandhurst, who were given commissions upon graduation.

To present-day Americans, the disadvantages of such a system are immediately obvious. The refusal of promotion to a good officer without money and the granting of promotion to any nincompoop with it seem calculated to undermine morale. Yet the purchase system did have some advantages. Many of the purchasers of commissions made good officers, proud of their regiments, supportive of their men, often providing them personally with the only small comforts available in a service in which the lot of the common soldier was abysmal. And the limitation of commissions to persons able to pay for them had the effect of keeping the army in the hands of the propertied classes; England was in little danger, unlike some other European countries in the nineteenth century, of a military coup headed by penniless officer-adventurers.

To leave the army, an officer might simply sell his commission, and to "sell out" in this sense had no negative connotation: No one was being betrayed. An officer who did not wish to sell out altogether might go on "half pay," withdrawing only from active service. This system worked as something of a retirement plan; the "half-pay officer," such as Dickens's Major Bagstock in *Dombey and Son* or Thackeray's Major Pendennis in *Pendennis* was a familiar figure in literature and life.

An officer's pay was quite low, especially in view of the fact that he had paid to get in. The low pay, like the purchase system itself, was left over from the earlier day when an officer had been essentially a recruiter and had been given what amounted to a bounty for every man he brought in; when the bounties were done away with, the pay was not raised to compensate for the loss. This fact, like the original purchase, had the effect of turning the officers' quarters into a kind of gentleman's club. Many young officers simply used the army as a fashionable social identity while they waited to inherit money or marry a wealthy woman, and in the meantime their pay might be augmented by an allowance from their fathers. Such men tended to sell out relatively early, so there was room on the lower rungs of the ladder for new candidates. Officers who made a lifetime career of the infantry or cavalry were those who particularly liked the life, whether or not they were any good at it, or who did not come into any money after all and found themselves stuck.

A MILITARY GLOSSARY

The definitions given here pertain essentially to the cavalry and infantry, since these are the services most frequently mentioned in Victorian fiction.

Company: in infantry, commanded by a captain, assisted by two to four (or more) lieutenants and ensigns. Composed of about one hundred twenty men. Eight to sixteen or more companies were included in a regiment.

Dragoons: originally infantry soldiers mounted for the sake of maneuverability. On arriving at the battlefield, they would dismount and fight on foot. During the nineteenth century the term often overlapped with the "heavy cavalry," trained for hard fighting in both attack and defense and trained especially in the charge.

Grenadier: originally a member of an infantry company especially trained to throw hand grenades. Unusually tall men were chosen for such training. When the hand grenade went out of use in the nineteenth century (to return in a more powerful form in the twentieth), the term "grenadier" came to be used for elite showpiece troops—extra tall.

Guards: "Household Troops," originally intended for the protection of the person of the sovereign. Preferred by fashionable young Victorians because these regiments did not normally leave the country; other regiments could be, and often were, sent to outposts of the empire for years at a stretch. Among the most prestigious Household Troops were the two regiments of Life Guards, a term that in any Victorian context should be associated by Americans with colorfully uniformed cavalry and not with the protection of swimmers. Well-known Household regiments included the Coldstream, Irish, Grenadier, and Scots Guards. The Household Troops, in their traditional uniforms, still protect the sovereign and perform the "changing of the guards" ceremony.

Hussars: light cavalry, trained in speed and maneuverability, especially useful for reconnaissance. Not usually used for heavy fighting—except when, as at Balaclava in the Crimean War, someone blunders.

Lancers: medium cavalry armed with lances used, rather surprisingly, throughout the nineteenth century. There

"Her Majesty reviewing at Woolwich the Royal Artillery returned from the Crimea"
(*Illustrated London News*)

Queen Victoria, confidently seated on a spirited horse, reviews the Artillery at Woolwich, near London, during the Crimean War. Since news photography was still in its infancy at the end of the century, current events were depicted by illustrators. This drawing appeared in the *Illustrated London News* in 1856.

were entire lancer regiments, and lances were often carried by the front rank of heavy cavalry formations.

Regiment: commanded by a colonel (sometimes by a lieutenant colonel). At the end of the century regiments consisted of two, three, or more battalions (each comprised of four to eight companies), as well as cooks, medical personnel, and so forth, attached to the regiment as a whole.

ARTILLERY, ENGINEERS, NAVY, and MARINES

The artillery and the engineers, both corps of the army, required in Victorian times more definite skills than did the infantry and the cavalry; consequently, officers in these corps held lower social prestige. Any outfit in which an individual's brains or other innate qualities could be more important than his family connections was bound to be suspect. Victorian readers thus accepted as quite realistic such artillery or engineer officers as Harry East, the protagonist's second best old school friend in Thomas Hughes's *Tom Brown at Oxford,* or Bernard Dale, a rural squire's nephew in Trollope's *The Small House at Allington*—sound, sensible, middle-class young men without much high-society glitter.

The artillery's big guns had great tactical importance in the era of the relatively inaccurate, short-range, smooth-bore muskets during the first half of the century; and for artillerymen to learn the correct placement and angle of fire for the guns was essential. Artillery guns with rifled barrels (grooved in spiral tracks on the inside) were developed in the 1850s, resulting in greater accuracy. But musket barrels were soon rifled also—the principle had been known for some time—and the infantryman's basic weapon became known as the "rifle." Artillery then became relatively less important, since a heavy gun cannot be as maneuverable as a group of infantrymen, until new types of projectiles, the time fuse and the shrapnel shell, were developed in the 1870s and put the artillery into the ascendant again. At all times, however, skill and ingenuity were required.

The engineers had to master the dual science of building up one's own fortifications and besieging or demolishing those of the enemy. The attention that had for centuries been focused on the art of siegecraft continued through the nineteenth century. Engineers also built bridges, surveyed and drew ordinance maps, and at the end of the century manned reconnaissance balloons and installed field telephones.

In order to attract and educate able men for these corps, the government early in the nineteenth century established the Royal Military Academy at Woolwich to train artillery and engineer officers. In neither corps were officers' commissions purchased, and promotion was consequently related to merit and experience.

The navy, despite its importance to the national defense, was a less usual middle-class career than the army, perhaps because its organization did not offer predictable advancement to anything like the same extent. In time of war, officers might win rapid promotion and cash bonuses by taking prizes—capturing or sinking enemy ships; Captain Wentworth, Anne Elliot's hero in Jane Austen's *Persuasion*, rises by this means. But at other times one could serve for years with no chance of promotion. The British, in fact, after the Napoleonic Wars took part in no major naval actions for the rest of the nineteenth century; and despite the nation's traditional supremacy at sea and such innovations as steam power and iron hulls, the navy remained something of a dead spot as far as the public image was concerned.

Another service the social status of which was dubious was the marines; the term in Victorian England denoted simply a soldier who served aboard ship. Generally, the Victorian marine was a matter-of-fact soldier who went about his duty in an unglamorous way. Sir Willoughby Patterne in Meredith's *The Egoist* is less than happy to welcome the "thick stumpy man," a middle-aged lieutenant in the marines who presents himself at Patterne Hall as Sir Willoughby's cousin (chap. 1); and although Sir Willoughby is a snob, his reaction may have seemed at least superficially understandable to the original readers.

THE ARMY OFFICER IN FICTION

In contrast to the curate and the barrister, both of whom usually appear in Victorian fiction (when destined to marry the heroine, at least) as upstanding and trustworthy, the army officer is at least potentially dangerous. Jane Austen's wicked Captain Wickham in *Pride and Prejudice,* who runs away with Lydia Bennet and has to be persuaded by a posse of the family's friends and relatives to marry her, did not surprise readers accustomed to this literary convention. Rawdon Crawley in *Vanity Fair,* who until his marriage indulges in gambling, drinking, and certain sexual escapades hinted at in chapter 30 and elsewhere, fits the image. George Osborne, serving in a less fashionable regiment and possessed of smaller means, imitates men like Rawdon as best he can. Captain Hawden in Dickens's *Bleak House* is the illicit lover of Lady Dedlock before her marriage and the father of Esther; and although he is not a deliberate villain, his profession makes the situation more plausible to the reader. And Hardy's Sergeant Troy in *Far from the Madding Crowd* is not a commissioned officer, but in this novel's reduced social scale he plays an officerlike role in his glamour and his seduction and abandonment of poor Fanny Robin.

However, there are some exceptions to this rakish sterotype. William Dobbin's role as an army officer in *Vanity Fair* is partly as a foil to George Osborne, yet he is himself a perfectly believable career soldier. And Jane Austen gives us a dependable officer and husband-candidate in Colonel Brandon of *Sense and Sensibility.*

Vanity Fair:
WATERLOO

Although Thackeray claims that as a novelist his "place is with the non-combatants" (chap. 30), his picture of the three-day Battle of Waterloo (June 16-18, 1815) does not violate historical fact. Napoleon's hastily gathered army met the combined forces of the Prussians under General Blücher and of the English under the duke of Wellington a few miles from Brussels. Napoleon, having caught his enemies by surprise in his first approach, was at first victorious in spite of the fact that he was outnumbered; but on June 18 the battle turned as Thackeray describes it at the end of chapter 32. George Osborne, lying dead with a bullet through his heart, was one of nearly sixty thousand men killed on the last day of the fighting.

Less dramatic aspects of the Waterloo chapters that may puzzle today's readers include such scenes as the officers' buying their own uniforms and swords (chap. 24); such equipment was not routinely issued. It was quite usual, too, for officers' wives to accompany their husbands' regiment not only to peacetime garrisons but actually to the battle or to the nearest city on the way. Thackeray's picture of socially whirling Brussels reflects historical fact, and the ball at which George Osborne drops a compromising note into Becky's bouquet is based upon an actual ball given on the same occasion by the duchess of Richmond.

The Life Guards, to which Rawdon Crawley belonged, ordinarily were not ordered to service abroad; the Battle of Waterloo was one of the few foreign actions in which they have ever served. Dobbin effectively expresses the extremity of the coming crisis when he tells George, "We're ordered to Belgium. All the army goes—Guards and all" (chap. 22).

The silver Waterloo medals by which old Mr. Sedley later recognizes veterans on park benches (chap. 37) were issued to all troops who took part in the battle and were an unusual phenomenon. Medals were not regularly issued for campaigns until the 1850s.

VII

Medicine

Few fields of human endeavor have changed so rapidly within the past hundred and fifty years or so as has that of medicine. Sound health care, accurate diagnosis of illness, and freedom from extreme pain are among our basic expectations of life; and our imaginations may feel a strain in trying to call up a medical picture that lacks so large a proportion of what we take for granted.

American doctors today are not only wealthy—to cite our culture's most immediate measure of status—but enjoy a personal aura, an almost priestly authority. In drama and fiction, the young doctor has become one of our most recurrent versions of the romantic hero—Byronic in his loneliness, his daring, his opposition to authority as represented by the older doctors with whom he comes in contact. And as a prospective husband for the fictional heroine, the young doctor is hard to beat.

This image represents a radical change from the past century. It is true that in the United States the medical doctor has always occupied a social position nearer to the top than he did in England simply because there was less top, so to speak; but in neither country in the early nineteenth century was he likely to be considered more than a competent practitioner of a dubious vocation. As the century progressed, this image shifted until in England it was just possible to include the highest ranks of physicians on the same social level with clergymen and barristers.

MEDICAL PRACTITIONERS
AND THEIR TRAINING

The Victorians recognized three ranks of medical men: the physician, who practiced internal medicine and prescribed drugs; the surgeon, who set broken bones, dug out bullets, and amputated limbs, performing all these acts well into the second half of the century upon fully conscious patients; and the apothecary, who prepared and sold drugs. The Royal College of Physicians, the Royal College of Surgeons, and the Society of Apothecaries, chartered bodies of ancient date, respectively oversaw these professions, gave examinations, issued licenses, and attempted to enforce standards.

A practitioner might be licensed in more than one of these capacities: Physician-and-surgeon and surgeon-and-apothecary combinations were frequent. Physicians, who did their best to make the art of diagnosis a mystique and prided themselves on their elegant bedside manner, tended to look down on their lower-ranking colleagues; and Trollope's Dr. Thorne, who "added the business of dispensing apothecary to that of a physician," incurs the scorn of medical Barsetshire (*Doctor Thorne*, chap. 3). Thackeray's senior Pendennis, an apothecary, is quite aware of the lowliness of his calling and abandons it as soon as he has made enough money to do so, buying a small estate and setting up as a country gentleman (*Pendennis*, chap. 2). But no illusion of modest behavior abashes Bob Sawyer of Dickens's *Pickwick Papers*, either as medical student or full-fledged apothecary; and Victorians encountering Sawyer's outrageous ventures in self-advertising, for example (chap. 38), may have confirmed their suspicions that from this class of medical man anything was possible.

Medical students' training shifted during the course of the century away from the old apprentice system, in which a young man was "bound over" to an established practitioner to assist him and learn his trade, toward the earning of specific degrees at accredited schools of medicine. Mr. Gibson, a country surgeon in Elizabeth Gaskell's *Wives and Daughters,* set in the first half of the century, quite plausibly keeps in his house "two 'pupils,' as they were called in the genteel language of Hollingford, 'apprentices' as they were in fact—being bound by indentures, and paying a handsome premium to learn their business" (chap. 3). An intermediate system appears in Dickens's *Bleak House* when young Richard Carstone enters the household of Mr. Bayham Badger on the understanding that Mr. Badger, a surgeon, will for a certain fee not only house and feed his protégé but will "superintend" his education, some of which will be obtained, presumably, at the hospital Mr. Badger attends in Chelsea.

Throughout much of the century, English medical training lagged behind that of the universities of Paris and of Edinburgh; these had attained preeminence in the study of anatomy and in the encouragement of research through the use of such new instruments as the microscope. In the 1830s the University of London was established, and its medical school soon became the best in England. Here Sherlock Holmes's friend Dr. Watson takes his medical degree, as he tells us, in 1878, and then "proceeded to Netley to go through the course prescribed for surgeons in the army" (Conan Doyle, *A Study in Scarlet,* chap. 1).

Today's readers might be reminded, incidentally, that the title "Doctor" did not have throughout the nineteenth century the particularly medical connotation it has today. Toward the end of the century the title became more usual for holders of medical degrees—as in the case of Dr. Watson—but at any earlier point a doctor was more likely to be the headmaster of a public school. For a medical practitioner in a novel to be called "Mr." does not reflect adversely on his standing or, rather, does not make it any lower than it already is.

THE BODY SNATCHERS

One of the reasons for the comparative backwardness of Victorian medical schools was quite simple—in the early part of the century students had great difficulty in obtaining human cadavers for dissection. Anatomy was taught with wax models, often small in scale, and the difference between these models and the real thing to the young surgeon confronted with his first case must have been considerable.

Yet to the English mind dissection was not only a revolting idea, clearly a desecration of the dead, but was troubling from a religious standpoint: How was one to assemble one's body for the Last Judgment if parts of it had been pickled in different bottles? Could the burial services medical schools said they gave to the remnants of the bodies actually be valid? Further, the old law in effect allowed dissection only of the bodies of persons executed for murder; the shame of dissection was in a sense added to the punishment for the crime, and this combination of ideas added to the average Englishman's horror of the whole prospect.

Medical students and the public were thus at cross-purposes. Since there were not enough executed murderers to go around and since medical students were willing to pay black market prices or to do the dirty work themselves, the result was that bodies were stolen from freshly made graves despite elaborate precautions—heavy iron grilles or "mort-safes" installed about the caskets, alarm systems, the hiring of guards to watch the graves. Nothing was foolproof. The surgeon Robert Liston, with the aid of a well-known "resurrectionist" (professional body snatcher) named Crouch, is said to have stolen the body of a hydrocephalic boy within a space of thirty minutes, even though a grave watcher was on duty.

The body-supplying business got out of hand in the notorious case of William Burke and William Hare, who, when they ran out of already-dead bodies, created their own by murdering the prospective subjects and selling them to anatomists in Edinburgh for sums of from eight to fourteen pounds. This case, along with rising pressure from medical schools and increased awareness on the part of the public of the need for medical students to learn firsthand about the human body, resulted in the early 1830s in an act of Parliament that greatly eased the situation. Bodies of the unclaimed poor in workhouses and hospitals were made available to anatomy students, and the trade of body snatching disappeared.

The popular image of the medical student and the experiment-prone doctor remained in the public mind a diabolical or even atheistic figure. Whether his knowledge of the mysteries of the body was obtained legally or illegally, there was something suspect in it. Mary Shelley's Dr. Frankenstein at the beginning of the century and Robert Louis Stevenson's Dr. Jekyll near the end of it make use of this stereotype as a starting point for fantasy. Even in the quite realistic novel, where a counterimage of the doctor as a trustworthy family attendant often prevailed, any undue professional curiosity could make the practitioner seem less upright. Hardy's Dr. Fitzpiers in *The Woodlanders* hints at the lightness of character he will later reveal by offering, early in the book, to pay old Grammer Oliver ten pounds for the right to dissect her brain after her death.

SURGERY AND CHILDBIRTH

The development of modern surgery provides one of the most dramatic differences between today and yesterday in the medical world. At the beginning of the century, neither anesthesia nor antiseptic procedures were known, and to present-day sensibilities a Victorian operating room would have many of the qualities of a sadistic nightmare. The majority of surgical operations were amputations of crushed, gangrenous, or tumorous limbs, performed on fully conscious patients held down by muscular attendants—often the medical students themselves. Since the best surgeons used their saws with great speed (Robert Liston, mentioned above as a determined dissector, was famous for the swiftness with which he could take off a limb), since methods of curtailing bleeding were understood, and since the wound was usually a clean one, patients often recovered from amputations. Operations requiring the opening of the body cavities were something else again. These were seldom attempted at all, and then only when the patient would have died in any case. Peritonitis usually set in and success was rare.

Anesthesia was first used for blocking pain in the 1840s, when an American dentist used ether to perform a painless tooth extraction. Considering the importance of the discovery, surgical practice was surprisingly slow to change its ways; anesthesia for operations became common only in the 1860s. The use of anesthesia during childbirth had a similarly slow acceptance. The pains of childbirth were thought to be ordained by nature and God (Genesis 3:6), and many felt it presumptuous to interfere. But ether was used in childbirth in the late 1840s, and in 1853 Queen Victoria gave birth to her eighth child, Prince Leopold, with the aid of chloroform and found the change very much for the better.

About twenty years passed between the introduction of anesthesia and the next major development, antiseptic surgical procedures, during which interval patients who had survived their operations died afterwards of infections. Joseph, Lord Lister, created a baron in recognition of his services to medicine, was in the 1860s the first to use carbolic acid in the treatment of surgical wounds. Lord Lister's operations, taking place in a cloud of carbolic acid steam, were so successful that his methods quickly became standard. Antiseptic procedures also saved the lives of many women in childbirth; puerperal fever (inflamation of the lining of the uterus) had killed thousands until it was learned that the midwife or doctor in attendance would do well to wash his hands.

VICTORIAN HOSPITALS

Hospitals in the nineteenth century were not at all a part of the middle and upper classes' ordinary way of life. Most people were born, underwent their illnesses, and died at home, cared for by their servants and members of their family under the direction of a local medical practitioner. The word "hospital" retained in many cases its older meaning of a charitable shelter for the poor; Hiram's Hospital in Trollope's *The Warden,* for example, had been established not for the medical care of its inmates but for the purpose of giving them a place to live.

Conditions in medical hospitals ranged, by present-day standards, from inadequate to abysmal. The army hospital in Sebastopol during the Crimean War, where soldiers with festering wounds lay for days on bare, rotting floors until the arrival of Florence Nightingale brought some degree of cleanliness and order, represents a low point. Medical hospitals in England improved slowly but fairly steadily, with an increasing emphasis on cleanliness for some decades before Lord Lister's discoveries provided a dramatic rationale. Municipal hospitals for the treatment of the sick (the poor sick) and of specific illnesses ("fever hospitals," for example) had been built throughout the eighteenth century and increased in number in the nineteenth; many of these hospitals were affiliated with the rapidly growing medical schools. For middle-class families, however, the idea of a hospital was a remote disgrace, like the parish workhouse. Betsey Trotwood's mysterious husband dies "in the hospital"—a disreputable end (Dickens, *David Copperfield,* chap. 54).

DISEASES AND PUBLIC HEALTH

Epidemic diseases familiar to the Victorians included typhoid fever, spread by the ingestion of particles of the feces of a human carrier of the disease (usually through the water supply), and typhus fever, spread by fleas. These two were not disentangled and their separate causes identified until the 1880s, and novelists sometimes confused them. The "typhus" that devastates Lowood School in Charlotte Brontë's *Jane Eyre* is more likely to be typhoid. Asiatic cholera, like typhoid, is spread by the ingestion of contaminated particles of human waste, but it is more virulent. During the nineteenth century, cholera appeared in terrifying epidemics, attacking

"Houndsditch" (Gustave Doré and Blanchard Jerrold,
    London: A Pilgrimage)

Everything is for sale. One of Gustav Doré's haunting engravings, published in 1872, of a poor street in London. Dickens'
Bleak House follows its characters into similar scenes of poverty—scenes which were in literature and life far from the experience of the typical middle class reader of novels.

rich and poor alike but, not surprisingly, doing most damage among the poor.

Effective preventive medicine developed only as people learned what to prevent. Some procedures, based on observation and guesswork, were effective for the monied classes that could afford to carry them out: Simple cleanliness would reduce the number of disease-carrying vermin, while the assumption that fever was caused by "noxious gases" from sewers and cesspools resulted in better constructed drains that could carry wastes farther from their point of origin and so decrease the likelihood of a contaminated drinking supply in the immediate neighborhood.

The poor in fact had little chance of escaping disease. Soap and water were often so expensive, in proportion to income, that anything like satisfactory cleanliness was impossible. In cities, human wastes went into cesspools dug under the houses or courtyards, from which seepage through the soil into nearby wells was easy: The more crowded the housing, the more likelihood of a merger between cesspool and well. The sewers that had been built simply poured raw sewerage into the nearest body of water—water dipped up in buckets by the poor and carried, untreated, into their houses. In the poorest sections, human waste was simply dumped into the streets, usually mixed with ashes and other household refuse, from which it was occasionally hauled away by "dustmen," who sold it for fertilizer. Conditions in rural villages were somewhat better: The poor lived in small, crowded cottages, often built adjacent to one another along the village street; and although the villagers were able to exchange diseases efficiently enough, their isolation often protected them from epidemics.

One major discovery in preventive medicine that had been made is that of vaccination for small pox, the result of the work of Edward Jenner in the late eighteenth century. When George Eliot's Dolly Winthrop advises Silas Marner to have little Eppie vaccinated (*Silas Marner*, chap. 14), she is not demonstrating a particularly advanced attitude for the first quarter of the nineteenth century; vaccination was by then so accepted that it took its place among Mrs. Winthrop's other items of folk wisdom.

TREATMENTS AND DRUGS

Victorian methods of treating disease show a mixture of common sense and superstition. Cleanliness and quiet, frequently recommended for middle-class patients, could hardly do harm. Bleeding, on the other hand, which seems to present-day readers a barbaric recourse, remained a quite matter-of-fact treatment for almost any complaint until the end of the century and beyond. A frequent method of bloodletting was to place live leeches on the patient's skin; and while the management of leeches was an art usually left to the medical practitioners, it was sometimes taught to unusually bright and responsible nurses. Leeches should be placed over a bony part of the patient's body so the bleeding can easily be stopped afterward, and they should never be pulled off but be allowed to fall away of their own accord. Leeches were sold in apothecaries' shops, often prominently displayed in large jars in the windows.

Wine, especially claret and champagne, was considered an effective medicine; the squire's lady customarily sent wine to any sick tenants on the estate, and physicians prescribed a glass or so daily for the invalids under their care.

Narcotic drugs, widely used in treating all sorts of diseases, were uncontrolled and could be bought fairly cheaply on the open market. Opium dens such as those described in Dickens's *The Mystery of Edwin Drood* (chap. 1) or Oscar Wilde's *The Picture of Dorian Gray* (chap. 16) were recognized by middle-class readers as part of the contemporary scene—a part they would be inclined to shun, not because such places were illegal (they were not) but because they were associated with low life and certainly did not fit the Victorian ideal of hard work, alertness, and vigor. Dr. Watson objects to Sherlock Holmes taking cocaine (Doyle, *The Sign of the Four*, chap. 1), but he seems satisfied with Holmes's explanation that he only indulges when there is nothing more interesting going on.

But even though opium dens were generally off limits, medicines containing narcotics were popular with the middle classes as well as with their social inferiors. Ladies were partial to Godfrey's Cordial and Batley's Sedative Solution, respectively preparations of morphine and opium. Nursemaids gave their charges narcotic soothing syrups to keep them from crying; a favorite was Daffy's Elixir, which Mrs. Mann cheerfully admits giving the parish orphans in Dickens's *Oliver Twist* (chap. 2) and which Amelia in Thackeray's *Vanity Fair* refuses to let her mother administer to little Georgy (chap. 38). This incident is presented as an example of Amelia's overdone maternal protectiveness; Victorian readers may have felt that she should have been more polite to her mother.

Some control of drugs was effected in the latter half of the century by laws regulating the sale of poisons. In the late 1860s, an act of Parliament forbade pharmacists to sell preparations of opium or morphine, along with other potentially poisonous drugs, to persons unknown to them unless the customer were introduced by a person who was known to them. Purchasers were required to sign for these drugs and to state the purpose for which they intended to use them. Unless someone in the purchaser's household died, however, the matter was investigated no further.

INSANITY

A useful thing to remember about insanity in the nineteenth century is that there were no public institutions for the constructive care of mental patients. The public lunatic asylums were more like prisons; their purpose was to prevent the inmates from harming the public and their care was of poor quality, to put it mildly. In middle-and upper-class families, the mentally ill were kept at home or in private asylums—usually quite expensive ones. Arrangements differed according to whether the patient was violent or simply moronic, but in either case the idea was to insulate him and to prevent his harming himself or others. Treatment or cure was seldom systematically attempted until the last decades of the century.

The number of those thought to be permanently insane in Victorian times thus included some whom we might consider temporarily incapacitated or might put into some other classification: victims of strokes, the educable retarded, mild manic depressives, or women afflicted with "puerperal mania," as mental disturbance after childbirth was often called. On the other hand, many Victorians whom we would see as badly needing help —the deeply distressed or anxious in particular—had to go on with their everyday lives because, not having seen hallucinations or foamed at the mouth, they were thought as capable as anyone else.

In the novels, Victorian readers found the treatment of the insane pretty much as it was in real life. Mr. Rochester's keeping his insane wife in the attic in Charlotte Bronte's *Jane Eyre*, was more plausible to the Victorians than it may be to us, though some of the original readers may have wondered why Mr. Rochester did not follow a frequent nineteenth-century custom and board his wife in a private asylum, perhaps somewhere in Europe. Lord George Gaunt in Thackeray's *Vanity Fair* is publicly presumed to be living in Brazil but is actually immured in a small house in the garden; this solution to a family embarrassment would not have been considered entirely farfetched. Neither was the prospect of being confined in a lunatic asylum by mistake or by someone's villainy, as occurs in Wilkie Collins's *The Woman in White*.

FIRST AID:
DROWNING

Today's fairly high level of awareness of first aid procedures has given readers a set of conditioned responses that should be put in abeyance when reading Victorian fiction.

Drownings are a particularly important example: When in Hardy's *The Return of the Native* three major characters are found floating about in Shadwater Weir (chap. 44/5.9) and none of their rescuers on fishing them out attempts to get the water out of their lungs and set them breathing again, today's readers are sometimes tempted to lose patience with the story. We should remember that lifesaving techniques as we know them are a fairly recent development.

The need to get drowning persons out of the water in the first place has, of course, always been apparent. The Royal Humane Society was established in the 1770s to set up life-saving stations supplied with poles and ropes and to give medals for those who rescued or tried to rescue drowning persons. (To the confusion of American readers, this humane society does not have anything to do with rescuing animals, although the R.S.P.C.A.—Royal Society for the Prevention of Cruelty to Animals—does.)

ILLNESS IN FICTION

It makes sense to assume that Victorian readers found the sudden illnesses, deaths in childbirth, and miscellaneous mishaps that so conveniently further the plots of their novels more plausibly aligned with everyday reality than these events seem to us. Readers who had spent long hours in their friends' and relatives' home sickrooms—since hospitals were avoided by the middle classes—might recognize symptoms: Oliver Twist's mother goes very pale and apparently dies of a hemorrhage immediately following the birth of her child (chap. 1); Mrs. Barton in George Eliot's "The Sad Fortunes of the Reverend Amos Barton" (in *Scenes of Clerical Life*) lingers several days after childbirth before dying of what the reader could thus assume to be puerperal fever. Pallor with a spot of red on each cheek signified tuberculosis or "consumption"; compound fractures or gunshot wounds were a serious matter, for "mortification" (unchecked infection and gangrene) could fatally set in. But in other cases the character simply sickens and dies or sickens and recovers with few symptoms or with confusing ones. Apparently the Victorian reader simply took what Providence dispensed in the way of bodily malfunctions in literature as in life.

Surgical operations appear in the Victorian novel hardly at all—a surprising omission in view of the potential for melodrama the operations certainly had. Perhaps such scenes were so far from the norm of middle-class experience that authors did not immediately think of them. Meredith's *Diana of the Crossways* includes an operation for what would appear, by the process of eliminating other possiblities, to be a breast or abdominal tumor: The operation lasts "about five minutes, four and a half" (chap. 26)—a necessary swiftness as the operation, correctly for the novel's setting in the first half of the century, is performed without anesthetic. The patient survives.

"Brain fever," a favorite affliction of heroines suffering an emotional shock—Catherine Linton of Emily Bronte's *Wuthering Heights* and Lucy Feverel of Meredith's *The Ordeal of Richard Feverel* are examples—is difficult to align with any present-day disease, though some form of encephalitis may have been given this label. The reading public and the medical world were unquestioningly confident of brain fever's real existence in mankind's catalogue of ills.

DOCTORS AS HEROES

The young doctor hero, so familiar today, appears in the Victorian novel only in a rudimentary form. Allan Woodcourt in Dickens's *Bleak House*, John Bold in Trollope's *The Warden*, and Edred Fitzpiers in Hardy's *The Woodlanders* have such heroic qualities as intelligence, self-confidence, and a desire to help the helpless. Yet their influence over others is obtained through their independent financial means or their good family connections; it does not come automatically because they are medical doctors. (Allan Woodcourt may be an exception here, since his mother's insistence on the excellence of his pedigree becomes a caricature and since he is esteemed for his medical skill. But his esteem, as Esther describes it, comes largely from the working classes, whom he would outrank anyhow.)

One Victorian figure who does display the passion for medicine that has become central to the doctor hero is George Eliot's Tertius Lydgate in *Middlemarch*. Lydgate in fact is so similar to the young doctors to whom we are accustomed in fiction and drama that the reader may need to remind himself of the differences between Lydgate's social setting and that of the present day in order to understand the extent and the irony of Lydgate's misfortune. The favorable impression Lydgate makes upon Middlemarch society is not due to his medical training, quite extensive for his period—he has served an apprenticeship with a country practitioner and then gone on to study in London, Edinburgh, and Paris—or his ambition to make important discoveries. What pleases the townspeople are Lydgate's manners, better, they feel, than those of most medical men, and the fact that he is the nephew of a baronet. The town beauty, Rosamond Vincy, is accordingly attracted to him in spite of the low prestige of his calling. "I do *not* think it is a nice profession, dear," is Rosamond's firm opinion of medicine, spoken some time after their marriage; none of Lydgate's attempts to make her see the importance of what he wants to do succeed in the least. This is the major conflict in Lydgate's life. Eventually Rosamond wins it, making the best of things by forcing her husband to become a fashionable doctor with a wealthy practice. To the original readers, Rosamond, though still rather villainous in her self-centered and obstinate way, might have been a more understandable character than she is to us; young middle-class girls had, after all, been conditioned to regard doctors as the opposite of a desirable catch.

NURSES IN FICTION

With the exception of members of religious orders devoted to the care of the sick, nurses for most of the nineteenth century were drawn almost exclusively from the lower classes. Dickens's gin-nipping Mrs. Gamp, one of the most memorable characters in *Martin Chuzzlewit,* represents a caricature of a type familiar to the original readers. Mrs. Gamp works as a private nurse and midwife, for neither of which occupations special training was considered necessary, and as a watcher of the dead, in this way uniting a number of functions the Victorians considered distastefully intimate. Mrs. Gamp's twelve-hour shifts, often sharing a round-the-clock job with her friend Betsey Prig (chap. 25), was part of the standard working conditions of the time, although one assumes that Mrs. Gamp was unusual in her habit of taking on two private patients simultaneously, going from one to the other and getting plenty of sleep on both shifts.

At the other end of the scale is Elizabeth Gaskell's Ruth of the novel of that name. Ruth takes up nursing after she loses a job as governess; since governessing was one of the few respectable occupations for women, the reader understands that Ruth has gone down in the world and that like Mrs. Gamp she can expect to enjoy no social prestige. Like Mrs. Gamp, too, Ruth has no training for the job, although she is complimented on her "gift of a very delicate touch" (chap. 29). But unlike Mrs. Gamp, Ruth has sweetness and integrity, and as she faces her troubles she also improves the fictional image of the nurse.

VIII

Farming and Rural Life

It is easy to overemphasize the importance of cities during the nineteenth century, since their dramatic growth and the problems they posed made up a phenomenon the English—or, in fact, the world—had never experienced on such a scale before. But we should not forget that the rural scene was still there and that it formed, as it had for centuries, the traditional and what often seemed the normal context for the kinf of life mirrored in the middle-class novel. The economic base was shifting from land to industry, but it did so slowly.

THE SQUIRE AND THE VILLAGE

The rural social unit traditionally centered around the "manor" or estate owned by the squire, who lived in the most impressive house on the property, the "manor house." The property usually included a number of separate farms, which the squire rented to tenants; and it sometimes included as well the entire nearby village—a street or two of small houses, shops, and an inn. The church and the parsonage did not belong outright to the squire, but since the presentation of the living (see chapter 4) often did, the effect was the same; the squire's landed property was in fact sometimes coterminous with the parish.

Socially and to some extent economically, the country village was often self-sufficient. Some villages remained isolated from the world far into the nineteenth century, especially if they had been by-passed by the main roads and the

141

newly built railroads. Hardy's description in *The Woodland-*
ers of Little Hintock, which only knowledgeable travelers
could find at all, represents an extreme case but one that
would not have seemed to contemporary readers beyond
belief.

LANDHOLDING

In theory, English law does not admit of absolute ownership of land. Under the feudal system, one held property as a
tenure under someone else; at the top of the pyramid, to
simplify the theoretical organization chart, is the king, holding his kingdom under God. I shall speak of freeholders as
owners, however, since by the nineteenth century the concept
of ownership had become an actual one in practice.

Freeholders owned their land in "fee simple," in absolute
possession or as close to this ideal as theory permitted; a
freehold belongs to the owner and his heirs forever. The
owner of a freehold cannot be put off it unless someone else
actually purchases the freehold in some way—as Heathcliff,
for instance, buys up the mortgage notes on Hindley Earn-
shaw's property in *Wuthering Heights*. Freeholders in the
nineteenth century represented what was left of the medieval
class of yeoman, men who worked a small landed estate but
ranked beneath squires and gentlemen. (The word "yeoman"
also refers to volunteer mounted troops, but this usage is not
related to landholding.)

Copyholders, by contrast, held their property on a permanent inheritable basis, but the property was legally part of a
lord's manor and some rent was paid. Copyholders occupied
what had been in the medieval world the class of the villeins,
ranking below the yeomen; villeins tilled their lords' fields
but were given successive life rights to a patch of ground for
themselves. Several acts of Parliament during the nineteenth
century allowed copyholders to be turned into freeholders, to
the improvement of (among other things) the forestry.
Copyholders were not allowed to cut timber on their holdings,

the timber rights belonging to the lords of the manor, and copyholders consequently had little incentive to plant or care for trees.

A closely related category of landholding, that of "life leasing," is an important part of the underpinnings of several Hardy novels and will be discussed below with reference to them.

LANDLORDS, TENANT FARMERS, AND LABORERS

To many Americans the term "tenant farmer" has a connotation of subsistence-level poverty that does not apply to the term as it is used in the English novel. The tenant farmer in Victorian England was often quite prosperous, though usually he did not rank with the gentry. Mrs. Lookaloft in Trollope's *Barchester Towers* is trying hard to close the gap (chap. 35-36); the humor of the scene depends upon the fact that her chances are pretty poor. Tenant farmers leased their land from the squire or from a nonresident landlord if there was no squire, often on a fixed-term basis. The Poysers in George Eliot's *Adam Bede* follow a quite usual practice, holding their farm on successive three-year leases from Squire Donnithorne.

The farm laborer was hired by the tenant farmer, and it is in the farm laboring class that we find the starkest levels of rural poverty. The laborer was the first to be affected by bad times, and he had few resources to tide him over them. A laboring family's diet was often made up of coarse bread, potatoes and other vegetables grown in the small plot attached to their cottage, and "drippings" (grease from roasted meat, bought from a middleman who acquired it from the kitchens of the better off). A country squire who voluntarily sent his drippings to be distributed among the laboring poor was considered a model of charity.

The squire was responsible for repairs to his farm buildings and fences, a responsibility he carried out to the greater or less satisfaction of his tenants, depending on his own

"TRIAL OF STEAM-PLOUGHS NEAR FARMINGHAM, KENT" (*Illustrated London News*)

An agricultural experiment: steam-powered plowing. The steam engines themselves were too heavy actually to move about the fields, so the plows were connected to them with lines and pulleys. Steam powered farm machinery was described by Thomas Hardy, in Tess of the d'Urbervilles, as an inharmonious intrusion upon nature.

priorities and the funds at his disposal. The squire was traditionally local and resident, his daily life made of much the same fabric as that of his tenants. In the Victorian novel, this figure typically represents a benevolent and natural order of things. The nonresident landlord, one who had bought up the estate as an investment and had no intention of living on it, increased in numbers during the Victorian period and was often considered a sign, or even a cause, of bad times.

The word "cottage," incidentally, had acquired by the nineteenth century two distinct connotations. The farm laborer's cottage was often small, damp, dark, and unsanitary, and the word might almost mean "hovel." But the term had also come into use as a small, tidy dwelling, quite picturesque, in the country or near the sea, occupied by members of the middle or lower-middle classes and not by farm laborers. Today's novel readers, like the original ones, must sort out the meanings according to the context. In *Sybil,* Disraeli describes "narrow and crowded lanes formed by cottages built of rubble. . . . The gaping chinks admitted every blast" (chap. 9/2.3). But when Mrs. Dashwood and her daughters in Jane Austen's *Sense and Sensibility* go to live in a rural cottage, they find their new home to contain two sitting rooms and four bedrooms (chap.6).

CROPS AND FARMING METHODS

The English farm was descended from the feudal domain in which fields were divided into narrow strips to be farmed by the lord's villeins, some for the lord's benefit and some for their own. By the nineteenth century, most of the old strips had been consolidated; the fields were comparatively large and were almost always individually fenced, sometimes with stone walls or hedges, whether used for crops or for pasture.

Major field crops were wheat (often referred to as "corn"), barley, and hay. Although the earlier practice had been to exhaust the land with successive grain crops and then to let the fields lie fallow until they recovered, by the nineteenth century the system of rotating grain with turnips or clover, both used to feed cattle, was established. Livestock consisted largely of cattle and sheep, the latter grown both for mutton and wool. The textile mills of northern England imported wool because the country did not grow enough, but an English farmer could sell all the wool he produced. Pigs and chickens were kept, though on a small scale. Draft animals included oxen, used mostly for plowing, and horses, which were more versatile. Garden vegetables were not grown on a large scale, although there were commercial market gardens on the outskirts of London. Since the public knew nothing about vitamins until after the turn of the twentieth century, eating vegetables was a matter of taste rather than of dietary prudence.

Agricultual improvements were stimulated during the nineteenth century by England's rapidly increasing population and a consequent pressure to increase the yield of the land. Boggy fields could be drained by a number of means, from digging open trenches to installing an elaborate system of buried pipe tiles (half-cylinders of clay put together into tubes into which the water seeped from the soil and was carried away by gravity before it could seep out again). Drainage counteracted the wetness of the English climate and caused such dramatic improvements in yield that many landlords were enthusiastic about it, despite the initial expense of the tiles. Elizabeth Gaskell's Squire Hamley in *Wives and Daughters* is old-fashioned in many ways but goes in heavily for tile drainage (chap. 30). A series of parliamentary acts in the latter half of the century allowed property holders to obtain loans at low interest for field drainage and other improvements.

Farm machinery gained in popularity during the century, but slowly; farm work is not as easily mechanized as, say, textile weaving. Plows were continually improved; the McCormick reaper was the first successful harvesting machine at about mid-century and was followed by various forms of reaper-binders. Horse-drawn contrivances for cutting, turning, and raking hay had become common by the end of the century. Steam power was sometimes used for such special operations as threshing and, more rarely, plowing—the latter a complex operation in which a plow was hauled along the furrows by cables attached to one or sometimes two steam engines or steam-propelled tractors. Hardy describes the steam engine used to drive the threshing machine in *Tess of the d'Urbevilles* with disapprobation: Neither it nor its operator harmonizes with the landscape, and the machine does not make the laborers' task easier but rather forces them to work at its own rapid and unwearying pace.

AGRICULTURAL TROUBLES

The unrest that characterizes much of the nineteenth century's changing economic scene did not leave the rural districts in peace. Before the repeal of the high tariffs on imported grain (the "corn laws") in the 1840s, local harvest conditions could mean riches or ruin for farmers and grain dealers, a state of things Hardy portrays in *The Mayor of Casterbridge.*

The most immediate sufferers from agricultural depressions were the hired laborers and their families, lowest on the economic totem pole, to whom unemployment could mean starvation. Their anger was frequently if illogically directed against the tenant farmers who had not hired them (usually because they could not afford to), and this anger often took the form of destroying the farm buildings and stock. Kingsley describes such a scene in chapter 28 of *Alton Locke.*

Another cause of resentment among farm laborers and the rural poor in general was the landlords' practice of "enclosing" or fencing in the "commons" (uncultivated land traditionally allowed to tenants of cottages for grazing their stock and gathering firewood) in order to convert them into fields or pastures for their—the landlords'—own use. Courts occasionally upheld the claim of villagers to such land, especially if the villagers were technically copyholders of the manor and thus had an ancient right to the manorial common; but more

his farmers happy, there is no hope of the Durbeyfields's obtaining any sort of renewal of their lease. The relentlessly modern world has thus thrown out the last remnants of the d'Urberville family, once owners of all the land in sight, to wander homelessly about on it.

Giles Winterborne in *The Woodlanders* has a similar but more complex landholding problem. The rights to a lease held under a sequence of lives have been transferred to him, but the length of the lease is still determined by the original lives. Winterborne's mother, a member of the South family, had been given these rights as a marriage portion and thus took the holding out of the family, even though the lives determining the length of the lease were still Souths. On her death, Mrs. Winterborne left the rights to her son; the holding includes several houses in the village of Hintock, the rental for which has formed the major part of Winterborne's income. The final life by which the lease is held is that of old South, Marty's father, who at the time the novel opens is ill enough to make Winterborne aware of the probably short span of prosperity remaining to him. An old document among his papers seems to offer hope in a way that can be explained more efficiently by Hardy himself than by a paraphrase:

> It bore a remote date, the handwriting being that of some solicitor or agent, and the signature the landholder's. It was to the effect that, at any time before the last of the stated lives should drop, Mr. John Winterborne [Giles's father], or his representative, should have the privilege of adding his own and his son's life to the life remaining on payment of a merely nominal fine; the concession being in consequence of the elder Winterborne's consent to demolish one of the houses and relinquish its site, which stood at an awkward corner of the lane, and impeded the way.
>
> The house had been pulled down years before. Why Giles's father had not taken advantage of his privilege to insert his own and his son's lives it was impossible to say.... (chap. 14)

Giles does not get around to having the lease extended to the end of his own lifetime before old South, "the last of the stated lives," dies. On asking the present landlord, Mrs. Charmond, to honor the agreement even though the time to act upon it has lapsed, he receives a negative reply: Mrs. Charmond intends to pull the houses down. Giles thus "loses his houses," as the characters put it, and, through his consequent lack of means, loses his chance to marry his childhood sweetheart, Grace Melbury.

IX

The Industrial Scene

Those works of nineteenth-century fiction concerned with industry are much taken up with the question of reform. This is a natural emphasis and a dramatic one. Victorian reformers dealt with a situation that had come into being without planning and the total picture of which not only the general public but the government and the industrialists themselves often did not see. The Industrial Revolution was unique. Nothing like it had happened before and the few decades between, say, the development of the steam engine at the end of the eighteenth century and the spread of factories over the north of England did not give the public time to find out what was going on, let alone make the kind of ethical realizations that, in slow and often discontinous patterns, became a significant part of the age. The right of employers to pay the lowest wages for which they could find takers had never been seriously questioned. The propriety of government interference in trade, to regulate working hours and enforce safety standards, was a new concept that, not surprisingly, went against the natural impulses of the factory owners in particular and of a large proportion of the upper and middle classes in general. The fact that reform movements achieved the success they eventually did is a credit to Victorian moral consciousness and energy.

The textile industry

It was in textiles that Britain first developed and held a world market. Raw cotton was imported from the United States and India to be woven into the calico, muslin, and other inexpensive fabrics that formed the bulk of the trade. Wool was partly homegrown, partly imported (especially from the British colonies of Australia and New Zealand); flax came from Ireland, Europe, and Russia; raw silk came from Europe and the Orient. Textile goods were sold in virtually every corner of the globe in which British merchants could get foothold. China, India, and Turkey became particularly important markets.

For several reasons, the textile industry was the focus of the nineteenth-century series of reform movements. As the first of the spectacular successes, it had, so to speak, a great deal of publicity; people were aware of the industry, no matter how obscure the living conditions of the workers may have been. Many textile mills were highly visible buildings, quite large, lighted by gas during the night shifts—"fairy palaces," to quote Dickens's ironic description in *Hard Times*—and within them was an easy-to-understand employment hierarchy: Owners, supervisors, and workers were distinguishable in a way many smaller and more complex industries did not permit. Official inspections and reports were more feasible here than elsewhere. Consequently, much of the country's reform legislation spoke specifically to the textile industries: Safety regulations and restrictions on child labor and on working hours were passed and enforced in the mills before spreading into the more elusive quarters of the industrial landscape.

Mining and ironworking

The textile mills ran by steam power, and the boilers of the steam engines burned coal. Since the most valuable coalfields were in Wales and northern England, the mills that

"Over London—By Rail" Dore shows the teeming slums, many of them newly-built by speculative investors, into which the cities' rapidly increasing populations were packed by the roomful. These houses had at least some space at the rear; others were built literally back to back.

sprang up near Manchester and Liverpool benefited from cheaply transported fuel. (Liverpool's increasing importance as a port, unloading cotton and loading textiles and other exports, was, of course, a factor in this choice of site.) Thus milling and mining might overlap within a single district: Dickens's Stephen Blackpool walks out of a cotton mill and falls, plausibly enough in terms of geography at least, into an abandoned mine shaft (*Hard Times*, chap. 34/3.6).

Coal mining was the most prevalent of underground operations, although the individual mines were usually small. Some were simply open pits, worked until the vein gave out. In underground mines, shafts and tunnels were often low, narrow, and steep; carts (in the early part of the century often drawn by women or children) took the coal to the main shaft, where it was hauled to the surface by horse-drawn rope-and-pulley contrivances or by steam engines.

Ventilation in the early mines was effected by furnaces installed at the bottom of the main shaft, which, when properly regulated, sucked in fresh air. The danger of such a furnace in a mine with pockets of coal gas may be imagined. Candles were used for lighting, under similar hazards, until the invention of the safety lamp—a metal case perforated with small holes through which the coal gas would not go, containing a candle.

Mining for iron ore was essentially similar to mining for coal. During the railway boom of the 1830s and 1840s, the industry grew considerably and developed new techniques. The Bessemer steel-making process, which came into use in the late 1850s, resulted in still greater growth.

Workers in iron and steel formed something of an elite: They were highly skilled, commanded sizable wages, and were fewer in number so that trade fluctuations in the iron industry, though quite capable of causing hardship, were less devastating than depressions in the textile or coal industries.

RAILWAYS

The coming of the railways changed the face of the land and changed the way of life of virtually every middle-class and urban inhabitant of Britain. Towns on the railway thrived; those far from the railway withered. The stagecoach disappeared overnight. Everyone took the train; even the working-class heroine of Elizabeth Gaskell's *Mary Barton*, whose family had walked from city to city in earlier times, makes a train journey, which for the original readers added to the realistic atmosphere of the book (chap. 26). The Toodle family in Dickens's *Dombey and Son*, finds the railway a source of new and welcome prosperity, while their run-down neighborhood, invaded by tracks and steam, becomes in Dickens's description a kind of temple to modern progress (chap. 15).

The first passenger line was the one Mary Barton rode on; it connected Liverpool and Manchester and opened in 1830. The great boom of construction then began, accurately reflected in the novels. George Eliot describes a conflict between a party of railway surveyors and a group of suspicious farm laborers (*Middlemarch*, chap. 56), and Trollope shows us in Sir Roger Scatchard (*Doctor Thorne*) the metamorphosis of a lower-class stonecutter into a wealthy baronet through the agency of a talent for railway contracting. The laborers who excavated the new lines, cutting through the high places and building up the low places, were called "navvies," short for "navigators," a nickname they had acquired during the building of the elaborate system of canals that preceded the railway era. The word "navvy" still denotes a laborer with pick and shovel. Picks and shovels were virtually the only tools with which the hundreds of miles of lines were dug; today's giant earth-moving machines had not been developed, and a work site looked like an anthill with swarms of toiling workers.

Like many parts of the nineteenth century industrial picture, the new network of railways did not cover the country according to some preset plan. Instead, competing companies built and ran their own lines between specific destinations, with a number of natural but inefficient results. Some routes were virtually duplicated in competition for passengers; rails were laid in different widths, using, of course, different rolling stock, and the development especially of efficient freight transportation was hindered until all the companies could agree on standard measurements. And, since each company built its own terminal in London from which passengers departed to wherever that particular company would take them, passengers coming into London on one company's trains and leaving on another's had to make an additional journey across town—a situation that still obtains. There were some advantages in the competition, however. An obvious one is that each company tried to outdo the others in service. (See chapter 14 below for a more detailed passenger's-eye view of the railways.)

LIGHT INDUSTRY: "SWEATING"

Much Victorian industry was literally hard to find. The manufacture of such objects as knives, nails, and pins, for example, frequently involved a series of middlemen who bought raw materials, sold them to workers, and bought back the finished product. The worker was expected to provide his own workroom (perhaps a corner of the cellar where he lived). The children of the working classes were quite at the mercy of their elders, and four- and five-year-olds might sit all day plaiting straw hats, basting hems, or making artificial flowers in order to bring in a few pennies a week.

Even when manufacturing was carried on under one roof, the organization was sometimes odd by present-day standards. The proprietor of a factory building might, instead of hiring workers, lease floor space and the power of his steam engine (which power was carried along the ceilings by rotating cylinders and transferred to the machines by leather belts) to what were in effect independent entrepreneurs, turning wooden table legs or cutting metal screws to fill contracts they had obtained on their own. Such establishments were difficult for Parliament to regulate with regard to working hours or safety standards, since the line between employer and employee was blurry.

Especially guilty of exploiting its economically helpless workers was the sewing and tailoring industry. Workers might sew in a tailoring or dressmaking shop, making clothes to the order of the shop's customers, or they might do piece-work at home; in either case earnings were abysmally low and the work was hard on the eyes. A system of "sweating" or subcontracting work in what could seem endless hierarchies until the person who actually did the work received only a fraction of what the middlemen were paid for a garment was prevalent. A middleman who hired out such work was called a "sweater," and his place of business was a "sweat shop." With the appearance of various types of sewing machines in the 1860s, garment work became more centralized and began to resemble textile weaving or other industries in which specific work is done in a specific place. The gaunt seamstress stitching away in her cold attic room became a less common phenomenon, but long hours and low earnings were still standard.

In Victorian fiction, the seamstress and tailor receive more attention than other types of piece workers, perhaps because the middle-class readers were more aware of clothes than of, say, nailmaking. Elizabeth Gaskell's *Ruth* and *Mary Barton* depict the lives of hardworking seamstresses. Kingsley's *Alton Locke* has a tailor for a hero and includes some scenes of "sweating" operations that horrified his readers: At one point, a "sweater" has literally captured a houseful of tailors, who stitch hopelessly away, getting more and more in debt to their employer for room and board but unable to escape because the only respectable portions of their clothing have been put in pawn by their employer (chap. 21).

WORKERS' LIVING CONDITIONS

Housing for the working class was basically of two kinds: middle-class houses grown dilapidated as the original tenants move to more fashionable parts of town or even to the suburbs and houses especially built for working-class occupation. The newly built houses, run up by speculators, were flimsily built, packed together side by side and back to back, with little ventilation (the window tax, levied since the seventeenth century on what then seemed an architectural luxury, was not repealed until the early 1850s). The older houses had been more sturdily built to begin with, but the owners had no interest in keeping them in repair and many were literally rotting.

Most working-class districts had no indoor plumbing: Water had to be carried in pails from an external and often distant source; human waste was thrown into the ditch or "kennel" that ran down the middle of the unpaved street, to be carried slowly down to the next block. Crowding was extreme: Houses were rented by the room and some tenants sublet their rooms by the corner. Basements and attics were full, despite dirt floors in the one and leaky roofs in the other, and a density of eight to ten people in a room was not unusual. Candles, even the cheapest kinds, and fuel for heating were often beyond the reach of the occupants. Under such limited recreational conditions, the popularity of gin, opium, and incest, not necessarily in that order, reinforced the prejudice of the comfortably-off that the working classes were a naturally low order of beings upon whom improved living and employment conditions would be wasted. Novelists sympathetic to the plight of the poor tried to show this environment as something the workers could not help and would change if they could, and descriptions of quite appalling interiors often have this motive.

INDUSTRIAL REFORM:
WORKING HOURS AND SAFETY

One of the earliest acts that attempted to regulate conditions in textile mills was the Health and Morals of Apprentices Act of 1802, which tried to protect the pauper children
working in the mills, theoretically as apprentices but in practice as little more than slaves, by forbidding employers to
work them longer than twelve hours a day. (The "morals" part
of the children's needs was to be supplied by religious instruction in the mills.) In the 1830s a bill limited children under
eleven to nine hours of work a day and provided as well for
systematic inspection as an aid to enforcement. In 1844,
women's daily working hours were limited to twelve, and an
act of the same year required factories to give workers compensation for preventable injuries due to unfenced machinery—an act that resulted, as was intended, in safer design. In
1847 came the long-sought "Ten Hours Bill," which made a
working day of that length standard for both sexes and all
ages.

Meanwhile, the less easy to inspect industries were being
regulated at a slower rate. Women were forbidden to work in
mines, though they would still work in open pits, by an act of
the 1840s that also kept boys under ten above ground. (Quite
young boys had been useful for opening and closing the doors
of the draft furnaces that pulled fresh air into the mines, for
tending donkeys and ponies stabled underground, and for
other chores.) Safety provisions were of obvious importance
in mining and were legislated frequently in the second half of
the century. Some smaller industries officially described as
"dangerous and unhealthy," such as potteries and lucifer
match factories, came under various degrees of control in the
last decades of the Victorian era.

CHARTISM

This political movement was to the middle classes almost, although not quite, as terrifying a sign of a disastrous social upheaval as the trade unions. "Chartism" referred to the "People's Charter" drawn up by the Working Men's Association, a group headed by the radical politician Feargus O'Connor and his newspaper, the *Northern Star*, in 1838. The Chartists felt that the Reform Bill of 1832 had not gone far enough and listed among their demands "manhood suffrage" (the extension of the vote to all male citizens of lawful age); the abolition of property requirements for and the payment of a salary to members of Parliament, both of which were necessary if working men were ever to give up their jobs and become legislators; the secret ballot, advocated on the ground that working-class voters could not otherwise escape intimidation; and annually elected parliaments, permitting closer control of national policy by the electors. Several of these points have now become political fact, but they were disturbing in the 1830s.

Even more disturbing to the middle classes was the advocacy by some Chartists of voilence as a way to make their policies known. O'Connor's *Northern Star* consistently advocated open sedition; when the heroine's father is seen reading this paper in chapter 8 of Elizabeth Gaskell's *Mary Barton*, the contemporary reader was expected to feel a presentiment of violence to come.

Two of several large-scale Chartist meetings are occasionally mentioned in fiction. Both were held in London, one in 1839 and the other in 1848, and both presented or attempted to present a petition to Parliament. That of 1839 was comparatively small, and neither the fifty official delegates nor the petition they brought was given any recognition by Parliament. It is this meeting that was attended by Mary Barton's father (chap. 9). In 1848, more elaborate doings were announced: The organizers planned a parade of five hundred thousand Chartists to march from Kennington Common, on the south side of the Thames, to Westminster to present to

Parliament a petition containing, it was said, six million signatures. Riots were expected; the royal family went to the Isle of Wight; soldiers were placed in readiness in public buildings; and thousands of citizens enrolled themselves as special constables. The result was something of a debacle: The crowd was quite small; it rained; and the procession was stopped by the police. The petition, when examined, turned out to contain numerous forged signatures, with that of the ultraconservative duke of Wellington a particular favorite. Chartism as a movement did not survive this embarrassment, although many of its principles lived on. In *Alton Locke*, published only two years after the Chartist meeting of 1848, Kingsley focuses in close-up detail on what to his original readers were quite recent events.

TRADES UNIONS

Victorian novels follow contemporary usage in speaking of "trades" unions, in the plural rather than the singular form to which Americans are accustomed. Such unions were also called "combinations," and in the early days of the century they were, as they had been through the history of English common law, thoroughly illegal. Working men who attempted to stipulate the wages they would accept or the number of hours or other conditions under which they would work could be found guilty of conspiring in restraint of trade and could be transported to Australia or to other penal colonies.

In 1824 Parliament, on the advice of a committee it had formed to investigate the antiunion "combination laws," repealed such laws on the ground that they did not serve their purpose and instead increased distrust and violence. But in the following year Parliament repealed the Act of 1824, so in a sense the situation was as it had been. It was now permissible, however, for working men to meet to discuss the hours, wages, and so forth that they would accept; only if they tried to force their employers to accept their decisions by means of threats, violence, or strikes did they become liable to punishment. Trades unions thus existed in a curious dimension: They were unlawful but not criminal. Workers could join them, organizers could travel about the country and talk about them safely enough, but if a union did something that could be interpreted as restraint of trade, its members became conspirators in the eyes of the law. This situation continued until the last quarter of the century, when Parliament legalized the trades unions and provided that no person might be prosecuted for conspiring to commit an act that would not be criminal if he did it by himself.

To the novelists and their middle-class readers, trades unions embodied the worst of their secret fears of a great revolt of the masses. The secret meetings, the conspiracies to do violence, and in particular the initiation ceremonies appear in the novels in an atmosphere that is quite diabolic: "Then came one of those fierce terrible oaths which bind members of Trades Unions to any given purpose" (Gaskell, *Mary Barton,* chap. 17). Since the early unions were helpless in many ways, secrecy and a certain amount of mysterious panoply were helpful in their attempt to survive, and the fictional ceremonies are realistic to some extent.

THE VICTORIAN "PROBLEM NOVEL"

Today's readers are fortunate to have a characteristic in common with the original readers of those Victorian novels that dealt with the problems of a society enmeshed in the consequences of the Industrial Revolution. Neither we nor the original middle-class reader is familiar with the daily life of the Victorian working classes. As a result, the novelists' descriptions and explanations continue to serve their purpose and we are able to understand the fictional goings-on more easily than we otherwise might.

These novels have in common an awareness of the sufferings of the working classes and an earnest, missionarylike desire to make the facts known and to get something done. Most of the fictional protagonists are educated members of the middle class, persons the reader could identify with, who happen to come into contact with the working classes. Charlotte Brontë's *Shirley*, Dickens's *Hard Times*, Disraeli's *Sybil*, Elizabeth Gaskell's *North and South*, and Kingsley's *Yeast* follow this pattern. Gaskell's *Mary Barton* and Kingsley's *Alton Locke* are exceptional in that each focuses almost exclusively on the working-class characters. In addition, many novels dealing primarily with the middle classes include episodes that dip sympathetically into the lower strata; Dickens's *Bleak House* is an example.

As stark and sordid as much of the description of the characters' lives may appear to us and as it appeared to the original readers, statistics and other objective sources show that these passages are realistic and might, in fact, have been even grimmer without exaggerating cases actually on record. However, two other aspects of the "problem" novel are frequently out of accord with reality: the extraordinary purity and goodness of the working-class characters and the solutions the novelists put forward to cure the ills they have described.

The first warping of reality is easily understandable. To earn the sympathy of the middle-class reader, especially if he is predisposed to consider the working classes as little better than animals, a character must seem unquestionably deserving: highly ethical, refined in natural sensibilities, and often remarkably well spoken. (Working-class characters in this type of novel sometimes occupy two distinct categories: the high-minded elite, so to speak, and the earthier, dialect-speaking "comic relief" figures, similar to the traditional rustics of fiction and drama.) Today's reader is more likely to be annoyed by this overdone purity than the Victorians were; fashions in the psychology of fictional characters have shifted.

The second discrepancy between the problem novels and reality, the vagueness or glibness of the formulae put forward by the author to solve the problems the book has depicted, results from a number of factors. One is that the author was emotionally committed to presenting his readers with a solution the reader could understand and accept—a goal that, from the complexity of the nineteenth-century industrial scene, would seem to preclude reality right there. A reversion to the simpler practices of the good old days or the cultivation of some quality intrinsic to right-minded individuals were ideas with great attraction. Thus Charlotte Brontë in *Shirley* shows the parish ladies saving unemployed workers and their families from starvation by making up a collection of food baskets; Dickens continually implies that social ills can be cured by the goodness of the human heart; Disraeli suggests that the poor should trust the aristocracy to do what is best for society; and Elizabeth Gaskell in *North and South* feels that better communication beween masters and men is the answer—that workers would not resent being laid off during a recession if they knew the economic facts of the case. Unsatisfactory as these solutions may be, they should not distract the present-day reader from the fact that the problem novels did have in large measure the results the authors intended. They did help awaken the middle classes to the conditions in which the working poor lived, and they made the public more receptive to reformers' attempts to relieve this distress.

X

Servants

Despite the Industrial Revolution and the increasing opportunities to work in factories, a large proportion of the nineteenth-century working classes continued to "go into service" (become domestic servants). The census of 1851 listed over one hundred thousand men and nine hundred thousand women engaged in domestic service—a larger total than was found for the workers in cotton, wool, linen, and flax mills combined.

An upper servant could earn considerably more than a factory worker and the job was in general more secure. One was less likely to be suddenly fired, assuming one's employers did not go bankrupt and one remained personally healthy, hardworking, quiet, and unpregnant. One would not starve or freeze in lodgings; one would be a part, however humble, of a social unit; and although the work was often strenuous, it did not require the monotonous standing and stooping that went with machine tending.

CATEGORIES OF SERVANTS

Servants in Victorian households fall into two general categories: upper and lower. This distinction does not have to do with the part of the house in which they were to be found but with the nature of their duties and the size of their wages.

Upper servants included the butler, housekeeper, parlor maid, cook, children's nurse, valet, and ladies' maid. (A household was not, of course, required to have a full set, and the areas of responsibility could be divided in different ways.) The first five on the list were administrators, supervising the echelons of lower servants beneath them: footmen, housemaids, under housemaids, kitchen and scullery maids, still-room maids, charwomen, nursery maids, pages, and so on. The valet and ladies' maid attended personally to members of the family and, as upper servants, expected their own rooms to be cleaned, their fires to be lighted, and the pitchers on their washstands to be filled by the under housemaids. Outside the house, the coachman and the gardener, both upper servants, had fairly autonomous control of the stables and the grounds. Either might have servants under him, often young boys learning to be coachmen or gardeners.

Upper servants enjoyed numerous perquisites: larger and better-heated rooms, more afternoons off, better uniforms, and better food. (Ladies' maids traditionally received as a special perquisite their mistresses' cast-off clothing, which the maids usually sold.) Upper servants might take their meals in the housekeeper's sitting room, separate from the lower servants, who ate in the servants' hall. In some households, this distinction was made at the end of a meal taken by all the servants in the servants' hall: The upper servants would rise and depart for dessert in the housekeeper's room.

Lower servants, who did the rough cleaning and waited on the upper servants, might be young but clever, more or less in training to become upper servants themselves. Others in the lower category might forever lack the skills or the poise required for responsible tasks and for contact with the family—a family a lower servant in a large household might hardly ever see. It was not only large households that had plenty of lower servants; unskilled servants were so numerous and would work for so little that even families who considered themselves poorly-off could have at least a maid-of-all-work. Dickens's impecunious Micawber family in *David Copperfield* quite plausibly enjoys the services of the "Orfling" (orphan), obtained from a nearby workhouse.

Middle-class households that could not afford the full range of butler, coachman, and all their subordinates made do with fewer servants—usually female ones; manservants were more expensive. A cook and scullery maid, house parlormaid and under housemaid, and a children's nurse and nursery maid might be an acceptable minimum, assuming that the family lived in a city and so had no grounds to maintain and could conveniently hire a carriage when it needed one. Some servants, laundresses, for instance, might be employed by the day, but most lived in the house. In many middle-class families, the lady of the house might take over some of the functions more luxurious households assigned to upper servants: She might act as her own housekeeper, doing the domestic accounts and paying the bills; she might brush her own hair and do plain needlework for herself and the children, saving a ladies' maid; she might undertake the education of the younger children instead of hiring a governess—a personage who was not exactly a servant but not exactly *not* a servant (see chapter 12). What the lady of the house could not respectably do was any work that would require her to change her clothes and abandon her ostensible role as a person of leisure: no scrubbing of floors.

SERVANTS' WAGES AND DRESS

Fifteen to twenty pounds a year, give or take a little and allowing for a rise in prices from the beginning to the end of the century, can be taken to mark the boundary between an upper and a lower servant's wages. (This sum is in addition to the board and room provided.) Manservants, less plentiful in domestic service than women and a greater status symbol, were the subject of a special tax: A footman in powdered wig and satin livery might receive forty pounds a year in salary and cost his employers an additional guinea in tax, besides the expense of the livery, the wig, and the hair powder (which was also taxed). A coachman could expect to receive thirty pounds a year, a butler or valet, forty to fifty. These sums are approximate and varied with the grandeur of the household. A good plain cook might be had for twenty-five or so pounds;

a male cook, especially a French one, would ask fifty. A footman in a less elaborate situation than the one described above would probably wear no wig and would spend more of his time carrying buckets of coal up the back stairs and less of it standing elegantly in the entrance hall. His salary in such a less sumptuous household would be twenty pounds a year or less. In the meantime, the annual expense of keeping a carriage and a pair of horses for a family living in town would be at least twice the salary of any of the upper servants.

Lower servants, or course, received comparatively minuscule wages. A girl might "go into service" when ten or twelve years of age and be paid six pounds a year, advancing in salary as she did in experience. A young boy hired as a page would expect about the same. An under housemaid, who cleaned fireplaces and emptied chamber pots, or a scullery maid, who washed pots and pans, would be paid ten pounds a year or less.

Uniforms (or, for men, "livery") varied with the position. The footman's eighteenth-century costume of knee breeches and white stockings was fairly standard, although the fabric could be more or less luxurious. Pages, who ran errands and made themselves generally useful, wore tight jackets with rows of buttons. A coachman throughout much of the century would wear an elaborate full-skirted coat and a "bag wig" of shoulder-length powdered ringlets, contrasting with the footmen's pigtailed versions. Women upper servants wore caps, aprons, and plain dresses in practical fabrics, cut in styles that followed the current mode at a respectful distance. Afternoon and evening uniforms were dark and unpatterned; morning uniforms might be lighter and gayer, lilac prints being a favorite choice. Lower servants were not seen by the family or guests, and their clothing was consequently not regulated.

WHERE SERVANTS CAME FROM

The traditional source of a family's servants, especially its upper servants, was the family's landed estate. The more tidy, quick, and obedient children of farm laborers or of village tradesmen would be taken into the squire's kitchen to be trained; the best of these would become permanent retainers and would go with the family to spend part of the year in the London town house. As children of the family grew up and established households of their own, they might take some of their accustomed servants with them—the vacancies in the parents' house being supplied by new faces from the estate.

There was some overlap between industrial workers and domestic service in that a factory worker's child might be put into service if an opportunity came along, rather than into the factory. Again, a servant who lost her job might go into a factory if she could find no other place, but the reverse was not usually true. Families were reluctant to hire factory workers, considering them rough and untrustworthy, except perhaps for the most menial chores.

Lower servants could be obtained for practically nothing from parish workhouses (sometimes called "Union" workhouses), which were happy to save themselves the room and board they would otherwise be obliged to lay out. If the servant was unsatisfactory, she could be sent back to the workhouse—a fate she would usually do her best to avoid.

In general, the servant class and their middle-class employers were separated by a distinct barrier of speech patterns, family origins, and expectations of life; but in some cases there was a crossing-over. The middle-class girl who was forced by circumstances to take employment as a governess or as a "companion" (in many respects a personal servant) was frequently encountered in life as well as in fiction. Middle-class women could descend even farther, to become housekeepers, the top of the hierarchy of upper servants, in households that did not keep a butler. Mrs. Fairfax in Charlotte Bronte's *Jane Eyre* is a distant relative of her master, although, as she tells Jane, "I never presume on the connection" (chap. 11). Mrs. Sparsit, Mr. Bounderby's housekeeper in Dickens's *Hard Times,* comes of a wealthy family. And Briggs in Thackeray's *Vanity Fair* has been a companion for many years when she is offered a job as housekeeper of Lord Steyne's country estate (chap. 52).

To go the other way, to rise from the servant class to the middle class by any means—marriage or somehow acquiring or saving money—was not usual. Former servants might go into trade in a small way, but they did not really enter the middle class.

SERVANTS IN THE NOVELS:
DICKENS ESPECIALLY

Servants in Victorian fiction are seldom seen from any vantage point other than that of their employers. Even those servants who function as first-person narrators—Nelly Dean in Emily Bronte's *Wuthering Heights,* for example, or Betterton in Wilkie Collins's *The Moonstone*—tell their employers' stories, not in any direct sense their own. And, since middle-class readers seldom came into contact with scullery maids or under gardeners, it is usually upper servants who appear in the novels.

Good servants in fiction, following the criteria set by their employers, are honest, dependable, and, above all, satisfied with their place in life and anxious to do their best in it. Dickens's gallery of hysterically loyal personal servants—Mr. Pickwick's Sam Weller, the Copperfield's Peggotty, Florence Dombey's Susan Nipper (of *Dombey and Son*), Esther Summerson's Charley (of *Bleak House*), Nicholas Nickleby's Smike, Martin Chuzzlewit's Mark Tapley, Mrs. Maylie's faithful crew in *Oliver Twist*—seem motivated exclusively by a compulsion to fulfill their employer's every wish and more: Sam Weller, overriding Mr. Pickwick's protests, at one point gets himself arrested for debt in order to join his master in prison, there to go on polishing Mr. Pickwick's boots. Bad

CAUTION.

ALWAYS LOOK TO YOUR OWN GIRTH, OR YOU MAY COME TO GRIEF LIKE YOUNG MILLWAY (WHO "SHOPS" FOR HIS SISTERS), WHEN HE MOUNTED IN THE HIGH STREET, JUST AS THOSE NICE GIRLS FROM THE GRANGE WERE LOOKING HIS WAY!

"CAUTION" (A. Corbould. Punch)

Opportunities for embarrassment before the opposite sex were many. The unseen villain of this picture, drawn by A. Corbould for Punch in 1877, is the servant who had neglected sufficiently to tighten the horse's girths.

servants display the opposite characteristics and are punished. Tattycoram in *Little Dorrit* rebels against the condescending pseudokindness with which she is treated and gains the present-day reader's sympathy, despite Dicken's quite contrary intentions.

Servants appear frequently in the novels as instances of their employers' follies and vanities. The wigged and liveried footman as a status symbol and vehicle of conspicuous consumption seemed more than Thackeray, for example, could bear; and his novels resound with the pompously "tremendous" knocks inflicted by footmen on the front doors of houses at which their mistresses have come to call. Dickens shared this antipathy; the unsympathetic Merdle in *Little Dorrit* has employed so many footmen to wait at table that the powder falling off their wigs "flavoured the dinner. Pulverous particles got into the dishes, and Society's meats had a seasoning of first-rate footman" (chap. 21).

BLACK SERVANTS IN *Vanity Fair*

Slavery had been abolished in Britain since the early 1770s; any slave who set foot on the soil of the British Isles became at once free. Laws passed between 1806 and 1811 put an end to the British slave trade, while slavery in the colonies had been gradually legislated out of existence by the 1840s. The Sedley's black footman, Sambo, in *Vanity Fair* (set in the first decades of the century) is not a slave, as he would have been in many of the United States at the same date, but a servant like the others in the household. The black population in England was then very small, and Sambo would have been regarded as something of a curiosity. He is, however, a well-trained upper servant and presumably finds another position after Mr. Sedley's financial ruin.

Joseph Sedley later brings home an Indian valet who is so incapacitated by the English climate that Joseph sends him back to India (chap. 50). The Indian, too, is a free man, in spite of Joseph's domineering manner with him.

NURSES AND NANNIES

Child care is virtually the only function of Victorian servants that present-day householders have been unable to replace with machines, indoor plumbing, or some other device of the modern age. Young children continue to require the supervision of a responsible person during their waking hours. To the Victorians, this problem was a comparatively small one, at least for the middle classes. They simply handed their children to a nurse who lived with her charges in a separate part of the house, supervised one or more under servants who did the heavy work of the nursery, and brought the children to visit their parents for perhaps half an hour at tea time. This state of things is accurately reflected in the fiction of the period; children who simply disappear until they grow up are not being disposed of by the authors in an unrealistic fashion.

The "nanny" developed as a type from the Victorian nursemaid, becoming something of a domestic tyrant, an authoritative but cherished voice on cleanliness, morals, and fair play. Originating, as had the nurse, in the working classes, the nanny adopted and promulgated the mores of her employers, usually in a didactically simplified form. The nanny was a late Victorian and Edwardian phenomenon, however, and does not appear in the Victorian novel in other than fragmentary form. Dickens's Peggotty in *David Copperfield* occupies a nannylike emotional niche, although technically she is a maid-of-all-work.

SERVANTS AND SEX:
The Way of All Flesh

An aspect of servant life that never, or hardly ever, appeared in the Victorian novel is the extent to which women servants might become the sexual prey of the gentlemen of the household, a fact of life for which considerable contemporary evidence exists. The cards were stacked in the gentlemen's favor. A servant had virtually no legal redress; one could sue one's seducer only if he had been rash enough to promise marriage and a rape, in the eyes of the law, had to involve threats of death or bodily harm on the part of the attacker, screams and struggles by the attacked, and a prompt report by the attacked to the authorities. To take a gentleman to court would require more money and more courage than a working-class girl was likely to have, and, in any event, few gentlemen would need to employ either rape or a promise of marriage. The large number of potential replacements in the labor market gave a servant no leverage in protecting her dignity or her right to make her own choice in sexual matters, for she could easily be turned away without a "character" (reference) to help her find another place. Moreover, a servant's monotonous and hardworking life gave incentive to any brief fun or drama, especially if gifts were included; and it appears that a servant would normally go along with her seducer and hope for the best. This best might include money and other gifts as well as a chance at becoming the gentleman's mistress, kept in lodgings with support provided for her and any children of the union. (Pregnancy was virtually inevitable, since birth control techniques were not widely known and were almost completely lacking, for much of the century, in the lower classes.) The worst was usually to become pregnant and to be dismissed by the lady of the house, a fairly likely eventuality.

One of the few fictional treatments of this theme, aside from such comic episodes as old Sir Pitt Crawley's infatuation with the servant Betsy Horrocks in *Vanity Fair*, occurs in Samuel Butler's *The Way of All Flesh*, published in 1903 but largely written before 1885. Ellen, the pretty housemaid, is found to be pregnant; the hero's mother wonders if her son might be the father. Ernest is innocent of seducing the housemaid, but it is significant that his mother should so automatically consider the possibility. In making *The Way of All Flesh* an indictment against the values of the Victorian middle classes, Butler has not been drawn by his own prejudices into a misrepresentation of the situation. Ernest is, in fact, as other scenes in the book make clear, an uncommonly naive young man for his social class; and his mother's assumption might in other cases have been correct.

XI

Crime and Punishment

A major difference between the Victorian criminal scene and our own is the lack of large-scale organization on either side. There was no Mafia or anything like it. The notion of a thieves' kingdom complete with royal hierarchy and secret language had been a property of romance for centuries; and various parts of the actual criminal class did, of course, form subcultures within the main society, but syndicated crime in today's sense had not come into existence. Nor was there a large-scale, well-organized body of law enforcement agents. The century saw considerable growth in this area, but at no time did the legal side of the cops-and-robbers game approach the strength with which we are familiar today. Criminals far outnumbered their pursuers. The extreme severity of the punishments in effect at the beginning of the century reflect this fact; if only a small percentage of wrongdoers could be caught, a punishment harsh enough to serve as a deterrent would have to take into account the law of averages.

If murder is put in a class by itself, it might be said that crimes against property were most important to the Victorians. Gambling, prostitution, or traffic in narcotic drugs were not energetically opposed or punished, although all three existed. Gambling had been regulated, more or less, through a complex series of acts dealing with gambling houses as public nuisances; but the betting on billiards and card games that takes up so much of the time of young men-about-town in the novels does not represent participation in an underworld. Prostitution, discussed below, was treated as a misdemeanor, while narcotics were openly available (see chapter 7).

THIEVES AND VALUES

It is useful to remember that the economic context of nineteenth-century England was a much tighter affair than our own. The masses of disposable use-once-and-throw-away goods we turn out so blithely would have been unimaginable to the Victorians. Almost everything had a secondhand value—often quite a good one. Articles of clothing, especially, made to individual order for upper- and middle-class customers, found their way when discarded to the secondhand shops with which some parts of London were crowded. There was a market for many of the contents of present-day garbage pails: "drippings" (the grease from roasted meat) were prized by the butterless poor for eating with bread; used tea leaves were saved and sold to dealers who called at the kitchen door. (These were used legally for cleaning carpets, illegally, for adulterating tea leaves sold as fresh.) Society seemed arranged in layers, with the discarded goods of an upper layer filtering down to the one below.

In such a setting, thievery was a considerably more varied undertaking than it is today. A silk handkerchief, which we would hardly consider tempting to a thief, might cost a buyer five shillings in the secondhand market; the thief who had stolen it would have received perhaps one shilling from the dealer to whom he sold it. Thus Oliver Twist's apprenticeship in handkerchief stealing has a definite economic rationale. This shilling (twelve pence) would take the thief a long way in street life, where a hot baked potato cost a half-penny, a piece of fried fish or a cup of coffee, a penny, and threepence paid for a night in a lodginghouse.

Watches and purses were highly desirable thieves' quarry, although they were usually more difficult than handkerchiefs to detach from their owners. A thief might receive some twenty-five shillings for a silver watch and four pounds for a gold one, according to an informant quoted by John Binney, one of the contributors to Henry Mayhew's absorbing compilation, *London Labour and the London Poor* (1849-1862). The small purse a lady wore fastened to her waist on a shopping expedition might contain twelve or fifteen pounds—a year's wages for a workman or a servant girl and a desirable haul for a pickpocket.

More difficult and dangerous forms of stealing, house-breaking and burglary, brought correspondingly greater rewards. Shops were usually more profitable than private houses but were harder to get into, especially as the shopkeeper and his family often lived upstairs. Binney's informant describes a burglary of an East End shop the proceeds of which brought forty-two pounds at the receiver's—a rather large sum. To reach this total, the burglars took virtually everything in the shop; and it is hard to imagine a present-day thief burdening himself with such items as this one gleefully lists: pencil cases, scent bottles, and postage stamps.

The dealer in stolen goods, the "receiver" or "fence," was a necessary middleman, since thieves seldom had the skills or contacts to do their own selling. Often the fence ran a pawnshop, a business that enabled him to mix stolen goods with those legitimately pawned. He might possess facilities for getting rid of identifying marks on stolen goods, including crucibles for melting down silverplate. In addition, a fence often had financial connections that enabled him to deal in stolen bank notes, offering the thief a high percentage of the face value in spite of the fact that the note, numbered and dated, may have been reported as stolen. Fagin in *Oliver Twist,* something of an archetypal fence, may have found Noah Claypole's stolen note a more negotiable item than he pretends: "Payment stopped at the Bank? Ah! It's not worth much to him [Fagin's imaginary friend]. It'll have to go abroad, and he couldn't sell it for a great deal in the market" (chap. 24).

MURDER

The murders that occur in Victorian fiction are fairly self-explanatory as to what is going on and the motive is usually made clear. The murderers are inevitably caught and punished by the hand of Providence or of human justice. *Oliver Twist* combines both these possibilities: Sikes, Nancy's murderer, manages accidentally to hang himself as he runs from his pursuers; Fagin is convicted as an accessory before the fact of the same crime and comes to his end as the focal point of a public hanging (chap. 50, 52).

The actual picture was quite different. Murderers often escaped detection. Many of the murder trials that so fascinated the Victorian public centered around extraordinarily gory jobs, fairly begging to be discovered; the criminals, representing a category still with us today, seem actually to have had a strong desire to be caught and punished. The murderer who simply wanted to get rid of someone had a fairly good chance, and examination of nineteenth-century evidence indicates that such chances were taken. Poison, for example, was a tempting alternative for the unhappily married; because of the frequency of disease and sudden death in all parts of society and the lack of routine scientific investigations, the murder might go undiscovered and the victim be buried with the rites of the church, the murderer attending as chief mourner. Newborn infants might be smothered, then said to have been stillborn. If one did not need to account for their deaths, infants made a particularly concealable category of corpse. A reader in an objective mood can see the ease with which Hetty Sorrel in George Eliot's *Adam Bede* could have hidden her baby's body had it died before she left it in its little hole and had Hetty herself been more callous and more clearheaded (chap. 43). The girl in Kingsley's *Yeast* who successfully pretends that the infant she has killed was born dead (chap. 16) would seem to be a more typical case.

The discrepancy between fiction and actuality in this emotion-charged category is not one that need influence the present-day reader's relationship to the Victorian novel. Like the original readers, we want evildoers to get their just desserts, and we are willing to accept a fictional environment in which the law of averages in this respect can be bent to the purpose.

KEEPING ORDER:
THE METROPOLITAN POLICE

Sir Robert Peel, as a member of Parliament, established the metropolitan police in London in 1828; and it is in honor of their founder, according to tradition, that London policemen are called "bobbies" (or, sometimes, "peelers"). Offices were set up in Scotland Yard, Whitehall, a name that has become synonymous with the police force and particularly with its detective branch. Policemen were also called "Bow Street officers" from the site of the chief metropolitan police court. It is by this title that Blathers and Duff are announced to the Maylie household (*Oliver Twist*, chap. 31), and it is to Bow Street that Trollope's Phineas Finn is escorted on a charge of having murdered his political enemy, Mr. Bonteen (*Phineas Redux*, chap. 47). (The "Bow Street Runners," a body sometimes mentioned in Victorian novels even though they belong to eighteenth-century London, were officers sent out by sitting police magistrates to investigate the crimes reported to the magistrates.)

The new force, replacing an inadequate system of parish constables, watchmen, and headboroughs that had not greatly changed since the time of Dogberry in Shakespeare's *Much Ado About Nothing*, was an immediate success. Its jurisdiction in and around London was widened and its organization was copied throughout the country. In the business district and many residential parts of London, policemen were so numerous that citizens felt a real increase of safety. The implication in Victorian novels that there is always a policeman around the corner ("Officer, would you step in here for a moment?"), which may seem to us so suspiciously convenient to the plot as to represent an exaggeration of fact, was an everyday part of life to many original readers.

Police courts in London and other large towns were presided over by salaried magistrates and were in continuous daily session except for Sundays and holidays. London had fifteen police districts, and consequently fifteen courts, in the last decades of the century. Magistrates had powers of summary jurisdiction and might commit offenders to houses of correction. Not all magistrates were as ferocious as Mr. Fang of *Oliver Twist* (chap. 11), although Dickens's character is supposedly based on a real person.

VICTORIAN PRISONS

Imprisonment for long terms was not extensively used as a punishment until the nineteenth century. In earlier times the housing and feeding of prisoners had cost more money than the society felt it could afford; torture was cheaper and might be expected to act more forcefully as a deterrent. By the nineteenth century elaborate tortures had gone out of use, along with mutilation (chopping off a hand or an ear) and branding; but several physical punishments were still used. Flogging, particularly, was often part of a prisoner's sentence. Hard labor was a popular sentence as well, and if no useful work could be found for prisoners, they might be set to frustratingly wasteful exertions such as walking a treadmill. (Some treadmills were designed to pump water or grind corn, but most prison treadmills just went around.)

Toward the middle of the century, long-term imprisonment began to attract popular interest on the assumption that a criminal removed from his usual environment and meditating on his misdoings would become more truly penitent than if he were given physical punishment and let out again. Solitude was emphasized; in such model prisons as Pentonville, built in the early 1840s, even the benches in the chapel had vertical partitions to ensure each prisoner's being alone with his thoughts and his view of the pulpit.

Earlier types of prisons still used in the Victorian age included jails (often spelled "gaols"), houses of correction, and hulks. The gaols housed persons awaiting trial or commitment; these were usually attached to police offices. Newgate, the chief gaol of London, attached to the Old Bailey police court, was the oldest, largest, and most notorious of these and stood in the public mind as an emblem of melodramatic crimes. Houses of correction, also called "bride-wells," housed offenders who were serving a comparatively short term: Two or three months was a typical first offense punishment for a pickpocket, for example. The original Bride-well Prison in London, where prostitutes were set the task of beating hemp (in order to extract the fibers, used in making rope), became a household word, immediately recognized in an after-dinner charade in Charlotte Brontë's *Jane Eyre* (chap. 18). The "hulks" were old and unseaworthy ships often used to house convicts awaiting transportation to Australia or elsewhere. It is from one of these, anchored in the Surrey marshes, that Magwitch escapes to terrify Pip in *Great Expectations*.

The term "penitentiary" was not used as it is in the United States to denote a prison for convicts sentenced to confinement and hard labor. To the Victorians, a penitentiary was a voluntary asylum, usually run by a charitable institution, for prostitutes who felt repentance, wished to begin a new life, and were in need of shelter. In Elizabeth Gaskell's *Ruth*, the mother of the young man who has seduced the heroine proposes "to procure her admission into the Fordham Penitentiary" (chap. 10); the suggestion is made as an act of condescending but practical charity, not as a threat to treat Ruth as a criminal.

Debtors' prisons constituted, in a sense, a class apart, as their inmates were not criminals and were not being punished, only detained (see chapter 2). Such debtors' prisons as the Fleet, the King's Bench, and the Marshalsea appear frequently in the Victorian novel. Dickens's characters have many dealings with them. Mr. Pickwick is taken to the Fleet on a matter of principle, having refused to pay the court costs in a breach-of-promise suit brought against him by his land-lady; and there he has his eyes opened to the harsher sides of life, which he has never suspected. Mr. Micawber in *David Copperfield* includes in his economic ups and downs a stay in the King's Bench prison, where he is joined by his family. As long as a debtor remained in prison, he could have what company he liked to visit or to move in with him.

Debtors were arrested at the suit of one or more of their

creditors; on paying these particular debts they would be freed, no matter how many others they might have. It was quite usual to pay the amount of the debt to the bailiff (sheriff or sheriff's officer) who made the arrest and stop the proceedings at that point. Mr. Micawber's departure for Australia takes place to an accompaniment of pursuit by bailiffs, whom David pays off (chap. 57). Imprisonment for debt and the whole scaffolding of social custom that went with it was made obsolete by an act of Parliament in the late 1860s.

CAPITAL PUNISHMENT

In earlier centuries, when the idea of punishment as a deterrent to crime was taken to the next step of making that punishment as horrible as possible, a condemned criminal might not only be executed but, if his offense were large enough, "hanged, drawn and quartered": He would be hanged until he were choken but not dead; he would then have his intestines "drawn", (pulled through a slit in his abdomen); at last he would be decapitated and "quartered", (cut into arm and leg sections that, with the head, would be taken away to various city gates and bridges to be hung up as a warning).

By the beginning of the nineteenth century, such barbaric extra touches had been dispensed with, but capital punishment was still the legal penalty for over two hundred crimes, many of them quite petty. Reform in this matter continued steadily throughout the century, until by the end of it only a handful of crimes—high treason, murder, piracy with violence, destruction of public arsenals and dockyards, and offenses against naval or military discipline—were punishable by death.

For the condemned criminal, hanging continued to be the usual method of execution, carried out by more humane techniques than had been the case in earlier times. The gallows with a trapdoor that dropped the criminal far enough to kill him by instantly fracturing his neck (provided the hangman had tied the right kind of knot) gained favor over earlier types of gallows, which merely allowed the criminal to strangle.

(Lead weights had been attached to lightweight criminals to shorten their suffering.) Until the late 1830s, prisoners condemned to death were usually hanged within two days of their sentencing, as is the case with Fagin in *Oliver Twist* (chap. 52); public interest thus went from the trial to the hanging without a gap. Hangings continued to be public spectacles until the late 1860s; thereafter hangings took place inside the walls of the prison (usually Newgate for London criminals). A vestige of the public ceremony remained in the tolling of the parish bell for fifteen minutes before and fifteen minutes after the hanging. A black flag was run up from within the prison at the moment of execution; in Hardy's *Tess of the d'Urbervilles,* Angel Clare and Tess's sister, Liza-Lu, watch from a nearby hill for this sign of Tess's end (chap. 59).

TRANSPORTATION

The idea of sending criminals out of the country instead of hanging them became popular in the eighteenth century, as readers of Defoe's *Moll Flanders* will recall. The practice seems to have accounted for a fairly large part of the population of Virginia. After the American Revolution, this site was no longer available and British authorities turned to Australia, which Captain James Cook had explored and claimed in 1770.

If a convict were transported instead of hung, he could not come back to England without, so to speak, reactivating the original sentence. Magwitch in Dicken's *Great Expectations* and Amory in Thackeray's *Pendennis* consequently have excellent reasons for avoiding at all costs capture and identification. Lighter transportation sentences were also used; convicts might be sent to Australia for a term of years, often seven or fourteen.

Once arrived in Australia, a convict might be hired out as manual labor to the free colonists who were building sheep ranches upcountry or as skilled labor (if he had any skills) to city dwellers. In this latter event, his life might become useful

and pleasant, the situation anticipating, although by accident, today's concept of the rehabilitation of prisoners as
functioning members of society. Transfer to any of the more
prisonlike penal colonies, such as the one at Botany Bay,
where conditions were savagely inhuman, was used as a
threat to encourage good behavior under the gentler modes of
convict life. A convict who behaved well in gang labor would
be given a pass that enabled him to seek work for himself;
then, as another step toward freedom, he would be allowed a
"ticket of leave" that allowed hom to come an go virtually as
he liked. Finally, if he conducted himself well, he would
receive absolute pardon and could become, in effect, a citizen
of Australia.

The transportation of convicts to Australia was sus-
pended in the 1840s; consequently, today's reader can assume
that a novel dealing with transportation is set before that
date—if, in fact, the novel in question observes a time setting
with precision.

PROSTITUTION

The large number of prostitutes in London openly seeking
customers and conducting negotiations in the public streets
was a matter of wonder to foreign visitors. Estimates of the
total number vary considerably. One of Mayhew's collabora-
tors in London Labour and the London Poor (1849-1862) cites
figures ranging from eighty thousand to a modest seven
thousand. William Acton, whose Prostitution (1857) is generally considered more reliable, suggests fifty thousand as a
total, but of these he finds only a little over nine thousand to
be known to the police as streetwalkers or occupants of
brothels. Whatever the statistics, the problem was a highly
visible one, and other English cities, such as Manchester and
Liverpool, felt themselves to be similarly overrun.

The social scale of prostitution ranged from the kept
mistress, provided by her lover with a house, servants, jewels, and a carriage in which to be driven about Hyde Park, to

the "twopenny upright," who plied her trade near dark alley-ways and whose categorical label pretty well denotes her earning power and the resources at her command. In between were numerous gradations. A reasonably young and healthy girl able to buy pretty clothes and plenty of food might work quite profitably in the Haymarket district of the fashionable West End, taking her customers to an "accommodation house" that rented rooms by the hour, then returning to the street in search of the next prospect. Her night's earnings might add up to three or four pounds—much more than she could earn as a factory worker, servant, or needlewoman, virtually the only other occupations open to her.

Prostitutes who worked in brothels were in a more help-less situation than the streetwalker. Contemproary reports about of women who were virtually imprisoned in brothels, their clothes taken away, kept perpetually drugged. In the brothels a high demand, with correspondingly high prices for the brothel keeper, existed for preadolescent girls of ten or twelve or so. Florence Dombrey's encounter with "Good Mother Brown," who in Dickens's *Dombey and Son* merely robs young Florence of her pretty clothes and turns her out on the street in rags, may have called up in presentable guise a deep fear in the minds of Victorian parents (chap. 6).

Despite the aura of deep moral sin that covered prostitu-tion in the public mind, prostitution in itself was not legally considered a serious crime. In English law, prostitution was regarded as a public nuisance; under a variety of acts in force during the nineteenth century, a prostitute could be arrested for disorderly conduct (drunkenness or assaulting a police-man or both), loitering, indecent exposure of the person, or, perhaps, side endeavors such as larceny or selling obscene pictures. Penalties were light, consisting of a fine or a term in a house of correction. This leniency may indicate a tolerant attitude on the part of authority toward what appeared a necessary social evil or it may simply suggest that prostitu-tion was so large scale a phenomenon that the police could not have eliminated it if they had tried.

PROSTITUTES IN FICTION

The fictional protrait of the Victorian prostitute would seem to differ considerably from reality. In the 1850s a medical doctor, William Acton, in his book, *Prostitution*, attempted to counter the popular image of the prostitute as a blighted being, consumed with remorse and disease. Prostitution, Acton argued, was often a temporary phase of a woman's life; many prostitutes married respectably; and the assumption that a prostitute's career led rapidly and inevitably downhill was not borne out by the facts.

Such a statement had little chance to prevail against Victorian moral didacticism. In middle-class fiction the prostitute is recognizable by her sunken cheeks, her ragged shawl, and the low moaning sounds she makes as she creeps barefoot through the snow to drown herself in the river.

An almost obligatory first stage for the fictional prostitute is her seduction by a dashing young gentleman, far above her in station, whom she sincerely loves and who she assumes will marry her. (Martha Endell in *David Copperfield*, who is close to the center of the stereotype, lacks this phase; but there are hints that Dickens at one point intended the seducer to turn out to be David's friend Steerforth.) Thus the folly of a girl's having anything to do with a man who is unlikely to marry her becomes part of the moral lesson. Little Emily, the fisherman's daughter whom Steerforth does seduce and whose attraction to him is blamed on her unrealistic desire to be a lady, would have descended to lower depths and Martha Endell not saved her from the brothel in which she has been immured. Elizabeth Gaskell's "poor Butterfly," the heroine's wayward aunt in *Mary Barton*, follows this pattern closely herself and desperately tries to warn Mary of the probable consequences of her infatuation with the mill owner's son.

XII

Education

Education in Victorian England was a much less standardized affair than it is in the United States today. There was less breaking down of the educational experience into small units to be counted up at intervals and rewarded with the appropriate diploma. Education represented a class distinction, as it does today, but emphasis was more openly on the manners the student acquired and the people with whom he or she associated. Higher education as a financial investment, with the expectation that a degree will effect some immediate dollars-and-cents increase in the graduate's income, was not traditionally a dominant concern.

WOMEN'S ROLE:
UPPER AND MIDDLE CLASSES

Women's education often consisted of "accomplishments," little impractical arts to make a man's home a bower of tasteful bliss when he returns home from the real world: Thus David Copperfield's wife Dora plays the guitar for him and sings "enchanted ballads in the French language, generally to the effect that, whatever was the matter, we ought always to dance, Ta-ra-la, Ta-ra-la" (chap. 26). Women's education might include some general information—geography, perhaps—to prevent young girls from becoming absolute ninnies; but since many pursuits were considered either too difficult for ladies or too indelicate for them, such studies seldom went far. Accomplishments were a safer bet, since these would not only entertain a husband once one had him but would lure him within range during the preliminary stages. And should the worst happen and a lady remain unmarried, she could always, if otherwise unprovided for, become a governess and teach her accomplishments to the next generation of girls coming up for their try.

GIRLS' SCHOOLS

Girls did not go to college and they did not in fact need to go away at all; to be educated at home, under a governess, with an assortment of visiting masters for special subjects such as drawing or dancing, was not unusual. Daughters of the upper classes and gentry typically followed this course. However, many middle-class families found that a finishing school could provide instruction in more accomplishments at a cheaper rate than might be possible with private lessons at home, taking room and board into account. The finishing school provided, as well, an assortment of fellow students occupying more or less the same rung of the social ladder with whom a girl might make friends and whose brothers she might meet.

These schools enjoyed local rather than national prestige; there was no feminine equivalent of Eton or Harrow in the sense of a taken-for-granted superiority. Once enrolled, a student did not earn a degree or follow a specialized course of study. One simply stayed at school from the age of thirteen or so until it suited one's family's convenience for one to leave, usually at seventeen or eighteen in order not to miss the period of one's husband-hunting bloom.

By the end of the century this picture had begun to change somewhat. Queen's College and Bedford College, both in London, were founded in the late 1850s for the purpose of giving a university education to women; Newnham and Girton colleges at Cambridge and Somerville and Lady Margaret Hall at Oxford were founded in the 1870s. In 1878 the University of London received a supplemental charter making all degrees and honors equally accessible to student of both sexes. Meanwhile, girls' secondary schools developed a trend toward qualified teachers and "real" subjects.

But this change involved only a small proportion of the population, and the novels continued for the most part to reflect the earlier and still typical situation. Thackeray's portrayal of Miss Pinkerton's establishment in *Vanity Fair* represents something of a norm for girls' schools in fiction. Dickens, critical enough of education in many aspects, lets these institutions go their superficial way: From the Wackles sisters' "Lady's seminary" in *The Old Curiosity Shop* to Miss Twinkleton's school in *Edwin Drood,* two novels that span thirty years of the author's career, Dickens cheerfully applauds the young ladies' establishments for producing nests of rosebuds. Maggie Tulliver in George Eliot's *The Mill on the Floss* protests the brainless content of her schoolwork and tries to learn her brother's Latin and geometry, but Maggie and her author represent a minority voice on the Victorian scene.

Public and private
boys' schools

Present-day American readers face a tangle of terminology at this point. In the United States, a "public" elementary or secondary school is supported by taxes and is regulated by state and federal as well as local agencies, under the basic idea that every child in the nation is entitled to attend such a public school without paying tuition. An American "private" school, on the other hand, may be established by a group or an individual but is not a direct part of a government-related system; and it does charge tuition, sometimes in fact so much of it that attendance becomes a mark of social status.

In Victorian England, the terms "public" and "private" had quite different connotations, and the social status is reversed. A public school had been endowed by its founder's will, sometimes centuries earlier; it was governed by a board

"Fourth-Form Room at Harrow School" (*Illustrated London News*)

This gloomy interior, with its hard benches and general lack of cheer, belongs to one of Victorian England's most prestigious boys' school, Harrow. Harrow's graduates, leaving at seventeen or so, customarily went on to Oxford or Cambridge.

as a nonprofit concern, although students did pay some tuition. In most of the public schools (Eton, Harrow, Winchester, Charterhouse, Rugby, to name a few), the emphasis was on the traditional Latin and Greek and the expectation was that upon leaving a boy would go on to Cambridge or Oxford. Students were upper and upper-middle class; the boundary was not crossed in large numbers by the upwardly mobile because a young man who did not fit in would feel acutely uncomfortable, even if he were prepared in classical studies and could afford to spend so many years in nonpractical concerns. Thus the term "public school" had a connotation of prestige for which the American reader of Victorian fiction should develop a sensitivity.

The private school, on the other hand, was the property of an individual who ran his establishment for profit, profit enough at any rate to support himself and his family. The student body might be the opposite of exclusive, especially if tuition rates were low. Curriculum sometimes imitated that of the public schools (classical languages) and sometimes attempted a more vocational program with emphasis, perhaps, on the simpler forms of mathematics.

A boy destined for an upper- or upper-middle-class life was taught at home to read and write and to understand the rudiments of Latin and sometimes of Greek as well. He went away to school, usually, from the ages of twelve to sixteen or so, and then on to a university. (The fact that many of the older public schools are called "colleges" may create confusion by sounding as if they served an older student body.)

A student was put into a "form," first through sixth, according to the progress he had made in his subjects. Each form mights be further divided into an upper and a lower section. Ernest Pontifex of Samuel Butler's *The Way of All Flesh* on entering Roughborough School at twelve years of age is put into the fourth form, having learned at home "every page of his Latin and Greek Grammars by heart" (chap. 27). Ernest is not a particularly industrious student, but in four years he has completed the sixth form and is ready for Cambridge.

Daily lessons usually required a student to construe, or to analyze for grammatical function, individual words or phrases within a passage of Latin or Greek and to translate the passage into English. This assignment is of the sort to which present-day students of languages are accustomed, but another exercise, much relied upon to develop the brain, may strike us as unusual: Students composed original verses in Latin, assigned according to subject and metrical form. Thus "making verses at school," an occupation occasionally mentioned in these terms in the novels, refers to this academic requirement rather than to some more spontaneous poetic outburst. *Tom Brown's School Days* contains a presumably authentic account of the methods the boys brought to bear upon this task (chap. 12/2.3).

Nonclassical studies made their appearance in the curricula rather slowly. At Harrow, for example, mathematics was required in the late 1830s, modern languages for the upper forms in the 1850s, and English history and literature, in the late 1860s.

Aside from the academic curriculum, a public school often stressed athletics, such as rowing and rugby football, which were supposed to develop the virtues of manliness and fair play. Rugby, where this type of football was developed and where Dr. Thomas Arnold served as headmaster in the 1830s, did most to foster this ideal; and both Rugby and Dr. Arnold figure without disguise in Thomas Hughes's *Tom Brown's School Days*.

UNIVERSITIES

As far as the novels are concerned, there are only two universities, Oxford and Cambridge. (University College, London, was founded in the late 1820s with the intention of providing an education for those barred from Oxford or Cambridge on religious grounds; but the novels, predominantly establishment-oriented, take little notice.) Oxford and Cambridge are equal in social status, aside from personal prejudice on the part of the authors, many of whom had attended one or the other.

Each university was composed of twenty-odd colleges, the earliest of which date from the fourteenth century; each college had its own buildings—library, dining hall, lecture rooms, and what Americans would call dormitories—and formed the tangible basis of university life. The college provided the student with a tutor and a course of reading through which, augmented by college- and university-sponsored lectures, the student proceeded to work toward his degree. Degree examinations were given by the university rather than by the college; thus student, tutor, and college were cooperatively in league, preparing the student for an evaluation to be made by a higher authority. There was no such thing as "taking" a course in some aspect of a subject, satisfying the professor, and receiving a grade that would remain a part of one's academic record. The closest thing to today's sequences of courses might be a reading list, and one's academic reputation depended upon the single culminating set of examinations that determined whether one received a degree.

These final examinations changed somewhat during the century, but usually they included written and oral sections and covered both classical and mathematical subjects. Bachelor's degrees were of two sorts, superior and average; the more impressive, the "honours" or "first class" degree, required extra work, usually in the form of additional reading. The less ambitious or energetic students tried for a "pass" (or, at Cambridge, a "poll") degree. A "double first" was a degree for which the holder had done honors work in two subjects, usually classical literature and mathematics.

The standard span of time a student spent reading for his bachelor's degree was three years. Sons of peers, however, who until late in the century wore a gold tassel on their caps, were allowed to take their degrees in two years. (In university slang, the gold tassel was called a "tuft" and so was the peer's son beneath it; a "tuft hunter" was a student who spent his college years trying to associate with the aristocracy.)

One could go on from the bachelor's degree to the M.A.

(*artium magister*) quite easily at Oxford or Cambridge: One simply retained one's name on the college books and paid a fee. No further academic work was required. The Ph.D, or Doctor of Philosophy, was not a degree native to the English university; the title "doctor" was given, rather loosely, to a man of learning—the headmaster of a public school, for example.

EDUCATION FOR EVERYONE:
THE RELIGIOUS OBSTACLE

The concept of universal elementary education in England was historically associated with the Protestant belief that every individual should have the opportunity to interpret the scriptures for himself. Consequently, a great deal of emphasis had been put on reading and on religious instruction; Bibles were sometimes the only texts used for reading lessons—as is the case with the village school operated by Mr. Wopsle's great aunt in Dickens's *Great Expectations* (chap. 10). The practical benefit in this world below of arithmetic, for example, slowly became apparent in the nineteenth century with the increasing number of opportunities for intelligent members of the lower classes. However, the traditional religious rationale lost none of its strength as the need for practical learning became clearer; arguments over denominational influence and control of schools, over textbooks (what creed and cathechism should the children learn?), and over the religious affiliation and training of teachers continued to entangle parliamentary debates and to delay needed legislation.

The solutions that turned out to be most workable were those that built upon the efforts of the varying denominations instead of trying to take everything down and start again in some sort of uniformity. Many elementary schools related to the Church of England had been built by the National Society for Promoting the Education of the Poor in the Principles of the Established Church Throughout England and Wales—the

"National Society" for short; schools related to the dissenting faiths (all denominations except the Church of England) were assisted by the British and Foreign School Society. In the early 1830s, Parliament voted sums of money for aid to elementary schools to be administered through these two organizations, and the thin end of the wedge for government support of schools had been driven in.

SUNDAY SCHOOLS AND VILLAGE SCHOOLS

Before the new idea of government-sponsored education for everyone entered the national consciousness, schooling for the lower classes had taken place on two levels as a charitable act and as a commercial enterprise. Victorian fiction often reflects these older patterns.

The concept of elementary education as a charity to be performed by middle-class ladies gained much of its focus from the "Sunday-school Movement" founded by Robert Raikes, a newspaper owner, in the late eighteenth century. Dissenting denominations and the "low" portions of the Church of England (see chapter 3), often more sensitive to the needs of the poor and working classes, took up Sunday Schools with great energy. The children met on Sundays before church services and sometimes on Saturdays as well or as often as they could be spared from their work in the fields or factories. For the most part, the teaching was religious, although secular subjects such as reading, writing, geography, and basic arithmetic were studied as well. Young ladies of good family were expected to spend a few of their leisure hours as volunteer teachers, and they need, of course, have had no special training. Gwendolyn Harleth in George Eliot's *Daniel Deronda* balks at this duty, and the original readers would have known from this and other clues that Miss Harleth was an unconventional and headstrong young lady, likely to come to grief.

Occasionally a parish school would become more ambitious and would hire a full-time schoolmaster or schoolmistress to teach the poor—or, usually, the more deserving classes of the poor. Girls and boys were usually taught separately, either in separate buildings or in separate parts of the same building. Wealthier members of the congregation that set up the school would act as patrons, subscribing toward the teachers' salaries and the cost of the building.

Elementary education as a private commercial endeavor still took the form, in the earlier part of the nineteenth century, of the old-fashioned "dame school" offering the barest of rudiments for a minimal fee. Mr. Wopsle's great aunt runs such a school in *Great Expectations* (chap. 10). A schoolmaster of a transitional type, part entrepreneur and part employee within a regulated system, is represented by Bartle Massey in George Eliot's *Adam Bede*: During the day Mr. Massey teaches children in the parish school; at night he presides over the efforts of grown men to learn to read or do accounts at sixpence a weekly lesson—thrice Mr. Wopsle's great aunt's charge, but, since Mr. Massey at least stays awake, worth the difference.

IN THE CITIES:
CHARITIES AND RAGGED SCHOOLS

Voluntary charitable efforts to educate the poor in the cities were so numerous that their failure to make more than a light dent in the mass of ignorance daily increasing with the population can be taken as evidence in itself of the size of the problem.

Charitable foundations often set up schools, many of which attempted to feed and clothe their pupils as well as to teach them. Young Toodle of Dickens's *Dombey and Son*, whom Mr. Dombey has caused to be admitted to the "Charitable Grinders'" school, wears the official uniform of a yellow cap and leggings. Such uniforms originated not as a mark of humiliation, though to Young Toodle this is the case, but simply as a replacement for rags. Mr. Dombey's impression that he has done the Toodle family a great favor has a foundation in fact: Even the worst charity schools had more applicants than places, and a boy often needed the influence of someone connected with the governing board to get in.

Another type of school for the urban poor, the "ragged" schools, which took their name from the usual condition of the scholars, operated on a shoestring and were run by the charitable ladies who in the more traditional rural settings would be establishing village schools. The ragged school movement was started early in the century by a Portsmouth shoemaker and spread rapidly; the schools charged no tuition, used only volunteer teachers, and in general did the best they could. Since the schools must have brought some glimmer of educational light to lives that otherwise would have been quite in the dark, the harshness with which Dickens describes such an institution in *Our Mutual Friend* (chap. 18/2.1) may have seemed to the original readers somewhat unjust.

THE MONITOR SYSTEM

In American schools a "monitor" is usually a student or teacher who has been given some temporary disciplinary responsibility, in particular those having to do with the administration of examinations. In Victorian England monitors, or pupil-teachers, as they were sometimes called, were assistants in the actual work of teaching. Their use was developed earlier in the century by two educators of opposing religious camps, working independently of each other: Joseph Lancaster, a Quaker and thus a Dissenter, and Andrew Bell, a Church of England clergyman. The problem both faced was that of a large number of pupils and a scarcity of able teachers; the solution was to let the older or more advanced of the children teach the others—sometimes after only a hasty briefing session.

The monitorial system as it was developed in the church-related schools, whether those of the Dissenters or of the established church, was taken into the system of nationally subsidized schools that developed in conjunction with the controlling religious societies. Eventually monitors were paid a stipend and treated as apprentice teachers, and they·were allowed to compete for the queen's scholarships to the teacher training colleges then being set up. Sue Bridehead in Hardy's *Jude The Obscure* pursues her career in this context (see the more detailed discussion below).

THE EDUCATION ACT OF 1870

Often spoken of as a milestone, the Education Act of 1870 coordinated and strengthened existing legislation and added new educational options in a way that made a great deal of difference in some districts and virtually none in others. The act provided for the formation of school boards in every school district that, in the opinion of the newly formed Education Department, was not sufficiently well served by the schools already in existence there. These school boards had authority to set up in such districts public elementary schools in which the religious problem was got around by allowing students to exempt, if their parents preferred, any religious instruction offered. All the schools, both the new "board" schools and the older church-related ones, were to be open at all times to "Her Majesty's Inspectors," and this post became a prestigious one in the new educational hierarchy that was taking shape.

These government inspectors set up "standards" or levels of achievement in the several basic subjects that children must reach in order for a school, whether church-related or established by a district board, to get its money from the funds authorized by Parliament. The first standard in reading, for example, consisted of "narrative monosyllables"— "See Dick run" or the equivalent. To reach the sixth standard, a student had to be able to read a paragraph from a newspaper, and one might add that Victorian newspaper paragraphs were usually longer and more complex than our own. Hardy's Tess Durbeyfield has "passed the Sixth Standard in the National School under a London-trained mistress" (chap.

3). Despite the confusion of strange terminology, American readers should distinguish between fictional characters who, like Tess, reach the "sixth standard" as students in lower-class schools teaching only the basics and those who reach the "sixth form" (have, in other words, as boys of the upper and upper-middle classes, attained a fair proficiency in Latin and Greek).

The Education Act of 1870 caused a shift in the meaning of the term "national school"; earlier, such an institution was one sponsored by the National Society and thus closely tied to the Church of England. The fact that Dickens's Ham Peggotty in *David Copperfield* "went to the national school, and was a very dragon at this catechism" (chap. 1) tells us that the Peggotty family belongs to the respectable church-going segment of the working class. By the end of the century, a national school, like the one Tess goes to, is one set up by a district board and supported directly by the government.

GOVERNESSES IN FACT AND FICTION

The humble figure of the governess, who was neither quite a servant nor a member of the family, continued to be a part of the Victorian scene and a mark of status for those who could afford her, even as the new school system grew. There was no abrupt shift from one to the other, partly because the new schools' identification with the poor and working classes made the middle class wish to avoid them if possible. The governess had almost always been born into a middle-class family and had fallen in the world, perhaps through her father's financial reverses or simply through her own failure to attract a husband. For a working-class girl to aspire to become a governess was uncommon. Even if she had acquired the necessary ladylike accomplishments, she would lack a major qualification: Mothers counted on the governess to correct any unacceptable habits of speech a child might have picked up from his working-class nurse.

The governess' many representatives in the novel depart

from reality chiefly in the fairy tale magic that frees a disproportionate number of them from their fate: Thackeray's Becky Sharp; Charlotte Brontë's Jane Eyre, Anne Brontë's Agnes Gray, Dickens's Ruth Pinch in *Martin Chuzzlewit*, Trollope's Lucy Morris in *The Eustace Diamonds*. Another group are saved before their bondage even begins: Hardy's Bathsheba Everdene in *Far from the Madding Crowd* has been found "too wild" for governessing (chap. 4); Dickens's Esther Summerson is educated as a governess but finds a happier career as housekeeper and wife in *Bleak House;* George Eliot's Gwendolyn Harleth in *Daniel Deronda* is on the point of accepting a situation as a governess when she is rescued by a marriage proposal; Jane Fairfax in Jane Austen's *Emma,* safe all the time in her secret engagement, is put under embarrassing social pressure when Mrs. Elton urges her to take the governessing post she has presumptuously found for her.

The real-life fact about governesses was that nothing much happened to them, and those governesses in fiction who do correspond to reality in this respect are consequently apart from the main action. Miss Wirt, the Osborne girls' governess in *Vanity Fair*, Miss Browning in George Eliot's *Middlemarch*, and Miss Merry in the same author's *Daniel Deronda* are representative.

SCHOOLS IN CHARLOTTE BRONTË'S NOVELS

Institutions of learning played a large part in Charlotte Brontë's life, and the schools that appear in her fiction—*Jane Eyre, Shirley, Villette*—are based largely on those she knew.

Lowood School, to which the heroine is sent in *Jane Eyre*, is modeled on the Clergy Daughters School in Lancashire, which the author and her sisters attended. (Two of these sisters died of typhoid fever contracted at the school.) In theory, though not in practice, the Clergy Daughters School represented a thoughtful attempt to provide an education for a class of young women without money or expectations of money, though of respectable clerical families, perfectly plausible candidates for the middle class, in short, given a little luck. The fortunate among the pupils might marry gentlemen and live a life of leisure; those who married tradesmen or others on the borderline of respectability would have been equipped by the school to do the work of upper servants for their households; and those who did not marry could become governesses or schoolteachers. The curriculum for the Clergy Daughters School included basic academic subjects, some ladylike accomplishments (music, drawing, and French), fancy needlework, "and the nicer kinds of household-work, such as getting up fine linen, ironing, etc." (This description, from the school's 1830 report, can be found in the Norton Critical Edition of *Jane Eyre*, edited by Richard J. Dunn.) Charlotte Brontë's portrait of the Clergy Daughters School emphasizes the cruelty and neglect with which the pupils were treated, and contemporary records show that this portrait is not greatly exaggerated. Yet the school's purpose was sound; after the typhoid epidemic, reforms were carried out to enable this purpose to be more nearly fulfilled. Charlotte Brontë did not return to the Clergy Daughters School, but Jane Eyre plausibly remains at the improved Lowood, benefiting from her studies.

In money matters *Jane Eyre* is aligned with reality, at least with regard to teachers' earnings. Jane's salary at Lowood on her becoming a teacher there is fifteen pounds a year, typical although on the low side. The salary is in addition to room and board. On advancing to a position as governess at Thornfield, she receives thirty pounds a year—again, a fairly usual salary. Later, as schoolmistress of the newly built parish school at Morton, her salary is again thirty pounds a year; this is quite high, but the patroness of the school, Miss Oliver, does things handsomely.

The accomplishments Jane has learned at Lowood School serve her in good stead. She could not have become a governess without them, especially as she must instruct a child whose native language is French. Her interest in drawing amuses her in her spare moments and attracts the attention of a gentleman, just as it should; at Moor House this talent indicates to her benefactors that she is more than a penniless waif and really belongs in the educated middle class, with them. Jane has no flair for singing or playing the piano, important accomplishments for most young ladies; but as Mr. Rochester does both, she need not compete.

In connection with the parish school depicted in Shirley, the reader needs to keep in mind that the distinction between the Church of England and the various dissenting denominations (Methodists, Baptists, Presbyterians, and so forth) was a deep and emotional one for each side. The established Church of England felt itself threatened by the energetic new congregations, just as the traditional manufacturing interests felt threatened by the danger of violence from their workers. In both cases a familiar order of things is challenged by what appears to be an invasion of brash newcomers from the lower classes. In Shirley, which deals with unrest among textile workers but which unlike many "industrial" novels is not sympathetic to the workers as a whole, the religious rivalry forms a counterpoint and a thematic bridge; the leader of the rebellious workers is a thoroughly unpleasant dissenting preacher.

This deep-seated class rivalry underlies what to the present-day reader may be the most puzzling episode in Shirley: a confrontation between the elementary school sponsored by the Church of England (one in which the middle-class young ladies of the parish are expected to serve as volunteer teachers) and its opposite number in the Dissenter camp. The parish pupils, marching in an orderly fashion to a picnic, encounter "the Dissenting and Methodist schools, the Baptists, Independents, and Wesleyans, joined in unholy alliance, and turning purposely into this lane with the intention of obstructing our march and turning us back" (chap. 17). The scene gains a musical background: The leader of the Dissenters "drew forth a hymn book, gave out a verse, set a tune, and they all struck up the most dolorous of canticles." The Church of England contingent, which happens to have a brass band with them, strikes up "Rule, Britannia!" The forces meet head on in the narrow lane, each marching smartly. Virtue, as the author and most of her readers would see it, triumphs, for the Dissenters break and run, their leader pushed into a ditch.

School doings in *Villette* (and in *The Professor,* written from the same experiences) are complex and curious, but, as they take place in Belgium and were consequently puzzling to the original readers, the author explains them.

DICKENS'S SCHOOLS AND TEACHERS

Dickens's fictional dealings with education are many and for the most part negative: The school Dickens most unreservedly praises, Dr. Strong's in *David Copperfield,* is a vaguely drawn rendition of an idealized public school, so clouded by generalizations that its impact on the reader is slight. Mr. Creakle's establishment is a more vivid part of David's experience. A significant aspect of Mr. Creakle's Salem House is that it was not, in the minds of Dickens's original readers, a scandalously bad place but merely a run-of-the-mill private school in which the owner is required to meet no standards, academic or otherwise, and that teaches or pretends to teach subjects imitative of those favored by the upper-class public schools: David is exposed to Latin and the Greek Testament. The masters' constant caning of boys who had not memorized their lessons was not unusual, either, although it is one of the virtues of Dr. Strong's school that such things never happen there.

Nicholas Nickleby sends its protagonist as an assistant master with a salary of five pounds a year (less than one would pay a scullery maid) to a private school that Dickens did intend for his readers to judge as intolerably bad; and indeed they did. Mr. Squeers's Dotheboys Hall is simply a depository for unwanted offspring. The abuses the school perpetrates, based on actual cases, appalled the original readers as much as they do the present-day ones; and *Nicholas Nickleby* was responsible for improved conditions in this murky area.

A private school the excesses of which are of a different sort appears in *Dombey and Son.* Little Paul Dombey, delicate son of a wealthy merchant, attends a school the proprietor of which is eager to impart knowledge but does so in the wrong way and for the wrong reasons. There is no physical cruelty, but relentless psychological pressure keeps the boys at their books, where they attain a superficial layer of intellectual accomplishment and enhance the school's reputation. The original readers would have found the establishment believable.

Mr. Gradgrind's school in *Hard Times* is quite different from the one Paul Dombey attends. It sets out to educate a considerably lower social class, and it ignores the elitist curriculum of Latin and Greek in favor of supposedly practical subjects, "nothing but Facts." Much of the grim, assembly-line atmosphere of Mr. Gradgrind's establishment really existed, for the earliest attempts to educate the hundreds of thousands of lower-class children in England required extreme measures. Most of the children had never developed self-discipline or powers of concentration, and tight regimentation had to be imposed as the only alternative to chaos. The fact-loaded curriculum, scornful as it might be of the things of the imagination, had the advantage of giving the students a set of tangible goals, while standardized teacher training kept the new system going in a predictable way. Dickens, however, sees in this mechanization a threat to individuality. Mr. Gradgrind's new instructor, Mr. M'Choakumchild, is apparently a graduate of one of the training colleges set up in the late 1840s under grants made by the Committee of Council on Education. In Dickens's view, Mr. M'Choakumchild has, with "some one hundred and forty other schoolmasters . . . been lately turned out at the same time, in the same factory, on the same principles, like so many pianoforte legs" (chap. 2).

Our Mutual Friend deals with essentially the same educational scene as does *Hard Times,* and Dickens's annoyance at a hierarchy in which mediocre minds can find a secure perch by conscientiously fulfilling precise requirements continues to make itself apparent. Bradley Headstone, who has acquired his information in a mechanical fasion, is in this way both a villain and a kind of counterfeit. Dickens includes a memorable description of the "ragged school" in which Charley Hexam, Headstone's pupil-teacher or apprentice, gets his first schooling. The problem with this institution, as Dickens perceives it, is that it is at the other extreme from the rigidly systematic new schools: "The teachers, animated solely by good intentions, had no idea of execution, and a lamentable jumble was the upshot of their kind endeavors" (chap. 18/2.1).

HARDY'S *Jude the Obscure:*
TRADITION AND INNOVATION

Jude Fawley spends his life trying to enter a traditional upper-class university, the shining vision of "Christminster" (Oxford), which inspires him as a child to set about learning Latin and Greek on his own and which later brings him to the town of Christminster to ply his trade as a stonemason while he tries to enter one of the colleges. Working one's way through a university is, for the present-day reader, a fairly feasible undertaking; but for a working-class Victorian, it was virtually impossible. Jude's failure to reach his goal may reflect on his common sense but not on the effort he puts in.

While the traditional road to learning has shut Jude out, a new one is opening: The new, post-1870 national school system now gave members of the working class a chance to gain an education for themselves and to hold teaching jobs within the system; and two of Jude's friends—his former schoolmaster, Richard Phillotson, and his cousin, Sue Bridehead——become a part of it. Phillotson has qualified for his post by attending "Wintoncester Training College," apparently one of the "normal schools" set up for the education of prospective teachers since the mid-1840s; when he takes Sue on as a pupil-teacher, Sue becomes eligible to apply for a queen's scholarship and, as Jude puts it, "go to a Training College, and become a first-class certified mistress" (chap. 15/2.1). Such opportunities were a new thing; earlier in the century Sue would have had to content herself with her original job as a shop assistant.

Sue fails in her attempt to rise in the educational hierarchy; she does obtain a scholarship to "Melchester Normal School," but she finds the rigidly restricted and supervised life of the school unbearable. In this part of her personality, Sue is closer to present-day attitudes than to those of the Victorians, and present-day readers must make adjustments in what may seem an unusual direction. To the Victorians, girls of any degree of respectability living away from their families and entrusted to a school must of necessity be protected from any scandal: No private excursions, no visitors besides relatives, and a dormitory curfew of 8:30 P.M. Sue's objections to this life made her appear to the original readers a person of questionable morals and not, as she might seem to us, a healthily independent young woman.

XIII

Courtship, Marriage, and Sex

To a middle-class Victorian woman, marriage was the only game in town. With it she would be considered, within limits, a human being; without it she would be an embarrassment, a superfluity, an object of ridicule. The situation was filled with irony. She could not appear anxious about this, the most crucial event in her life, for visible anxiety would make her a less desirable choice. And she must remain passive, never pursuing, even though the necessity of marriage was for her many times stronger than it was for the careless bachelor she hoped to attract.

Propriety was essential. The middle-class young lady must be chaperoned, must be treated with ceremonious respect, or her value in the marriage market would fall. That she must be sexually chaste goes without saying, and she must avoid as well a long list of stylized situations in which her reputation might be compromised: going on any sort of journey, dining, or going to a play or concert alone with a man. Even to have frequent drawing room conversations with a man to whom one was not engaged, however crowded the drawing room, could have an adverse effect, for the young lady is in a sense being trifled with—her admirer is enjoying her company, monopolizing her charms, with no apparent intention of advancing the courtship to its next stage. A girl might reach a point at which every day that passed without the trifler's proposal brings her nearer to being laughed at. And such an eventuality would, of course, lessen her chance of attracting a subsequent gentleman.

KIND AND CONSIDERATE.

Maud (who, with Ethel, has just been invited to go for a Cruise in a friend's Yacht). "NOW, THE QUESTION IS, WHOM SHALL WE ASK TO CHAPERONE US?—OLD MRS. BUSBEE, OR OLD MISS MAJORIBANKS?" *Maud.* "MRS. BUSBEE."

Jack (who is to be of the Party). "WHICH IS THE WORST SAILOR?" *Maud.* "MRS. BUSBEE."

Jack. "O, THEN ASK HER! FOR THE SOONER SHE GOES DOWN BELOW THE BETTER, YOU KNOW."

"KIND AND CONSIDERATE" (George Du Maurier. Punch)

A *Punch* cartoon by George Du Maurier, 1874. The chaperone was necessary to the prevailing code of etiquette; two young ladies did not go sailing alone with two young men. The present drawing suggests that such a custom could be hard on the chaperone.

"MAKING LOVE"

Today's reader of Victorian novels might think the supposed requirement of physical chastity at odds with the amount of physical sex that seems to be going on: People are constantly making love, even in crowded drawing rooms. The explanation is that the language has shifted. To "make love" meant simply to flirt, to make playfully amorous conversation. Mr. Sedley in Thackeray's *Vanity Fair* observes of Becky Sharp's conversation with Joseph at the dinner table, "Here is Emmy's little friend making love to him as hard as she can" (chap. 4). Adolphus Crosbie, visiting a rather dull country squire in Trollope's *The Small House at Allington*, behaves himself in a way that is more proprietous than it may sound: "He had . . . as a matter of course, taken to such amusements as the place afforded. He had shot the partridges and made love to the young lady, taking these little recreations as compensation for the tedium of the squire's society" (chap. 23).

Similarly, a "lover" is simply a suitor or admirer. Dickens's Lady Tippins of *Our Mutual Friend*, who "is always attended by a lover or two" (chap. 2), is a model of respectability.

NO "DATING"

One of the greatest differences between the Victorian courtship context and our own is that young men and women of good family did not "go out" together. The poor and the working classes did. A servant girl might "walk out" with her suitor on her Sunday afternoon off, and the couple might be said to be "keeping company" until—often for obvious obstetrical reasons—they were married. In cities the very poor often did not bother to marry but lived in what the sociologists of the day called "irregular unions." It was partly to distinguish itself from these strata of society that the middle class insisted on treating its young ladies with stately respect and on viewing all male and female friendships as

leading in a straight line to the altar. Such a ritualistic perfor-
mance meant that all preengagement conversations must take
place in the full view of the lady's friends and family.

This restriction seemed more natural because, for the
most part, the social life of middle-class young people was an
appendage to that of their elders. Parties were not segregated
according to age, and it was the older generation who gave
them. A young man calling on a young lady would usually
make a pretense, at least, of meaning to visit her parents. In
Dickens's *David Copperfield*, Dora Spenlow's best friend en-
courages David's courtship of Dora with the news that "Dora
is coming to stay with me. She is coming home with me the
day after tomorrow. If you would like to call, I am sure papa
would be happy to see you" (chap. 33). To be left alone in the
family parlor with the object of his affections, unaccom-
panied by mother or sister doing embroidery, was for a young
man a rare and in some ways a disquieting experience; the
sudden privacy might turn out to be a maneuver expected to
result in a marriage proposal.

COURTSHIP ETHICS

To set up and maintain a respectable domestic establishment cost a great deal of money, easily four or five times what
a bachelor might spend in keeping up a single life. One had to
have a house and servants; large numbers of children were
virtually inevitable. Because of the expense, the majority of
middle-class men married late, in their thirties and often
beyond. The discrepancy in age of the typical Victorian husband and wife results from this economic fact, in combination
with the groom's natural tendency to choose the prettiest and
happiest of the woman available. An old maid of twenty-five
had usually lost ground in both these categories, and her
eighteen-year-old sister had much the better chance.

The rigidities of this situation led to the general feeling
that it was unethical for a man to appear interested in, let
alone propose marriage to, a woman whom he was unable

within the immediate or foreseeable future to marry. It is important for a present-day reader to realize the degree to which this principle had worked its way into the Victorian mind, for it explains the seeming diffidence of many a fictional suitor who today might plausibly have married the girl at once. The danger of long engagements was greater for women. Should a woman fall in love with a man who could not afford to marry her and then settle back to wait for him, years and years if necessary, she might overstay the brief period of bloom during which she might have caught another and more prosperous husband; and the original man might get away—never reaching a point at which he could marry at all, perhaps, or preferring a bachelor existence or falling in love with a younger and prettier girl.

Just as a young man should not monopolize a young lady's attention unless he planned to propose, a young lady was thought to have no business leading a man on to a proposal she did not intend to accept; to be called a flirt was an insult, not a compliment. It was even assumed, when a women did refuse a proposal, that she must have "encouraged" it and was consequently to be blamed. To an even greater extent, a broken engagement decreased a young woman's marital value regardless of whether she or her fiancé had done the actual jilting: Something was fishy, in either case.

Secret engagements were frowned upon as a violation of society's trust. People could hardly operate efficiently if they were not told what was going on, and other contenders in the marriage arena might waste their time in preliminary maneuvers with one or the other of the secretly engaged couple. The remorse of Jane Fairfax, in Jane Austen's *Emma* springs from her conviction, shared by the original readers, that by agreeing to a secret engagement with Frank Churchill she has entered, as she puts it, into a "life of deceit" (chap. 52/3.16).

THE BACHELOR'S PERIL:
BREACH OF PROMISE

The fact that it was possible to bring suit in a court of law for breach of promise to marry serves as an acknowledgment of the Victorian woman's helplessness in a society in which her only respected and comfortable identity was that of a wife. A man who had falsely promised marriage, especially if he had used this promise as a lure in seducing the woman, could be made to pay damages assessed by a jury for injury to the plaintiff's feelings. (Formerly the ecclesiastical court involved could simply force the defendant to marry the plaintiff, but this practice was stopped in the middle of the eighteenth century.) The promise to marry need not have been in writing, although love letters were considered useful courtroom evidence, nor need there have been witnesses to the declaration.

To be named in a breach of promise suit, whether or not the plaintiff were or had been pregnant, could be highly embarrassing for a young man who hoped to rise in the world. The mere threat of legal action by the prospective bride or her mother could sometimes suffice to bring the groom to the altar. But the proceedings were equally embarrassing, if not more so, to the woman; and women of the solidly respectable class did not indulge in them. Lily Dale, for instance, in Trollope's *The Small House at Allington* does not dream of bringing suit against Adolphus Crosbie, to whom she is quite firmly engaged when he jilts her. But Madelina Demolines, a woman of questionable social position, includes the threat of breach of promise in a quite outrageous plot against Johnny Eames (Trollope, *Last Chronicle of Barset*, chap. 80). Fiction, in fact, usually treated an actual or potential breach of promise action with a comic touch. Dickens's Mr. Pickwick, attempting to tell his landlady that he plans to hire a manservant, somehow gives her the impression he has proposed to her, and the trial of Bardell versus Pickwick is the result (*Pickwick Papers*, chap. 12; 34). Thackeray's Major Pendennis undertakes to get his lovelorn nephew's letters out of the hands of the lady and her father lest the letters show up in court and consequently in the newspapers, and the episode is described in a nostalgic, amused tone.

FORBIDDEN MARRIAGES:
CONSANGUINITY

Numerous characters in Victorian fiction marry their first cousins (Catherine Linton in Emily Bronte's *Wuthering Heights,* for example, successively marries both her first cousins), and the practice was perfectly legal in the eyes of both civil and religious authorities. The "Table of Prohibited Degrees" in the Church of England's Book of Common Prayer listed thirty relatives whom one might not marry (fathers, sisters, and so forth), but first cousins were not on the list.

A difficulty that exercised England throughout the nineteenth century but that rather surprisingly, seldom appears in fiction was that of the "deceased wife's sister": A man was not supposed to marry a woman in this category on the grounds that his former wife's relatives had become literally his own—husband and wife being "one flesh"—and that to marry her sister would constitute incest. This ban was not lifted in England until 1907. If, after Tess's execution, Hardy's Angel Clare did marry Liza-Lu Durbeyfield, as the last chapter of *Tess of the d'Urbervilles* implies, he would have been more than fifteen years in advance of the law permitting him to do so. Tess herself, in suggesting the marriage, meets Clare's objection that Liza-Lu is his sister-in-law with a reassurance to the effect that life in an obscure country village has its advantages: "That's nothing, dearest. People marry sister-laws continually about Marlott" (chap. 58).

MARRIAGE PROCEDURES

One could be married either by banns or by license; the ceremony itself might take place in a church in either case, although after 1836 the holders of a license might instead choose a civil marriage in a registry office. The "crying" of banns—the announcement in the parish church of the intention of a couple to marry—was the traditional method. Banns had to be read on three successive Sundays before the marriage took place.

A license to marry without banns was theoretically granted by the archbishop of Canterbury, although in reality it became a fairly routine affair. The fee for a license was one pound, and this drawback might be weighed by engaged couples against the publicity and the time required for marriage by banns. An additional option was provided by the Marriage Act of 1836 in the substitution of a certificate from the superintendent of registrar for the usual license; the procedure was essentially the same, but Dissenters were relieved from the implied authority of an archbishop.

Church marriages could be performed only during the "canonical hours," a stricture that added considerable drama to the necessity of getting to the church on time. During most of the century the hours were from eight in the morning until noon; in the 1880s the hours were extended to 3 P.M.

CEREMONIES AND CUSTOMS

Perhaps the most noticeable difference between the weddings that take place in Victorian novels and those to which American readers are accustomed is the comparative lack of pomp. One did not reserve a church and put on a private parade for one's invited guests: the churches were open to everyone and irrelevant people might be all over praying or looking at the tombstones and memorial tablets, while the ceremony is taking place. This state of affairs was required by law; because of the centuries-old danger of a woman's (or man's) being in effect kidnapped into a legal union, no marriage ceremony could take place behind closed doors. Thus, in Jane Eyre, the stranger who interrupts the marriage of Jane and Mr. Rochester has wandered in from the churchyard and has caused no presentiment of alarm until the fatal moment. In *David Copperfield,* David's marriage to Dora brings into the ceremony the tone of playful grotesquerie that has characterized the courtship: David dimly remembers "some other people strolling in . . . an ancient mariner behind me, strongly flavoring the church with rum" (chap. 43). When in Hardy's *The Return of the Native* Thomasin and Wildeve finally marry, after a sequence of misadventures with both banns and license, Wildeve's earlier love attends the ceremony disguised in a heavy veil—a melodramatic but feasible exploit, since it was not customary to restrict the church to invited guests (chap. 19/2.8).

Wedding rings were put on the bride's finger during the ceremony, as they are today, but the double ring ceremony in which the groom, too, receives a ring, to the accompaniment of phrases added to the marriage ceremony, is a twentieth-century innovation. Nor did the Victorian bride-to-be wear a diamond solitaire ring, unless she happened to own one already; throughout most of the century, the engagement ring had not yet taken on its present role as the necessary sign of a coming marriage.

The white wedding gown gained favor during the century and by the 1870s was customary and had taken on the supposedly traditional significance (that the wearer is a virgin) - that it still possesses. However, brides in the earlier decades wore other colors with no shadow of stigma. Amelia in *Vanity Fair,* for instance, is married in brown silk (chap. 22); and although Amelia's passion for her husband is the strongest sexual attraction in the novel, readers need have no suspicions about her premarital propriety.

ELOPEMENTS

Couples who wanted to marry without the delay of banns or license went to Scotland, most notoriously to Gretna Green, a village just over the border. Here the pair need only declare before witnesses their wish to marry to have the marriage made legal; in Gretna Green this ceremony, such as it was, was traditionally performed by the blacksmith. The mention of Gretna Green thus refers to an elopement and often to the machinations of a fortune hunter. Miroblant, a presumptuous French cook in Thackeray's *Pendennis*, has decided to marry an Englishwoman—any Englishwoman— "and fly with one to Gretna Grin" (chap. 23).

Realistic fiction almost always presented an elopement as a bad idea that the participants would soon regret. Isabella Linton's runaway marriage to Heathcliff, for example, turns bitter at once.

MIDDLE-CLASS SEX LIVES

There is no doubt that a double standard of sexual morality was in force for the Victorians. Women were expected to remain chaste until marriage and faithful thereafter. With men it was quite different. "Adventures" with actresses, milliners, prostitutes (high-class ones, preferably), or even kept mistresses were not considered irrevocably disgraceful during the long interval between a man's sexual maturity and the point at which he could afford to marry. A young man was said to be "sowing his wild oats"; the assumption was that he would then settle down and sow some domestic ones. After marriage, keeping a mistress or just general philandering did not gain quite the acceptance that wild oats did, but such activities were far from unknown. Adultery in men was considered less serious than in women, as the era's divorce legislation indicates (see below). A man's adultery did not threaten the authenticity of his heirs while that of a woman might be the means of her passing off "spurious offspring," as the saying was, upon her husband.

According to popular belief, the natural sexuality of men and of women were quite different, and this difference gave support to society's double standard. Men were possessed, exclusively, of the sex drive for the species, helpless before the unfortunate (if enjoyable) necessity to find relief. Women, farther from the animals and closer to heaven, not only had no sexual feelings but actively disliked sex, submitting to it in obedience to their husbands and in hopes of the compensating joys of maternity. It was, of course, middle-class respectable women to whom this stereotype was administered; some prostitutes—"abandoned women," abandoned, that is, to their own senses—appeared to enjoy sex.

The degree to which this generalized view was or was not valid in individual cases would be very difficult to ascertain, especially from the woman's side. No pornography was written for women, and no class of people made a living fulfilling their sexual needs or acting out their fantasies. Had women desired such things, they could not have paid for them, and consequently the Victorian feminine libido could be said to have left little trace. Certainly we might assume that uniform conditioning will not always produce uniform results and that a great deal depends upon the individual personality; the repressive atmosphere that converts one middle-class woman in her marriage bed into a dutiful zombie, paralyzed with shame and quite numb below the waist, might in another woman result in a stubborn if secret determination to experience the forbidden. If she then had the good luck to marry a man who did not think of his own sexuality as a beastly and deplorable need, she might have a chance of a satisfying sex life. Such a combination of fortunate events would seem against the odds, however.

Something of an optimistic note with regard to the sexuality of Victorian women might be found in the horror with which the middle classes regarded the "vice" of masturbation: Little girls were considered sneakier in this endeavor than little boys, since the evidence was harder to find; and Victorian mothers' guidebooks listed symptoms to watch for: nail biting, circles under the eyes, and a fondness for heavily spiced foods. If feminine masturbation were so emphatically on the public mind, then women must have known about it, might have been tempted to try it, and might then, if they could overcome the guilt with which the act was laden and which they were dutifully instilling into their daughters, have had some chance of orgasmic enjoyment.

In fairness to the masculine side, it should be added that the perils of masturbation were made just as melodramatic, if not more so, for little boys. Insanity and debility were regularly predicted as a result, and one of the beliefs that marred masculine sexuality in general—in this case, that semen was an irreplaceable bit of vitality and that every ejaculation shortened one's life—added its bit of horror to masturbation as well as to more sociable exertions.

CONTRACEPTIVE TECHNIQUES

Birth control techniques were known to some extent in the nineteenth century, especially in the upper and upper-middle classes; and the age saw several attempts to spread this knowledge in the poorer classes, where a large family in hard times could starve or succumb to diseases that would not have killed them if they had been fewer in number and consequently better nourished. Francis Place, a member of the working class who became active in radical politics, distributed in the 1820s a series of handbills explaining the desirability and some of the known techniques of contraception. Place himself was not energetically persecuted, but some of his successors were; and the impact of such teachings upon the population is hard to gauge.

Two of the techniques most frequently recommended by Place and others were those of coitus interruptus, the man's withdrawal before ejaculation, and douching by the woman after intercourse. Neither was at all foolproof; all one could hope for was a slightly smaller family than one would have otherwise. A pleasanter and more effective method, also frequently recommended, was the insertion into the vagina of a small sponge, about the size of a walnut, attached to a narrow ribbon for easy retrieval (to follow the descriptions in Place's handbills). The sponge absorbed enough semen to make its effectiveness rank comparatively high; it was cheap and reusable (it had only to be washed out); and it could not be felt by either partner when in use.

In the last decades of the nineteenth century the increasing availability of vulcanized rubber allowed the development of several types of rather effective cervical caps. Rubber also became the material of much more efficient condoms, manufactured at a price low enough for the working class to afford them. (Condoms had been in use for centuries, made of such materials as fish skin and soft leather; but they had had a small and elite market.)

It should be emphasized that information about the techniques just mentioned was circulated in Victorian times in a clandestine, underground manner and many people knew nothing of any of them. The Catholic Church had consistently opposed birth control and the spread of information about it. The typical Victorian, whatever his religion, tended to think with moral repugnance of contraception as a means of gratifying the baser passions while unnaturally preventing the consequences of such gratification. The only means of reducing the size of one's family of which the Victorian consciousness could fully approve was abstinence.

In the novels, the size of families is not a reliable guide to speculations on whether or not the parents might be practicing birth control; to do so is probably to consider too curiously. It is true that large numbers of children, especially if the father has a small or uncertain income, is consistently associated with comic-relief irresponsibility: Dickens's Micawbers, Trollope's Quiverfuls, and Hardy's Durbeyfields are a few examples. And the more respectable fictional families tend to have only one or two children—fewer, in fact, than one would have been likely to find, on an average, in real life. However, this situation may result from the authors' simply declining to add supernumerary siblings who would play no part in the plots; or it may be that the link between respectable parents and small families had to do, in Victorian minds, not with protected sex but with less sex.

WOMEN'S PROPERTY RIGHTS

Throughout most of the nineteenth century, married women could not own or dispose of property separately from their husbands, and a husband had a right to any property his wife inherited or earned. (Marriage settlements comprise something of a qualification here, but these were a phenomenon of the upper reaches of the middle class and beyond.) This situation is reflected in the novels in a way the original readers would have taken as a matter of course. Mr. Murdstone, the protagonist's stepfather in *David Copperfield*, who makes a career of marrying docile young women with a bit of money, perpetrates his domestic villainy with the full approval of the law. Poor Mrs. Tulliver in George Eliot's *the Mill on the Floss* loses her cherished household goods when her husband goes bankrupt and his property is sold; these teapots and tablecloths were of her own purchase, bought "before I ever though o' marrying your father!" (chap. 22/3.2).

In 1882 the Married Woman's Property Act, which consolidated several acts of the preceding decade, gave women considerably more power over property they inherited or acquired. Legally a married woman became a *feme sole*, a status greatly differing from that earlier assigned to her by the common law, in which husband and wife had been legally one person. This act changed many women's lives, not surprisingly, and had a significant effect on the public image of women as individuals. In George Gissing's *New Grub Street*, set in the middle and late 1880s, the protagonists's wife inherits a comfortable sum and offers to share it with her husband, even though the couple has been living apart. Mrs. Reardon's offer is a genuinely good natured one, as Gissing's original readers would have recognized; she was under no obligation to share the money with her husband.

DIVORCE

For the Victorians there were two types of divorce: judicial separation, in which the parties concerned might live apart but could not remarry, and the more absolute divorce in which the parties could remarry. The first type, divorce *a mensa et thoro*, "separation from bed and board," could until 1857 be granted by an ecclesiastical court and was a simpler business all round. The second type, divorce *a vinculo matrimonii*, "divorce from the bond of matrimony," required until the same year an act of Parliament, following preliminary suits in ecclesiastical and common law courts.

The Matrimonial Causes Act of 1857 created a special lay court for all matters connected with divorce, the Court for Divorce and Matrimonial Causes, having invested in it the powers formerly exercised in matrimonial cases by the ecclesiastical courts, the courts of common law, and the House of Lords. The act did not broaden the grounds for divorce (listed below). It did, however, reduce the cost of obtaining a divorce, so the existence of one law for the rich and another for the poor was no longer so obviously the case.

Judicial separation, as divorce *a mensa et thoro* was called after 1857, could be obtained by either husband or wife on grounds of adultery, physical cruelty, or desertion for two or more years. Usually the court would direct the separate maintenance of the wife at the expense of the husband.

The Victorians' double standard of sexual attitudes shows up clearly in the grounds allowable for absolute divorce, one in which the parties might remarry. An action could be brought by a husband on grounds of his wife's adultery alone; in an action brought by a wife, however, a charge against her husband of adultery had to be joined to a second charge of physical cruelty or of desertion for two or more years. Thus a husband's adultery, in a sense, was protected by law, while a wife who did the same thing could lose her children, any property she had brought into the marriage, and, of course, her identity as a member of respectable society.

A feature of Victorian divorces that may strike American readers as odd is that a husband might bring suit against the man who has, in his opinion, alienated the affections of his wife. A jury finding in favor of the husband might then order the defendant to pay damages to the husband.

Victorian divorce procedures had to have a guilty party and an innocent party; two guilty parties—two adulterers, say—could not by the principles of the law obtain a divorce and would therefore be condemned to live with each other, so to speak. A court looked hard for evidence of collusion: A husband and wife conniving to get a divorce through a set-up adulterous affair, for example, would have to be unusually clever to avoid detection. And if the injured party had at any time in the past forgiven the defendent, or "condoned" the midbehavior in question, divorce became unobtainable.

The question of what could and what could not, in the eyes of God and the law, be forgiven was in fact central to divorce legislation. For a husband to forgive an erring wife was considered dangerously immoral, threatening to the stability of other families and, in fact, to the country; a wife, too, was allowed a scorecard upon which a husband might eventually run up enough abuses to be declared officially unforgivable. This view of marriage, not limited to the Victorians and in fact still central to many states' divorce laws in the United States, may seem to present-day readers savagely inhumane, almost a kind of institutional sadomasochism. But we should keep in mind that the concept of the happiness of the individual as a high social priority is a relatively new one and that such a concept may be (as it has been) variously interpreted.

WIDOWHOOD

To be left a widow with a comfortable jointure and a good social position might not have been a consciously articulated hope among Victorian wives, but the simultaneous independence and respect enjoyed by widows represent a combination hard to find elsewhere in the social landscape. A great deal of a widow's comfort and social standing would depend on the amount of her jointure, the income left to her for her lifetime from her husband's estate, the bulk of this property having in the usual course of things gone to the eldest son. Since the amount of this income represented the husband's decision at the time he made his will, a widow was in a sense still dependent upon her husband's benevolence for her status in the eyes of other people, as she had been during his life.

Elderly or middle-aged widows, if "well left," might command the prestige enjoyed by Lady Russell in Jane Austen's *Persuasion* or Mrs. Mountstuart-Jenkins in Meredith's *The Egoist*. Younger widows were expected to remarry, especially if they had children in need of a father's guidance. Thackeray's Amelia in *Vanity Fair* acts in accordance with the reading public's expectations when she finally marries Dobbin. And Eleanor Bold in Trollope's *Barchester Towers* becomes an object of terror to her friends and family because of the array of unsuitable men whom it appears she might marry. Only when Eleanor is safely united with the exemplary Mr. Arabin does her family relax and regard her once again as her amiable self.

COURTSHIP AND MARRIAGE IN THE NOVELS

In Victorian fiction, centrally concerned as it is with women's need to get married in the first place and happily married if possible, the topography over which these campaigns are fought is presented for the most part accurately. What is not realistic is the high degree of success. Statistics show that as many as one in four middle-class Victorian women never married; some of these became governesses, if they had to earn their living, while the majority became "maiden aunts" in the households of their married brothers or sisters—self-effacing, apologetic, eager to please, often supervising the servants and otherwise acting as unpaid housekeepers. A variation of the maiden aunt was the unmarried daughter who lived with and cared for her aging parents. Statistics are less useful in questioning the second premise of the novels' view of courtship—that the heroine will marry a wonderful man and live with him happily thereafter—but one may feel dubious nevertheless.

Occasionally a novel will show some awareness of the fact that the heroine's fortunate fate does not accord with the laws of probability. Jane Austen often adds to her narrative tone a playful awareness of the fictional conventions upon which she and her readers are agreed. In Charlotte Bronte's *Shirley*, the coheroine, Caroline Helstone, is warned by other characters against the psychological damage to be incurred by reading novels and getting one's hopes up; but Caroline falls in love nevertheless, managing luckily to suffer so sweetly and with such integrity that her lover comes to his senses and Caroline is saved.

THE POWER OF SCANDAL:
ELIOT AND HARDY

Many Victorian plots depend heavily on the heroine's consciousness of public opinion, an opinion that was always ready to pounce upon the least appearance of sexual guilt. To the original feminine readers these taboos were not puzzling, for they obeyed them themselves.

In George Eliot's *The Mill on the Floss*, Maggie Tulliver finds herself in a thoroughly Victorian dilemma: The young man whom she loves and who loves her, but who is engaged to her cousin Lucy, takes her for a row on the river. First through absentmindedness and then through design, Stephen Guest lets the boat go so far downstream that they cannot get back the same day. It would be impossible for Maggie to return after a night spent unchaperoned in the company of a young man, whether or not sexual intercourse had occured, and retain any fraction of her good name. Complete disgrace must follow. The only recourse, as Stephen knows, is for Maggie to agree to marry him and to return home, after a trip to Scotland for the ceremony, as his bride (chap. 55/6.13). Maggie chooses, however, not to do so great a wrong to her cousin Lucy; she returns home alone and finds herself the town castaway.

When Hardy's Bathsheba Everdene in *Far from the Madding Crowd* pursues Sergeant Troy to Bath (chap. 32), she sets out with the conscious intention of informing him that she has given him up and that he is to stay away from her. But she underestimates the distance, and her horse goes lame when she arrives in Bath. When she does return home, the horse having recovered, she is married to Troy. Even Bathsheba, careless as she often is of convention, would not have dared come home alone after an absence of several days.

Divorces in Fiction:
Thackeray, Meredith, and Hardy

Social disgrace was the inevitable consequence of divorce, in life as well as literature, despite the legal reforms that made the obtaining of a divorce less financially harrowing. This disgrace fell largely on the woman, regardless of whether she or her husband had played the part of villain. She could not ordinarily get custody of her children; children were considered the property of their father, and a woman who had managed to divorce her husband for a combination of adultery and physical cruelty, say, might find that the circumstances did not affect the law's view of a father's rights. Furthermore, a larger number of husbands brought divorce actions against their wives (usually for adultery) than the other way round—a discrepancy that resulted from the greater difficulty wives found in proving acceptable grounds and from the fact that wives were less able to pay the initial costs of a legal action. The idea of divorce, then, was associated in the public mind with adulterous women, and respectable society had no place for a divorcée.

In Thackeray's *The Newcomes*, Lady Clara Newcome escapes from her sadistic husband to becoms the wife of the man she loves—and must then live an isolated life, shut out from respectable dinner parties and feminine friendships (chap. 58). Either Sir Barnes Newcome's abuse of his wife was not sufficient for her to divorce him or Lady Clara lacked the initiative or the funds to begin such an action. The course she does take, that of leaving her husband's roof for the protection of the man who has loved her from afar, automatically makes her the guilty party. Sir Barnes goes through the steps that were standard before 1857, when Parliament streamlined the procedure. He first obtains a divorce *a mensa et thoro* (a judicial separation) from an ecclesiastical court, presumably in Doctors' Commons; Thackeray does not mention this rather perfunctory step, but it would have been required at the time. Sir Barnes then brings an action in a court of common law against Lord Highgate, the man whom he charges with the alienation of Lady Clara's affections. The jury, sympathizing with Sir Barnes, "consoled the injured husband with immense damages, and left him free to pursue the farther steps for releasing himself altogether" (chap. 58). The case is then taken before the the House of Lords, where it attracts a great deal of newspaper publicity—another factor in Lady Clara's disgrace. After the House of Lords passes a special bill, the divorce is final and Lady Clara is able to marry Lord Highgate. And, as Thackeray insists, the ending is not really a happy one.

An exceptional Victorian protagonist in that she survives the threat of a divorce and is not ejected from good society is Diana Warwick of Meredith's *Diana of the Crossways*. The author does make it clear that for Diana even to go to a dinner party under this shadow is an act requiring great courage. Circumstances are on Diana's side with regard to gaining the sympathy both of the characters in the book and of the original readers: She is innocent of adultery with Lord Dannisburgh, the cabinet minister with whom her husband accuses her of misbehaving; and the divorce action fails, the court finding that Mr. Warwick has not proved his charge (chap. 14). (Meredith based his episode on the attempt of the husband of Mrs. Caroline Norton to bring an action against Lord Melbourne, then prime minister, for the seduction of his wife.)

Divorce or the idea of divorce appears in Hardy's *The Woodlanders* and again in *Jude the Obscure*. In *The Woodlanders*, the Matrimonial Causes Act of 1857, which simplified divorce procedure though it did not enlarge the traditional grounds for divorce, is the cause of an unfortunate misunderstanding. The heroine's father, having heard rumors that the new court will make "un-marrying . . . as easy as marrying" (chap. 37), tells his daughter she can easily divorce the husband who has left her and take up with a former suitor. This hope is broken when it is found that the husband "had not been sufficiently cruel" to his wife and that she had after all no grounds for divorcing him. The fact that Melbury, the father, is not worried about social disgrace attaching itself to his daughter through any connection with divorce is ironically characteristic of Melbury: A timber merchant in an isolated area, he is himself barely within the lower ranks of the middle class. Although he sends his daughter to a boarding school to learn refinement and is anxious to live a higher-class life, he does not really know the rules.

The plot of *Jude the Obscure*, set in the last decades of the century when divorces were no longer too expensive for the working class, is made up of symmetrical marital complications. Jude and his cousin Sue, in love with each other, obtain divorces from their respective spouses; they live together but do not marry; eventually, on separating, each remarries the previously divorced spouse. The divorces are obtained in each case by the husbands on grounds of adultery and desertion. Jude's wife, who has left him and gone to Australia, writes asking him to divorce her: "it would be a kindness to her, since then she could marry and live respectably" (chap. 34/4.6). Sue's husband, Phillotshon, also divorces Sue at her request.

Phillotson's attitude toward his wife differs considerably from the standard Victorian reaction of horror at extramarital attachments, and Hardy makes an ironic point in the consequences of Phillotson's understanding: When he allows Sue to leave him and join her lover, Phillotson is fired from his job as schoolmaster because, as the town sees it, Phillotson has scandalously condoned his wife's adultery.

XIV

Transportation and Communication

These two crucial ingredients of present-day life—the ability to move oneself from place to place and to communicate efficiently with persons at a distance—were as valuable to middle-class Victorians as they are to us. The means differed, but not the motives.

HORSEBACK RIDING

For the upper and middle classes, horseback riding was for the most part a recreation; one hunted in the country or rode in the parks of London. Mr. Carker of Dickens's *Dombey and Son* rides to work instead of having himself driven in a horse-drawn vehicle, but this habit is presented as an unusual thing to do, one of Mr. Carker's unpleasant eccentricities. Dr. Fitzpiers in Hardy's *The Woodlanders* also rides a horse to visit his patients, but, as he points out, he lives in a heavily wooded area and can follow shorter routes through the trees than he could if he drove a gig. The automobile was, of course, undreamed-of; the first specimens appeared at the end of the Victorian age and were looked upon simply as toys for the wealthy.

Ladies always rode sidesaddle—facing ahead, of course, not sideways, with the right leg hooked over a curved support and the left leg in a stirrup. The seat itself was usually flat, shaped something like an elongated pear, and covered with quilted leather. In the 1830s an important modification was made to the sidesaddle with the addition of a prong that

"HEREDITARY SPORTSMEN: THREE GENERATIONS" (R. Caton Woodville. *Illustrated London News*)

On a well-trained horse, a woman riding side saddle could keep up with the field. Trollope's Lizzie Eustace, in *The Eustace Diamonds*, pictured herself in this elegantly self-confident role when she set out to join the hunt.

curved from behind around the rider's right calf. The older saddle had supported the rider's leg just above the knee with an in-curving piece on either side of the pommel; and although the rider could stay on a quiet horse at a moderate pace, her seat was not very secure. The new "leaping head" allowed a rider actively to grip the saddle with her leg, holding herself on by the pressure she could exert against the left pommel piece and the new one farther down the left side; and although she could not really control the horse as one can when riding astride, she had a much greater chance of staying on and could even jump fences and go foxhunting. (As the new design became popular, the pommel support to the right was omitted, since it was not needed. The newer saddles thus had two supports curving away from each other, while the older ones had two supports curving toward each other.)

The ladies' riding habit, usually a tailored jacket and a skirt with a train, was considered quite becoming, especially in the days of the "crinoline" or hoop petticoat, when the riding habit provided a refreshing change of outline. Lady Alexandrina De Courcy in Trollope's *The Small House at Allington* often wanders about in her habit when she comes in from riding, even though the jacket is too tight to allow her to play a good game of billiards (chap. 23). And Lady Eveleen de Courcy (no relation) in Charlotte Yonge's *The Heir of Redclyffe*, getting up an impromptu ball on a lawn, "actually set them quadrilling in spite of adverse circumstances, dancing better, in her habit, than most people without one" (chap. 7).

The necessity of the sidesaddle as an adjunct of feminine modesty is very much taken for granted. Even Hardy's rebellious Bathsheba Everdene, an accomplished rider on any saddle, "quite at home anywhere between a horse's head and its tail," is deeply embarrassed to find that Gabriel Oak has seen her riding astride (chap. 3).

As a matter of etiquette, gentlemen rode on the ladies' "off" side (to the right); since both the lady's legs were on the left side of her horse, another horse jostling close on that side could give her a painful squash. It was taken for granted that all gentlemen could ride. David Copperfield's ascent into the middle class is helped by his friend Steerforth, who teaches him riding, among other gentlemanly accomplishments (chap. 21); and David is thus able to make a dashing appearance at Dora Spenlow's picnic by hiring a "gallant gray" for the occasion (chap. 33).

HORSE-DRAWN VEHICLES:
PUBLIC AND PRIVATE

Public vehicles for long-distance travel included primarily the stagecoach, familiar to American moviegoers since the English design was similar to those used in the American West. The teams of horses were changed at frequent intervals and performed most of their journey at a trot. Passengers paid less for "outside" seats, on the roof; Mr. Squeers, the tyrannical schoolmaster in Dickens's *Nicholas Nickleby*, fetches his new pupils from London to Yorkshire on the outside of the coach even though it is snowing—a fit introduction of the pupils to their new and economical mode of life. Gentlemen might ride outside, to enjoy the view and smoke cigars, but ladies did not.

Coaching had become a way of life, with a network of roads and inns and a hierarchy of skilled drivers, when in the 1830s the railroads made the coaches obsolete. A coach averaging ten or eleven miles an hour could not compete with a train making the same journey at thirty or forty and charging its passengers a lower fare. Novelists during most of the Victorian age tended to speak of the stagecoaches in a tone of elegiac nostalgia; the opening chapter of George Eliot's *Felix Holt, the Radical* provides a colorful sample of this pleasant indulgence, as does Tom Pinch's journey to London in Dickens's *Martin Chuzzlewit* (chap. 36). As a general rule of thumb, a reader can establish the time setting of a novel on one side or the other of the mid-1830s according to whether the characters travel by rail or by stagecoach.

A slower and cheaper form of public travel was provided by the carriers' vans that regularly transported parcels but

DETAIL FROM "THE ATHENEUM CLUB PALL MALL" (*Illustrated London News*)

A hansom cab and driver. The passenger entered through the doors, here opened, at the front of the vehicle; the driver sat at the rear, the reins passing over the roof. Despite its having only two wheels, the hansom was well balanced and speedy—elementarily, the best mode of transportation for Sherlock Holmes.

into which passengers might fit. Mrs. Dollery's van in Hardy's *The Woodlanders*, provides the only public transportation to the environs of Little Hintock. Dickens's working-class characters include the carriers Jarvis of *David Copperfield* and John Cheerybingle of *The Cricket on the Hearth.*

The horse-drawn omnibuses introduced in London in the late 1820s became the most successful form of mass transportation in the cities. The omnibuses were drawn (slowly) by only two horses, or sometimes three, and carried sixteen or more passengers; their "double decker" design was continued in the gasoline-powered buses of the twentieth century. Middle-class Victorians usually preferred cabs to buses, but the novels show a few exceptions: Miss Bunion, an unpretentious poet in Thackeray's *Pendennis*, is delighted to find an omnibus to take her all the way to Brompton for sixpence, and Mr. Harding in Trollope's *The Warden* proceeds humbly about his London errands by the same means.

Other vehicles for public hire included hackney cabriolets, also called "cabs" or "four wheelers," which were weighty and dignified and might be used, for example, to convey the bride and groom from the church after a wedding. Hansom cabs were two-wheeled, one-horse vehicles that, in comparison to hackneys, conferred little status. They were, however, well designed for balance (the driver sat on an elevated seat behind the passenger compartment, the reins passing over the roof), comparatively cheap, and quite fast. It is not surprising that they should be the favored means of transportation for Sherlock Holmes: "A minute later we were both in a hansom, driving furiously for the Brixton Road" (Doyle, *A Study in Scarlet*, chap. 3).

"Coach" was a fairly general term; when applied to a hired vehicle, it usually meant a closed carriage such as a hackney cab. David Copperfield "stopped an empty coach that was going by" and got into it with Martha Endell, the prostitute who aids in the search for Little Emily (chap. 50).

The "fly" was an unusually elegant four-wheeled carriage with a collapsible top, often found for hire at railway stations. One such fly, with its driver, Flitch, figures importantly in the

"A 'block' in Park Lane," by M Jackson. *Illustrated London News*, December 17, 1864, p. 604.

A Victorian traffic jam. A passsenger atop the horse-drawn bus, upper left, appears to be attacking with his umbrella a hansom cab driver; a donkey cart, pedestrians and sheep mix in the lower layers.

complex logistics of Meredith's *The Egoist*. Flies were expensive to hire, but they were admitted to the parks; one could not drive round the fashionable "ring" in Hyde Park in a hansom cab—furiously or otherwise.

Uppermost in prestige among private vehicles were the heavy family carriages, broughams, chariots, barouches, varying in style but all drawn by two or even four horses, closed or closeable for the privacy and comfort of their occupants, and with places outside for the accompanying servants: a seat (called a "box," although it was not enclosed) for the coachman and steps or rungs in the back for the footmen. Families entitled to bear coats of arms had them painted on the doors of their carriages, where they aided identification and occasionally enabled a family to be represented in a funeral procession by the simple procedure of sending the coach, empty, with the blinds drawn.

The various light and open gigs, curricles, and pony carts are associated with young people, who might even do their own driving. Eleanor Harding of Trollope's *The Warden* has a pony carriage; Becky Sharp, on becoming Mrs. Rawden Crawley and setting up housekeeping in Mayfair, drives her own open carriage in Hyde Park.

When traveling on the Continent, people often took their own carriages and hired horses for them, stage by stage, as they went. During the crossing of the English Channel, the carriages were kept on deck where their owners might make use of them as private deck chairs.

RAILWAYS

Novelists found the railway of great use. The question of who is in what train, bound whither, for what purpose becomes pivotal to the plot in Dickens's *Hard Times*. Thackeray's Clive Newcome is suspected of kissing his cousin Ethel while going through a tunnel (*The Newcomes*, chap. 42), and one wonders, in fact, why this opportunity for mild scandal was not used in fiction more often. Perhaps it had already been done to death in family jokes. A railway train provides a sudden and melodramatic end for Dickens's Mr.

Advertisement for Ogden's Guinea Gold Cigarettes. *Illustrated London News,*

An unrealistic dialogue. Smoking in a woman's presence was not considered polite, nor did people mention the brand names of products in casual conversation. Advertising in 1898, as now, sought to create a world of its own. However, the railway car's passenger compartment is a typical one.

Carker, villain of *Dombey and Son*, who is run over and his "mutilated fragments" cast into the air (chap. 55). Trollope's Ferdinand Lopez commits suicide by stepping in front of an express train in *The Prime Minister* (chap. 60). Captain Brown in Elizabeth Gaskell's *Cranford* is run over while rescuing a child who has wandered onto the tracks (chap. 2). Mrs. Henry Wood gets rid of two characters and radically reroutes her plot in a single-paragraph railway accident in *East Lynn* (chap. 14).

Railway scenes in novels occasionally require the reader to keep in mind the layout of the passenger car that evolved during the Victorian era. The earliest passenger compartments were literally horse-drawn carriages, the wheels modified and of course minus the horses, strung together; and this small-scale coziness was preserved in the later versions. For some time, in fact, one could put one's own carriage onto a flat-bed railway car and sit inside the carriage; Mr. Dombey travels in this way to Leamington (Dickens, *Dombey and Son*, chap. 20).

Most of the railway companies—each of which designed its own cars—distinguished strictly between first-, second-, and third-class compartments. Roughly, first class was for the gentry, second class, for the gentry's servants and for unpretentious tradespeople, and third class, for working people, with prices and accommodations scaled accordingly. (Some of the earliest third-class carriages were open boxes, without roofs or seats, in which the passengers stood and marveled that they could travel so fast so cheaply.)

A first-class compartment held six or eight passengers in two facing seats. In early carriages, the compartment had a door to the outside (or two, one on each side), so that passengers could get in and out at stations, but had no connections with the other compartments. The "corridor" plan, a great improvement, retained the door that opened directly from each compartment to the station platform but added a corridor on the other side.

The dining car was a late development, and passengers became accustomed to rushing in and out of station restaurants or taking hampers of food with them.

THE UNDERGROUND RAILWAY

The underground railway, a form of transportation Londoners now call the "tube" and Americans the "subway," dates from the early 1860s, when a line was opened that conveyed passengers a distance of almost four miles and made use of steam-powered trains. Although new lines continued to be built, this innovation remained for some time a conveyance for the working classes and for the more threadbare members of the middle classes. It is consequently seldom mentioned in the novels. Frank Greystock in Trollope's *The Eustace Diamonds*, planning to marry a woman with no money, mentally lists what he considers a grim set of changes in his life: He must give up his comfortable bachelor lodgings, rent a house in an unfashionable part of town, and—crowning indignity—travel to and from his law chambers by the underground railway (chap. 18).

Early underground lines were constructed on the cut-and-cover principle: The laborers dug a trench and then roofed it over. (Portions of what are now the Circle, Central, and Metropolitan lines date from this early phase of construction.) Since London is largely underlaid by blue clay, an excellent kind of soil for deep tunnels, methods of constructing circular tunnels developed rapidly. The underground system was able to remain solvent in spite of, or perhaps because of, the low fares it charged; and the use of electric engines made the air more breathable, but the underground's social status as a mode of transportation did not improve until the First World War brought about a general shift in values.

SHIPS

The major change in travel by water a reader of Victorian fiction needs to remember is that wooden sailing ships were replaced by iron steamships during the century. The shift was more gradual than that from stagecoach to railway, since there were more types of boats and the technical choices were more complex.

The sailing vessels were smaller and slower; getting a trip underway in one took days. A ship leaving London would proceed down the Thames to Gravesend, two days away with favorable tides, there to unfurl her sails and face the ocean. Thus the emigrants to Australia in *David Copperfield* receive farewell visits for some time after they have actually cast off in London, the visitors coming and going in small boats (chap. 57).

Sailing vessels and steam-powered ones shared the sea for some time. Dickens's Martin Chuzzlewit, after crossing the Atlantic in a sailing vessel, is taken ashore in New York in a steamboat, apparently one with a paddle wheel; it looked, "as it worked its long slim legs, like some enormously magnified insect or antediluvian monster" (*Martin Chuzzlewit*, chap. 15). When Mary Barton takes her first look at the harbor of Liverpool, she sees both "white-sailed ships . . . gliding with the ensigns of all nations" and "puffs and clouds of smoke from the countless steamers" (Elizabeth Gaskell, *Mary Barton*, Chap. 27). Steam-driven paddle wheels were in use for some time before the development of the screw propellor; screws were known to be better—among other things, they were less affected by the tilting of the ship in rough seas—but they required a more powerful engine to drive them, the invention of which took time. It is a paddle-wheeled steamer that runs over Magwitch as he attempts to drown Compeyson in Dickens's *Great Expectations* (chap. 54). Iron was used for shipbuilding in the second half of the century.

LETTERS, TELEGRAMS, AND TELEPHONES

Today's readers might be suspicious of the fulsomeness and frequency with which characters in Victorian fiction write letters; the convenience of such habits for an author's storytelling purposes seems as if the author might be stretching reality. It is true, however, that the Victorians wrote a great many letters. With no telephones and with travel (though greatly improved since the previous century) still not efficient enough to allow face-to-face conversations at a moment's notice, letters were the natural resort. The pace of life was slower; to spend one's morning dealing with one's correspondence was not unusual. Ladies in particular took pride in a reputation for writing entertaining letters, and this form of expression was in fact one of the few outlets for verbal creativity in which they could indulge with society's approval. Finally, the Victorian postal service was remarkably efficient, with four home deliveries a day in some parts of London, and one could send lengthy missives or brief notes back and forth quite easily.

In the early decades of the century, letter writing was a more expensive and less frequent undertaking. Postage was expensive and was usually paid by the recipient of a letter rather than by its sender. To use more than one sheet of paper was to incur an extra charge, so a letter writer might "cross" the sheet, that is, fill it up, then turn it at right angles and fill it again in that direction. The results could be read, though not easily.

The postal reform of the late 1830s and early 1840s made numerous changes. Postage stamps were invented (among them the famous "penny black" of 1840), so that letters were paid for in advance by the sender. Postage was reduced, restrictions on the weight of letters and the number of enclosures were eased; correspondents could write at length without resorting to "crossing"; and the post office made so much money that it was able continually to increase its services, with additional deliveries and rolling post offices in railway cars, where letters were sorted en route for delivery upon arrival.

Telegrams had less impact than letters upon middle-class domestic life and consequently upon the fiction of the period. They were of importance to the railroads and to the business world, and in the novels private news of an official nature is sometimes communicated by telegram. In Trollope's *Barchester Towers*, the prime minister is told of the death of the bishop of Barchester when Mr. Harding sends him a telegram.

The Victorians had no telephones, even though the technology was understood in the 1870s. The post office, which controlled the telegraph interests, feared the competition the telephone would bring to other forms of communication and fought its development whenever it could.

XV

Houses and Hospitality

Victorian etiquette, as it appears in fiction, may seem to today's reader an elaborately stylized dance without a predictable pattern. Two things will help: learning enough about the setting of Victorian daily life to visualize fictional scenes as the authors intended and keeping in mind the great importance of class distinctions in such matters as houses, furnishings, and entertainments. Each of the many layers of the Victorian middle classes strove to imitate the class above and to repudiate the class beneath—especially if this last were the class from which the family in question had risen. These tendencies are not undetectable in our own society.

TOWN HOUSES:
GENERAL PLAN

Upper- and middle-class housing existed in two basic categories: town and country, an architectural distinction resulting from the fact that land in a town, especially in London, was very expensive and building lots were small. The typical town house was consequently squeezed upward.

The best rooms, used for entertaining, were on the ground floor and the first floor. (Americans would call these the first floor and the second floor, respectively, a difference in terminology that can give rise to considerable confusion.) Family bedrooms occupied the next floor or two up, along with nurseries and schoolrooms for the children. Servants slept in the garret and sometimes in the cellars as well.

The kitchen was almost always underground, with a stairway leading down to it at the front of the house. The hole with the stairs in it was called the "area" and was usually protected by railings to keep people from falling into it from the sidewalk. One of the Jellyby children in *Bleak House* gets his head caught between two of the area railings (chap. 4).

Also underground was the servants' hall; "hall" here does not mean a corridor but one or several rooms providing dining and sitting space for the servants. Also "below stairs," part of or adjacent to the servants' part of the house, were the "scullery" for washing pots and pans from the kitchen, the pantry or larder, and storage rooms for coal, candles, soap, and so on. A system of back stairs allowed the servants to circulate from their underground headquarters through other parts of the house without intruding on the stairs and corridors used by the family.

The ground floor contained the entrance hall opening from the street, often a large and handsome room in itself, and the dining room; food then need be brought up only one story from the kitchen. Some householders saved work for their servants by installing a dumbwaiter, which ascended from the kitchen to a butler's pantry just off the dining room. The study (or "library") belonging to the father of the family was often on this floor as well, located perhaps on the other side of the entrance hall from the dining room. This is the plan of the ground floor of Sir Pitt Crawley's town house in Thackeray's *Vanity Fair*. Lady Jane, finding that Rawdon Crawley is visiting her husband in his study and hoping to detain him for breakfast, manages conveniently to come out of the dining room as the brothers are leaving the study (chap. 54).

On the first floor ("second" to Americans), reached by the main staircase from the entrance hall, were the drawing rooms, often a suite of them, separated from one another by double doors and equipped with the pianos, harps, thick carpets, sofas, potted plants, and other accoutrements that made life pleasant. To receive her guests, a London hostess stood at or near the top of the stairs leading from the entrance hall up to the drawing rooms; she did not need to open the front door or take her guests' coats, for the servants did that.

Except for some differences in furniture styles, the bedrooms of Victorian houses were not greatly different from those of Americans today. Beds were smaller, heating depended on fireplaces, and there were fewer closets ("cupboards" in British) than we might think standard; but the general function of the room would be the same. What we, and present-day Englishmen as well, would be likely to miss from the bedroom floors of the house are the bathrooms and water closets.

Plumbing of every sort made its way into the Victorian house slowly and in separate stages. Mrs. Proudie in *Barchester Towers* was in advance of her times (the 1850s) in insisting that the bishop's palace ought to be supplied with hot water above the ground floor: "Surely there should be the means of getting hot water in the bed-rooms without having it brought in jugs from the kitchen" (chap. 5). To Trollope's original readers, Mrs. Proudie's eloquence may seem as preposterous here as it does elsewhere in the Barchester novels. The government was trying to encourage the building of municipal water works that would supply water at a high enough pressure to reach taps above ground level, but for Barchester to build such works and for the bishop's palace to install the necessary pipes and water heaters was another matter. Throughout most of the century maids continued to carry jugs of hot water up to the bedrooms for the family and guests to use in washing up. Whole pailsfull were carried for baths, usually taken in a portable metal tub brought into the bedroom. This custom is useful to Rachael Verinder of Collins's *The Moonstone;* when annoyed by her evangelical cousin, Drusilla Clack, Rachael asks her maid to bring her bath and thus, as the prudish Miss Clack observes, "hit on the only possible way of forcing me to leave the room" (chap. 29/2.7).

The "bathroom," as it evolved in well-to-do houses in the closing decades of the century, was a separate room with a fireplace, containing one or more of the usual round, high-backed metal tubs (often bought in a set of graduated sizes to fit the family) and sometimes containing, as well, a shower bath in which the bather stood beneath a tank into which a sufficient number of bucketsfull of water had been poured. In some houses, the portable metal tubs were replaced by an elaborate affair of stone, set in a hooded cabinet of mahogany panels and equipped with ornamental faucets and other hardware. Often the bathroom had a drainpipe to carry away used water, but until late in the century the water's journey upstairs was usually performed by servant power.

Not surprisingly, the middle-class novel ignores the existence of other sanitary arrangements for the necessary functions of the body; but as today's readers may wish to envision the Victorian scene in all its details, this indelicate subject may as well be covered. Bedrooms were equipped with chamber pots and under housemaids were expected to cope with them, carrying them downstairs (down the back stairs, needless to say) and emptying them into an earth or water closet on the first floor or into a privy in the back yard. (The "back yard" or "back garden" was a service area, seldom incorporated with the presentable parts of the house.) Indoor "closets" were often located near the dining room on the ground floor so that gentlemen who had finished their dinners with a large quantity of wine could join the ladies upstairs in greater comfort. Country houses, benefiting from a more expansive floor plan, sometimes installed such closets in a cloakroom just off the entrance hall; a guest could thus take care of his personal comfort before having the servant who answered the door announce his presence.

Several types of "earth closets" were in use; one model used the ashes taken from the household grates, ingeniously screening out the large cinders, and was operated by pulling a handle. Water closets evolved from curious primitive arrangements into the form familiar today, becoming increasingly common as more and more houses were connected to main sewers rather than to individual cesspools, which sometimes overflowed and in any case had to be cleaned out. Toward the end of the century, as greater water pressure allowed indoor plumbing to advance upward through the house, water closets were installed in odd corners, frequently just off stair landings. The location was often determined by the most efficient disposition of the pipes.

The early Victorian house was heated almost entirely by open fireplaces; consequently, almost every room had one. A number of inventions for using fewer pieces of coal and for throwing more of the heat out into the room instead of up the chimney made the fireplaces less wasteful than they had been in previous centuries. The iron stoves used for heating so many nineteenth-century American houses were not popular in England, and the word "stove" was in Britain often applied to the grate of an open fireplace.

Fires did not burn all night, of course, and to light a new one in each bedroom so that the family could get up and dress was one of the duties of the underhousemaid.

By the end of the century, gas was used to some extent for heating; in Wilde's *The Picture of Dorian Gray* (1891), the scientist Alan Campbell undertakes secretly to get rid of a dead body in an upstairs room heated by "a gas-fire with asbestos" (chap. 14)—a convenient installation for this purpose, since to carry in other fuel might have aroused suspicion.

LIGHTING

The streets of London were lighted by oil lamps at the beginning of the century, but the results were minimal and pedestrians who wanted to see where they were going depended on "linkboys" carrying torches to accompany them. In 1812, after processes for handling coal gas had been worked out, the Chartered Gas Light and Coke Company was formed and had pretty well illuminated the main streets of London by 1816. Burners were constantly improved, and at the end of the century the incandescent mantle gave many times the light the earliest models had. Gas fittings were increasingly installed in private houses, particularly in the lower stories, to light the dining room and the drawing rooms; in some houses this extravagence was carried no further, and the family were still taking lighted candles up to bed with them at the end of the century.

Electricity made its appearance in private homes quite slowly. Large power companies were authorized only at the end of the century. Wiring was complicated and expensive; practical incandescent bulbs were a long time being perfected; and in general the late Victorians seemed to feel that the light they already had would do well enough.

COUNTRY HOUSES

The country houses of the upper and upper-middle class differed from town houses in having more space and a great deal more flexibility in architectural plan. A country house drawing room might be on the ground floor rather than on the next floor up and might have floor-to-ceiling French windows giving access to a terrace outside; thus a character described as entering such a room "through the window" should not be envisioned clambering over the sill. The grounds might include flower gardens and a "park," formerly a private game preserve but by the Victorian age simply an ornamental woodland, often with walls around it. A device that functioned as a wall in a gentleman's park was a kind of ditch called a "ha-ha,"often used to separate the park proper from the adjoining pasturelands. Two other potentially confusing country house landscape terms are the "plantation," not a large farm but a group of ornamental trees, and the "shrubbery," a lawn planted with shrubs, often in ornamental patterns. Victorian ladies said to be "out in the shrubbery" are walking along carefully tended paths, not creeping through the bushes.

Country houses were more useful for long-term entertaining than town houses. There were more bedrooms, more room for servants, and more things for guests to do on the premises. Guests might be invited with their horses, lap dogs, and personal servants for a visit of weeks, particularly in the late summer and autumn, when the men were expected to

"THE CHAMPION LAWN TENNIS MATCH" (*Illustrated London News*)

Tennis became popular in the 1880s and was played, as here, with vigor and with considerable inventiveness in the way of ground strokes.

shoot game birds on the estate. Numerous Victorian novels are set partly or entirely in such a country house party, and to the original readers such an entertainment was matter of course, either in their own lives or in the lives they would not have minded leading.

DINNER PARTIES:
BASIC PATTERNS

The dinner party was not the only Victorian social occasion, by any means; but it was one of the most important, and it is frequently encountered in the novels. The readers are assumed to know the etiquette. In Dickens's *Martin Chuzzlewit*, the humor of the dinner at Todger's boarding-house (chap. 9) depends on the fact that the scene is a thoroughgoing parody of a fashionable dinner party, from the landlady's elaborate preparations to Mr. Pecksniff's final oration on the scandalous topic of legs.

The customs in force at a formal dinner party were also followed, on a reduced scale, in the everyday family dinners of the upper and middle classes. There was a sequence of courses, servants did the waiting, and the ladies retired after dessert to the drawing room while the gentlemen enjoyed after-dinner port or claret around the table.

The dinner hour in polite society throughout much of the century was five o'clock—a schedule to which Lockwood in Emily Bronte's *Wuthering Heights* is unable to convert his old-fashioned housekeeper. In the 1880s and 1890s the dinner hour leaped rather abruptly farther into the night, to eight o'clock or even nine, although many families continued to dine earlier. To take one's main meal in the middle of the day rather than in the evening was considered countrified; in Elizabeth Gaskell's *Wives and Daughters*, poor Mrs. Gibson is so eager to prevent her aristocratic luncheon hosts from thinking she is eating her main meal of the day that she sends her plate away untouched, although she is really quite hungry (chap. 25).

One always dressed for dinner, retiring for this ceremony to one's room and the services of one's maid or one's valet. Evening dress was expected; ladies wore jewels and low-necked dresses.

Family and guests gathered in the drawing room before dinner, as one does now, although the predinner cocktail was not a part of the pattern. "Going down to dinner" was a carefully structured procedure in which the ladies were conducted down the stairs to the dining room on the ground floor, each on the arm of a gentleman. Precedence was carefully observed in the arrangement of this procession according to rank, as was the seating of the guests in the dining room. The rules for precedence are too complicated to be given here, but novel readers might keep in mind that the host "takes down" the lady of highest rank, while the others arrange themselves or are arranged by the host or hostess in the proper gradations. Thus Mr. Merdle in Dickens's *Little Dorrit* "took down a countess who was secluded somewhere in the core of an immense dress" (chap. 21). Mr. John Paul Jefferson Jones, an American newspaperman somehow invited to a dinner at Lord Steyne's, is innocent of this custom and cannot understand why the lady to whom he has offered his arm should be carried off instead by the earl of Southdown (Thackeray, *Vanity Fair*, chap. 49).

Guests were usually seated at a single long table, with the host and hostess at either end. The successive courses were brought in and served by servants—at formal dinners by footmen with powdered wigs. A dinner usually began with soup, often turtle soup, made of sea turtles and considered a great delicacy; then fish; then game, perhaps grouse or pheasant. Next came one or more entrees or "made dishes," elaborate concoctions, often of chicken, with accompanying side dishes of vegetables, then a "joint," usually roast beef, and finally a dessert course of fruit (oranges were a favorite), ice cream, or pastry. The tablecloth was taken up before the dessert course, revealing the mahogany tabletop, which the housemaids had spent hours polishing. Appropriate wines, in their appropriate glasses, accompanied each course; with fish, for example, "hock" (rhine wine) was served in especially ornamental, high-stemmed pink- or green-tinted glasses.

This riotous pageant of calories might lead the present-day reader to picture the Victorian diner as more than pleasingly plump, by modern standards. This picture would be in many cases correct. Fashionable ladies, their waists indented by their corsets, were admired for their fine arms and shoulders—round, smooth, and undeniably heavy. Gentlemen inclined toward the portly. Victorian etiquette did allow, however, a few loopholes for the slender. A hostess's duties did not include urging her guests to eat; one was served matter-of-factly by maids or footmen, and one was under no obligation to partake of a course at all or to clean one's plate if one did.

AFTER DINNER

At the end of the dessert course, perhaps two hours after the meal had begun, the ladies left the dining room: The hostess caught the eye of the feminine guest of honor, nodded, and all the ladies immediately rose, abandoning in midsentence any conversation in which they might have been participating. The highest-ranking lady went out of the dining room first, the hostess last, a gentleman near the door having in the meantime got up to open it for them.

Left to themselves in the dining room, the gentlemen would reseat themselves by gathering around the host (the ladies' departure having left them seated in every other chair) and drink claret or port for an interval of from thirty minutes to an hour. In some houses the gentlemen would indulge in cigars at this point, but in others cigars were considered suitable only for strolls in the open air. This was the time for discussing politics, business, or any other topic that had been displaced by polite small talk in the presence of the ladies. The host's most treasured wines might be brought up from the wine cellar; in Meredith's The Egoist, Sir Willoughby Patterne makes use of this part of the evening and the famous

ADVERTISEMENT FOR JOHN BRINSMEAD AND SONS, PIANOS
(*Illustrated London News*)

The accomplished young lady, surrounded by the rewards of
her diligence. The illustration is from an 1888 piano advertisement aimed, one suspects, at the parents of daughters.

"Patterne port," bottle after bottle of it, to induce old Dr. Middleton, the father of Sir Willoughby's restless fiancee, to prolong his and his daughter's visit (chap. 20).

Upon the host's ritual question—"Gentlemen, shall we join the ladies?"—the gentlemen were expected to proceed upstairs to the drawing room, where tea and coffee would be served and the ladies would provide musical entertainment. Indeed, they may have been hard at this endeavor for some time, as if for the purpose of drawing the gentlemen upstairs by siren tactics. Becky Sharp's first attempt to fascinate Joseph Sedley ends badly when Joseph, leaving the paternal dining room, turns not up the stairs to the drawing room but out the front door to a cabstand (Thackeray, *Vanity Fair*, chap. 3).

BALLS AND DANCES

Except among characters who lead a high-society life and take such things casually, a ball is a special highlight, much looked forward to, in the lives of the heroines of Victorian fiction. One needs to keep in mind that young ladies did not go to balls with a "date." They might be escorted by brothers or other male relatives or be chaperoned by an older lady, but to arrive as part of a group of family or friends was the usual thing. Young men asked for dances in advance, and one generally and to keep the list in one's head, although it was possible to write the names of one's partners on the ivory spokes of one's fan. The refreshments provided—champagne, chicken, and what not—were called "supper"; the music was, of course, live, there being no other kind of music; and the dancing could go on until past midnight.

In novels set near the beginning of the century, the characters perform "country" dances similar to the square dances, and reels brought by English settlers to America in the eighteenth century. Like their American counterparts, the English country dances were lively and sometimes quite elaborately patterned. To "open" a ball was to perform, with one's partner, as head couple in the first dance of the evening.

A more complex and formal dance, done in sets of four couples each and consisting of five different "figures" in sequence, was the quadrille, which became popular in England early in the century. In the United States during the nineteenth century the quadrille was called a "cotillion," a term that then became the generic name for a formal ball.

The waltz, preceded by its music, arrived in England in 1816 and caused a furor: To dance and to embrace simultaneously and in public struck many people as unthinkable, and parents declared they would not allow their daughters to waltz. Such resolutions seem to have made no noticeable impact upon ballroom fashions, and the waltz retained its popularity throughout the nineteenth century.

The bouncy and irreverent polka became the rage in the early 1840s, having traveled across Europe from Prague. Trollope's Griselda Grantly, later Lady Dumbello, is a cool and self-possessed young lady, but she dances the polka until she gasps for breath (*Framley Parsonage*, chap. 20).

PRESENTATION AT COURT

To be presented to the sovereign at one of the official "drawing rooms" or "levees" held periodically during the year was a highly desirable mark of status to the upper-middle classes. (To the aristocracy, naturally, the event was more a matter of course.) Queens had drawing rooms at which these presentations took place; kings and princes had levees; but as far as the novels are concerned there is no essential difference.

One could be presented at court only by a person who himself (or herself) was entitled to attend, having been presented at some earlier date. The Lord Chamberlain checked the guest list, and certain categories of persons had no chance at all. Lawyers were sharply categorized: Barristers could be presented but solicitors could not. Bankers and merchants could be presented only if they were involved in large-scale commercial enterprises and could not possibly be looked upon as clerks or shopkeepers.

The ceremony itself, rather anticlimactically, consisted of kissing the queen's hand while curtesying to the other members of the royal family. Gentlemen bowed instead of curtseying. Peeresses and their daughters did not kiss the queen's hand but instead were kissed by her on the cheek.

Dress was carefully regulated. Gentlemen wore "court suits," conservative in that they represented the fashion of the eighteenth century: knee breeches, powdered wigs. Alternately, a gentleman might appear in a military uniform, as long as he was entitled to wear it. Ladies were required to wear white evening dresses with trains and low necklines. White feathers were the stipulated head ornament, and of course one wore all one's jewels. *Vanity Fair's* Becky Sharp Crawley has obtained the diamonds she wears to court by questionable means—they are the gifts of Lord Steyne, who presumably expects payment of a certain kind—and she has stolen the white brocade of which her dress is made, having found it in an old wardrobe belonging to the Crawley family (chap. 46). However, as Thackeray delights in pointing out in this atmosphere of larceny, her presentation at court puts the final stamp of respectability on Becky's social standing. Another satiric view of this ceremony occurs in Elizabeth Gaskell's *Mary Barton*, when John Barton innocently describes the carriages bound for the queen's drawing room as a circus parade (chap. 9).

CALLS AND CARDS

The paying of morning calls upon one another was one of the duties of ladies in fashionable life. For the most part, these customs as they appear in the novels are self-explanatory to American readers, with the exception of the fact that "morning" here has the connotation of "before the main meal." As the fashionable dinner hour receded, the morning went along with it; and Victorian "morning calls" were generally paid between one and five in the afternoon.

A lady might tell her servant to say that she was not at

home even if she was; the term simply meant that she did not want to receive visitors. And often a lady out paying calls did not want to come in at all but simply to leave her card, which her footman would take to the door and hand to the servant who opened it while the lady sat comfortably in her carriage. The "calling" ritual could thus be reduced to a quite efficient sequence of gestures. Eleanor Bold in *Barchester Towers* sets out to visit the Stanhope family in a state of some curiosity, since she "had never been in the house before, though she had of course called" (chap. 19).

CUTTING

This social custom sounds as if it might have something to do with duelling and is, in fact, on a psychological level perhaps equally devastating. To "cut" an acquaintance is to pretend not to see him, to fail to respond to any greeting he may extend. One may cut someone in a rather wishy-washy way, pretending to look someplace else or even turning towards a shop window; to "cut someone dead," a more savage procedure, is to stare straight into the other person's face without a sign of recognition. For either party of an acquaintanceship to cut the other is, of course, the end of the acquaintance.

Cutting is one of the standard issues of weapons to the inhabitants of *Vanity Fair*. When old Miss Crawley and Mrs. Bute Crawley, meeting Rawdon and Becky in the park after their clandestine marriage, "cut their nephew pitilessly" (chap. 20), the couple correctly concludes that reconciliation is far away.

FUNERALS AND MOURNING

Victorian mourning customs may seem to today's readers so elaborate and so directed toward outward display as to become blatantly hypocritical. The funeral processions—the hearse with its black horses and waving black plumes, the mourners (some of whom may have been provided by the undertaker) wearing long crepe headbands—seem to bear out this impression; and satirical comments in the novels are frequent enough to indicate that some sense of falsity was apparent to the Victorians themselves. Yet elaborate mourning etiquette may have been psychologically beneficial, for the outward display gave whatever sincere grief the mourners may have had a thorough exercise. There was always some correct ritual to follow: David Copperfield, after breaking to Steerforth's mother the news of her son's death, goes through the house closing the window blinds (chap. 56).

To "go into mourning" for someone, even a fairly distant relative, was quite usual, but the most ritualized mourning costume was observed by widows. A widow was expected to wear black for a year and a day after the death of her husband; she might then go into a "second mourning" of muted colors trimmed with black and, after a year of this, might wear bright colors again. In the meantime, she has gone through a succession of widow's caps, beginning with an immense crepe bonnet and evolving slowly into smaller and more becoming versions. In George Eliot's *Middlemarch*, Dorothea's decision to shift into a lighter phase is welcomed by her personal maid: "There's a reason in mourning, as I've always said; and three folds at the bottom of your skirt and a plain quilling in your bonnet . . . is what's consistent for a second year" (chap. 80).

XVI

Fashions in Dress

There is not a great deal of difference, basically, between Victorian fashions and our own. Our clothes make statements about our social class—perhaps not always the statements we intend. Expensive fabrics and high-status styles are still sought after. We have evolved several variations on the nineteenth-century values, chiefly the much greater comfort of our garments and the anti fashion of wearing shabby clothing originally made for workmen; nevertheless our motives for choosing the clothes we do are much the same.

GENTLEMEN'S CLOTHING

Americans might begin by visualizing the contrast between eighteenth-century men's fashions, as exemplified by the signers of the Declaration of Independence, and nineteenth-century men's fashions, as exemplified by Abraham Lincoln. This instant view leaves out a great deal, but the basic shift in silhouette, fabric, and colors is accurate.

In the early years of the nineteenth century the knee-breeches-and-boots look was still current, along with colorful brocaded fabrics, lace trimmings, and gold braid. Joseph Sedley's wardrobe in *Vanity Fair*, "of the most brilliant colors and youthful cut" (chap. 3), was typical of the period, although Joseph's taste was somewhat extreme. Powdered wigs had already been set aside, except by judges, barristers, and bishops as part of their professional costume and by some servants—coachmen and footmen—who wore a traditional livery.

It was in the second decade of the century, with the fading of Joseph Sedley's splendor, that men's fashion began its descent into the drabness that characterized it for the subsequent hundred years, to be relieved only in the later part of the twentieth century with the emergence of high-status leisure clothing. "Beau" Brummell, a commoner who went to Eton, became known as a wit, amused the Prince of Wales (later George IV), and eventually set the fashions and reigned over the high society of Regency England, had much to do with changing the direction of fashion from gilt-and-lace gorgeousness to the subdued colors, scrupulous cleanliness, and impeccable fit of the upper- and middle-class Victorian ideal. Buff, blue, and "bottle green" coats for daily wear with white trousers, shading into gray and black harmonies for more formal occasions, together with immaculate starched linen neckcloths and kid gloves, typified the Brummell look. Embroidery and lace were out; fabrics were costly but subdued, decoration subordinated to the proportion of the whole.

To bestow upon an established area of competition a whole new set of criteria is no small accomplishment, and Brummell should not be discredited as an innovator. Yet the times were ready for a change. Cleanliness in particular had never before been a status symbol; eighteenth-century gentlemen and gone to court in embroidered coats stiff with sweat and had carried lace handkerchiefs soaked in cologne to counteract the effects of the belief that bathing was bad for the health. But the nineteenth century had seen the emergence of a crowded, jostling middle class, eager for respectability, the varying strata of which could be distinguished to some extent by the amount of laundering its members could afford. A look of understated simplicity, with all the irony of reverse snobbery, was what the times welcomed.

Coats for indoor and town wear in the earlier years of the century were cut away in front, tailed behind, and had a nipped-in waist. Gradually the coat became longer and fuller, until the "redingote" of the 1830s had become double-breasted and was not cut away. In later decades the "frock coat" (almost always black) showed the voluminous lines implied by its name.

The cut of trousers varied from almost skin tight styles to the fuller "pantaloons" and back again to something slimmer. Trouser legs often fastened with straps about the insteps of the wearer's low, thin-soled shoes, the delicacy of which was supposed to indicate that the wearer did not have to walk about in the mud. Thackeray's dandified Pendennis, newly arrived at "Oxbridge," is nonplussed to find himself outdone in mathematics by "one or two very vulgar young men, who did not even use straps to their trousers so as to cover the abominably thick and coarse shoes and stockings which they wore" (*Pendennis*, chap. 18).

The embroidering of fancy waistcoats for brothers and cousins was a popular branch of young ladies' needlework. It was in these garments that some remainder of eighteenth-century gorgeousness was allowed to persist. Fashion plates of the century, nevertheless, show increasingly plain waistcoats; and one cannot help suspecting that the young ladies' handiwork spent most of its time stored away in the gentlemen's dressing rooms.

Headgear was dominated by the "top" or "stove pipe" hat; early versions were awkwardly cylindrical, but the oval form that had evolved by the end of the century was quite graceful. Eventually silk replaced beaver as the material of the top hat, and the "silk hat" for formal wear did not go out of fashion until the third decade of the twentieth century. A variety of other headgear was worn for special occasions; Sherlock Holmes's "deerstalker" cap was originally worn, as its name implies, for shooting. (In cities, caps were worn by the working classes but seldom by the middle classes.) The derby was a comparatively low felt hat that came into style in the 1880s.

"Greatcoats," many-layered cape affairs, were worn outdoors, for driving a curricle on a frosty morning, perhaps. The "Mackintosh" of rubber-coated fabric was manufactured on patents obtained by the inventor of that name in the 1820s and gradually replaced the greatcoat in situations in which expense or weight made a difference—cycling, for example.

Gentlemen started the nineteenth century smooth shaven, although sideburns and even curling side whiskers were permissible. Moustaches were associated with the military during the Napoleonic wars and again during the Crimean War in the 1850s, when civilians took up the fashion. By the end of the century, a full beard had become a necessity of manliness and respectability.

WOMEN'S FASHIONS

Feminine fashion shifted more frequently and more dramatically than men's, perhaps because a woman's fulltime job as her husband's status symbol both allowed and encouraged her to spend more time on matters of dress. Despite all the changing of furbelows, however, there were in the nineteenth century only four basic silhouettes: the high-waisted "empire" look of the early part of the century, the tiny waist and increasingly full skirt of the 1830s through the 1860s, the "bustle" outline , typical of the 1870s through the 1890s and finally, almost at the turn of the century, the flowing skirt-and-blouse "Gibson girl" look.

The "empire" fashion of the early 1800s emanated from France, where its theoretical inspiration was a return to the simplicity of ancient Greece and a repudiation of the vanities of the aristocratic classes, now overthrown by the French Revolution. The English had a horror of anything reminiscent of the French Revolution, and their political opposition to France at that time was quite visible in the Napoleonic wars; but this attitude did not alter France's position as fashion arbiter of Europe. The English ladies rushed to buy light muslins and pretty ribbons and to have them made up into high-waisted, flowing dresses. Jane Austen's characters are frequently preoccupied in this manner. French women wore no corsets beneath their light attire; English women usually did, but the construction did not pinch the waist. The emphasis was on the bust, which was smallish by today's pin-up standards but was lifted quite high and enhanced by a low neckline. White was a favorite color.

Year by year these simple styles became more elaborate,

"Paris fashions for March." *Illustrated London News.*

Frills and furbelows. The latest Paris fashions for March, 1872. Nineteenth-century silhouettes moved from the simple, high waisted "empire" styles worn by Jane Austen's characters to the bell-shaped hoop skirts of the 1840's and '50's. In the 1860's fullness was shifted to the back of the skirt.

adding ruffles and tucking, until the original simple lines became cluttered. Eventually the waistline dropped to a more natural point of indentation and skirts became fuller. During the 1830s and 1840s, enormous puffed sleeves balanced this fullness; in *The Mill on the Floss,* set in the 1830s, George Eliot observes of one of Maggie Tulliver's aunts that "at that period a woman was truly ridiculous to an instructed eye if she did not measure a yard and a half across at the shoulders" (chap. 7).

By the 1840s, skirts had become so full that layers of horsehair petticoats were needed to hold them out to the proper silhouette; and by the mid-1850s the hoop petticoat called, rather confusingly, the "crinoline" had come into use. Sleeves lost their fullness, and the emphasis shifted to the contrast between the small proportions of the lady from the waist up and the great balloon of her skirt. Getting about could be something of a problem. Trollope's Signora Neroni has her own way of finding large skirts inconvenient; she often invites gentlemen to sit beside her on her invalid's couch, "though, as she declared, the crinoline of her lady friends was much too bulky to be so accommodated" (*Barchester Towers,* chap. 11).

In the late 1860s the crinoline petticoat suddenly went out of fashion; because dresses were still made with full skirts, they were gradually swept up and to the back. The bustle, early versions of which were called the "dress improver," became an important unseen part of the wardrobe. Corsets remained as tight in the waist as they had been, or tighter, and molded the bosom into one bulge rather than two—a curious phenomenon that continued until the early years of the twentieth century. Necklines rose quite high in an elaboration of tucking, ribbons, and lace; evening necklines, though lower, were modest in comparison to those of earlier decades. The puffed sleeve returned in several versions, and trains appeared on formal dresses and sometimes even on street and traveling costumes.

The last decades of the century saw an increasing participation of women in sports—croquet (considered in its

"On the Parade, Southsea," by Seppings-Wright. *Illustrated London News.*

A young lady and her dog stroll beside the sea in 1893. Outdoor exercise and loosened-up fashions were typical of the final decade of the Victorian era.

earliest days to constitute a violent challenge to the female powers of endurance), tennis, golf, bicycling, even roller skating. Either for this reason or because the silhouette had been rigid for so long that fashion demanded a change, women's clothing loosened up; the skirt became wider, looser, and shorter. The waist was still pinched, but by the end of the century women could take normal strides whenever they wished to do so.

Vocabulary

The following words, encountered with some frequency in the Victorian novel, have become obsolete, have never crossed the ocean to become part of the American language, or have taken on additional and different meanings more familiar to Americans. The latter category may present a special hazard.

ARTICLES. Often refers to the legal agreement by which an apprentice is bound to his employer.

BASIN. A plate or bowl, filled not with soapy water but with soup.

BATHING MACHINE. A seaside phenomenon. A bathhouse on wheels in which ladies and children changed into their bathing clothes and were towed by a horse out into waist-deep water. Sometimes had an expandable awning to give the bathers more privacy.

BEDESMAN OR BEADSMAN. An almsman or inmate of an almshouse, supported by charity. The old men who live in Hiram's Hospital in Trollope's *The Warden* are called "bedesmen."

"BLUE." Short for "bluestocking," a woman with intellectual interests. Derogatory. One of Harry Foker's cousins in Thackeray's *Pendennis* is "blue, and a geologist."

BLUE BOOK. An official parliamentary report, often filled with facts and statistics. A "blue book" may also be a social or professional directory. It is not, as it is in the United States, a notebook in which to write examinations.

BOTANY BAY. One of the penal colonies in New South Wales, Australia. A character in George Eliot's *Middlemarch* expresses suspicion of another character with the observation that "if everybody got their deserts, Bulstrode might have to say his prayers in Botany Bay."

CHEMIST. Pharmacist. Still the British term.

CITY. The financial district of London, full of banks.

COMMONER. Anyone who does not belong to the royalty or the peerage. (Peers include dukes, marquises, earls, viscounts, and barons.) Baronets and knights are commoners and so are the highest government officials if they do not hold a peerage. Not derogatory.

COMMUNIST. One who, in some quite theoretical way, believes in the abolition of private property. Not a member of a specific party organization.

CORN. Grain (wheat, oats, rye) or wheat in particular. Not "maize" or "Indian corn."

COUNTING HOUSE. A business office.

COVENTRY. To be "sent to Coventry" is to be socially ostracized. The phrase is used of Stephen Blackpool in Dickens's *Hard Times* when his coworkers refuse to talk to him. Rawdon Crawley is appointed governor of "Coventry Island" when Lord Steyne wants to get him permanently out of the way.

CRUMBY. A slang term for "pretty." Alex d'Urberville exclaims of Tess (chap. 5), "What a crumby girl!" and means nothing derogatory.

DEMOCRAT. Usually refers to belief in universal suffrage as a means of direct government by the people. Not associated with the American political party of that name.

DESK. Often a portable box or case in which writing materials, letters, and valuables could be stored. Not necessarily a large piece of furniture.

DIRECTLY. "Right away," but really means it—not "by and by," the usual American meaning (especially if pronounced "terreckly").

DIRTY. Often meant "muddy." Catherine Moreland in Jane Austen's *Northanger Abbey* plans a walk with friends and hopes the morning's rain will not have made the lanes dirty (chap. 11).

DRAUGHTS (pronounced "drafts"). The game of checkers.

FRONT. A woman's false hairpiece, comprising what Americans would call "bangs" and present-day Englishmen, a "fringe."

FUNDS. The national debt, in the aspect of an opportunity for investors. Mr. Osborne of *Vanity Fair* goes down to dinner in such a bad humor that his daughters and their governess "suppose the funds are falling" (chap. 13).

GAZETTE. An official government publication listing appointments and promotions (military ones, for example), names of bankrupts, and other notices of changed status. To be "in the Gazette" as a bankrupt was a disgrace; to be "gazetted to" such-and-such an infantry company could be a sign of advancement. The names of officers killed in battle were also listed in the Gazette.

GOVERNMENT. Often only the members of the cabinet, the "ministry."

GUY. A ragged, grotesque-looking person. Refers to the effigies of Guy Fawkes, originator of the Gunpowder Plot in 1605 and thus a national villain, which are carried about by children on the fifth of November. A derogatory term.

HOCK. Rhine wine: white, light, sweetish. Mixed with soda water, supposed in the nineteenth century to be a cure for hangover.

HOME COUNTIES. Those counties nearest to London: Middlesex, Surrey, Kent, Essex, Hertford, and Sussex. Usually mentioned in a political context.

INSTANT. The current calendar month. A letter might begin, "I have received yours of the fourteenth instant." Abbreviated "inst."

LEVELLER. An extreme democrat, in the broad sense; one who would get rid of all social distinctions. A term of opprobrium in the Victorian novel.

NEGUS. Hot spiced wine. In *Wuthering Heights*, Mr. Linton mixes a tumbler of negus for Catherine after she has been bitten by the bulldog.

NURSING A CHILD. Could mean breast-feeding him, the sense in use today, but is just as likely to mean simply holding him. In Dickens's *Great Expectations*, Mrs. Pocket's baby is taken away from the table and "nursed by little Jane," another of the children (chap. 23).

OFFICES. In the plural has a domestic connotation: parts of a house where specialized work is done, such as the laundry, pantry, scullery, and so forth; may include stables and gardening sheds. In the singular can mean a place of business, as in the United States.

"OURS." In military slang, "our regiment." "Captain Dobbin of ours."

PAIR OF STAIRS. What Americans would call a flight of stairs. To climb three pairs of stairs is to go up three stories, not six.

PATTENS. Clogs, often raised from the ground on iron rings; worn by women over their indoor shoes. Useful for muddy weather and regularly worn by laundresses.

PLATE. Silverplated dishes and utensils—elaborate candlesticks, for example. Not crockery. The "family plate" was usually kept polished and on display in the dining room, especially during dinner parties.

PORTER. Dark beer; not "port," a dessert wine.

POST-OBITS. A form of borrowing money on one's future financial expectations; the debt is to be paid when the inheritance comes through.

QUIZ. To tease or joke with someone; to have light bantering conversation. As a noun, an odd or eccentric person or thing. Need not have anything to do with asking questions.

RATES. Property taxes, locally assessed. The "poor rates" benefited the poor of the parish in which the tax was collected.

SENATOR. A general term for a member of a governing body. Can be applied to a member of either the House of Lords or the House of Commons. Not a member of the upper chamber, as is the case in the United States.

SHOOTING. What Americans call "hunting"—going after such game as birds or hares, usually on foot, or standing still while servants drive the game toward the sportsmen. ("Hunting" in the Victorian novel refers to the elaborately choreographed sport of fox hunting.)

SHOVEL HAT. A broad-brimmed hat, turned up at the sides, worn by old-fashioned parsons and consequently associated with them.

SPONGING HOUSE (or spunging house). A private prison for debtors, usually kept by a bailiff. Not a public bath.

STATE. Used in the sense Americans express with the term "federal"; associated with the national government, not with that of any participatory unit. A "state-supported school" in Britain is authorized by the national body. The word "state" does not have the connotation of a legislative unit smaller than the national one.

STRAWBERRY LEAVES. Part of the design of a ducal coronet; thus associated with a dukedom.

TURNPIKE. Essentially the same meaning it has today except that one could ride, drive, or walk on it. The toll was usually levied only on cattle (any sort of hoofed animal, including horses or sheep); walkers went free. Well-kept turnpikes had a gravel surface.

UNION. A number of connotations, determined by context. (1) Political union of the parliaments of Great Britain and Ireland, which occurred in 1801. (2) Combination of two or more parishes for the administration of the Poor Laws; the workhouse itself was sometimes called the "union." (3) Debating societies at Oxford and Cambridge. (4) A "trades union," in the sense with which Americans are familiar.

WINKING. What we would call "blinking," shutting both eyes. Linton Heathcliff describes his reaction to the sight of his father striking Cathy: "I winked . . . I wink to see my father strike a dog, or a horse, he does it so hard" (Emily Bronte, *Wuthering Heights,* chap. 28). Linton is withdrawing from the scene, not demonstrating his approval of it.

WORK. For ladies, the denotation of this term in the novel is almost entirely limited to needlework such as embroidery. It may include knitting or other portable endeavors that require no mess or concentration, will fill empty time, but can be put down at a moment's notice.

Annotated Bibliography

The following list, by no means complete, comprises a starting point for students of the Victorian novel who are interested in other aspects of the period.

POLITICAL HISTORY

BRANTLINGER, PATRICK. *The Spirit of Reform: British Literature and Politics, 1832-1867.* Cambridge, Mass.: Harvard University Press, 1977. Relates Victorian literature (including essays and poetry as well as fiction) to such issues as Chartism and the reform bills. Illustrations. Documentation, bibliography, index.

GRAVES, CHARLES LARCOM. *Mr. Punch's History of Modern England.* 4 vols. New York: Stokes, 1921-22. *Punch,* though a comic magazine, took stands on serious issues—often in opposition to the status quo. Covers 1841 through 1914. Illustrations, mostly from *Punch.*

HALEVY, ELIE. *History of the English People in the Nineteenth Century.* Trans. from the French by E. I. Watkin. 6 vols. London: Ernest Benn, 1924-1934. Several reprinted editions available. Most thorough and detailed, with scholarly apparatus.

THOMSON, DAVID. *England in the Nineteenth Century, 1815-1914.* Baltimore: Penguin Books, 1950. Vol. 8 of the Pelican History of England. Concise and clear one-volume overview. Documentation, bibliography, index.

ESPECIALLY FOR PICTURES

BENTLEY, NICOLAS. *The Victorian Scene: A Picture Book of the Period 1837-1901.* London: Weidenfel and Nicolson, 1968. Informative text and plentiful illustrations.

EVANS, JOAN, ed. *The Victorians.* Cambridge, England: Cambridge University Press, 1966. Quotations from contemporary works (novels, essays, menus, and so forth), with relevant illustrations. Documentation.

JUDD, DENIS. *The Victorian Empire, 1837-1901: A Pictorial History.* New York: Praeger, 1970. England all over the world. Factual text, bountiful pictures. Bibliography, index.

PRIESTLEY, J. B. *Victoria's Heyday.* New York: Harper and Row, 1972. The decade of the 1850s, year by year. Large proportion of illustrations in color. Text gives solid background for events described. Documentation, bibliography, index.

WOOD, CHRISTOPHER. *Victorian Panorama: Paintings of Victorian Life.* London: Faber, 1976. Realistic, narrative paintings crowded with detail, which the author explains. Documentation, bibliography, index.

MANY-SIDED SURVEYS

ALTICK, RICHARD D. *Victorian People and Ideas: A Companion for the Modern Reader of Victorian Literature.* New York: Norton, 1973. Learned and lively; a clear view of the literature's cultural context. Illustrations. Documentation, bibliography, index.

BEST, GEOFFREY. *Mid-Victorian Britain, 1851-1875.* New York: Schocken Books, 1972. Clearly written with well-arranged statistical information. Illustrations. Documentation, bibliography, index.

BURN, WILLIAM L. *The Age of Equipoise: A Study of the Mid-Victorian Generation.* New York: Norton, 1964. Scholarly yet vivid. Documentation, bibliography, index.

DODDS, JOHN W. *The Age of Paradox: A Biography of England, 1841-1851.* New York: Rinehart, 1952. Year by year through the decade. Documentation, bibliography, index.

REED, JOHN R. *Victorian Conventions.* Athens, Ohio: Ohio University Press, 1975. Deals with such literary conventions as disguises, deathbeds, and orphans. Refers to broad cross-section of Victorian fiction and in doing so connects the literature of the period with its real-life context. Documentation, index.

SCHNEEWIND, JEROME B. *Backgrounds of English Victorian Literature.* New York: Random House, 1970. Politics, religion, morality. Illustrations. Documentation, bibliography, index.

YOUNG, G. M., ed. *Early Victorian England, 1830-1865.* 2 vols. New York: Oxford University Press, 1934. Essays on many topics by many authorities. Illustrations. Documentation; especially sharp-focused index.

RELIGION

ARMSTRONG, ANTHONY. *The Church of England, the Methodists, and Society, 1700 to 1850.* New York: Rowman and Littlefield, 1973. Discusses not only the rise of Methodism but its context in the Victorian scene. Documentation, bibliography, index.

CHADWICK, OWEN. *The Victorian Church.* 2 vols. London: Oxford University Press 1966, 1970. Authoritative and detailed. Documentation; bibliography and index in each volume.

CROWTHER, M. A. *Church Embattled: Religious Controversy in Mid-Victorian England.* Hamden, Conn.: Archon Books, 1970. Deals with, among other matters, the "Broad Church" attempts to bridge the gap to the new German (historical) biblical criticism. Documentation, bibliography, index.

CUNNINGHAM, VALENTINE. *Everywhere Spoken Against: Dissent in the Victorian Novel.* New York: Oxford University Press, 1975. Shows stereotyping of view of Dissenters found in Dickens and others. Documentation, bibliography, index.

MCLEOD, HUGH. *Class and Religion in the Late Victorian City.* Hamden, Conn.: Archon Books, 1974. Covers 1880-1914; concentrates on London. Illustrations. Documentation, bibliography, index.

MAISON, MARGARET M. *The Victorian Vision: Studies in the Religious Novel.* New York: Sheed and Ward, 1962. (English title: *Search Your Soul, Eustace.*) Documentation, bibliography, index.

ROSENBERG, EDGAR. *From Shylock to Svengali: Jewish Stereotypes in English Fiction.* Stanford, Cal.: Stanford University Press, 1960. Documentation, bibliography, index.

ETIQUETTE, FASHION, AND TASTE

BEETON, ISABELLA MARY ("Mrs. Beeton"). *The Book of Household Management.* London: S. O. Beeton, 1861. Reprints and later editions available. Compendious and detailed: cookery, servants, hospitality. Illustrations.

EVANS, HILLARY, AND MARY EVANS. *The Party That Lasted 100 Days: The Late Victorian Season: A Social Study.* London: Macdonald and Jane's, 1976. Sprightly text and contemporary illustrations of this ritual of the upper-middle class. Points of etiquette explained. Bibliography, index.

GERNSHEIM, ALISON, AND HELMUT GERNSHEIM. *Fashion and Reality.* London: Faber, 1963. Juxtaposes fashion plates with contemporary photographs. Knowledgeable commentary. Documentation, index.

GLOAG, JOHN. *Victorian Comfort: A Social History of Design from 1830-1900.* New York: St. Martin's, 1973 (1961). Affectionate, lively descriptions of Victorian status symbols. Illustrations. Documentation, index.

The Great Exhibition, London, 1851. New York: Crown Publishers, 1970. Facsimile of the original catalogue. Prestigious products of art and industry, originally displayed in the Crystal Palace. Numerous engravings.

HAYWARD, ARTHUR L. *The Days of Dickens: A Glance at Some Aspects of Early Victorian Life in London.* Hamden, Conn.: Archon Books, 1968 (1926). Much about fun and frolic, some attention to seamier sides of London life. Illustrations. Index.

MOORE, DORIS LANGLEY. *Fashion Through Fashion Plates, 1771-1970.* New York: Clarkson N. Potter, 1971. Fine illustrations, many in color, and knowledgeable text. Documentation, index.

PALMER, ARNOLD. *Moveable Feasts: A Reconnaissance of the Origins and Consequences of Fluctuations in Meal Times, with Special Attention to the Introduction of Luncheon and Afternoon Tea.* New York: Oxford University Press, 1952. Informative and witty.

QUINLAN, MAURICE J. *Victorian Prelude: A History of English Manners 1700-1830.* Hamden, Conn.: Archon Books, 1965 (1941). Relevant to the Victorian scene; special emphasis on religious attitudes. Bibliography, index.

The Random House Collector's Encyclopedia: Victoriana to Art Deco. Introd. Roy Strong. New York: Random House, 1974. Numerous illustrations giving a sense of the taste of the period. Bibliography.

WOMEN'S LIVES

BANKS, JOSEPH A., AND OLIVE BANKS. *Feminism and Family Planning in Victorian England.* New York: Schocken Books, 1964. The violently controversial issue of birth control. Documentation, bibliography, index.

BASCH, FRANCOISE. *Relative Creatures: Victorian Women in Society and the Novel.* Trans. from the French by Anthony Rudolf. New York: Schocken Books, 1974. Detailed study, with frequent reference to major novels. Illustrations. Documentation, bibliography, index.

CALDER, JENNI. *Women and Marriage in Victorian Fiction.* New York: Oxford University Press, 1976. Sharp perceptions, references to major novels. Bibliography, index.

HOLCOMBE, LEE. *Victorian Ladies at Work: Middle-Class Working Women in England and Wales, 1850-1914.* Hamden, Conn.: Archon Books, 1973. Increasing opportunities for gainful employment (and exploitation) in such fields as nursing, teaching, and civil service.

VICINUS, MARTHA, ed. *Suffer and Be Still: Women in the Victorian Age.* Bloomington, Ind.: Indiana University Press, 1972. Nine essays on varied topics. Illustrations. Documentation, bibliography, index.

PROSTITUTION AND SEXUALITY

ACTON, WILLIAM. *Prostitution, Considered in Its Moral, Social, and Sanitary Aspects, in London and Other Large Cities, with Proposals for the Mitigation and Prevention of Its Attendant Evils.* London, 1857, rpr. St. Clair Shores, Mich.:

Scholarly Press, 1976. Acton went against popular opinion by claiming that prostitution more often represented a temporary phases of a woman's life than a road to inevitable ruin but confirmed the middle-class view that a respectable woman was by nature devoid of sexual urges.

MARCUS, STEVEN. *The Other Victorians: A Study of Sexuality and Pornography in Mid-Nineteenth Century England.* New York: Basic Books, 1966, revised edition, 1974. Much quotation of original sources.

PEARSALL, RONALD. *The Worm in the Bud: The World of Victorian Sexuality.* New York: Macmillan, 1969. Voluminous compendium; deals authoritatively with birth control, homosexuality, and much more. Documentation, bibliography, index.

TRUDGILL, ERIC. *Madonnas and Magdalens: The Origins and Development of Victorian Sexual Attitudes.* New York: Holmes and Meier, 1976. Emphasizes the Victorian perception of sexuality as a danger. Illustrations. Documentation, bibliography, index.

"WALTER." *My Secret Life.* New York: Grove Press, 1966. The ultimate Victorian libido. Originally published in a limited edition in the 1880s.

ECONOMICS, INDUSTRY, RAILROADS, AND ENGINEERING

ARTELL, V. T. J. *Britain Transformed: The Development of British Society Since the Mid-Eighteenth Century.* Baltimore: Penguin Books (Penguin Education), 1973. More than half the text deals with the nineteenth century, in particular with industry. Numerous illustrations. Bibliography, index.

CHAMBERS, J. D. *The Workshop of the World: British Economic History from 1820 to 1880.* New York: Oxford University Press, 1961. Concise and factual. Documentation, bibliography, index.

ELLIS, HAMILTON. *British Railway History.* London: Allen and Unwin, 1954. Illustrations. Documentation, index.

KELLETT, JOHN R. *The Impact of Railways on Victorian Cities.* Toronto: University of Toronto Press, 1969. Illustrations. Documentation, index.

ROLT, L. T. C. *Victorian Engineering.* Baltimore: Penguin Books,

1970. Relates engineering achievements to general background of the period. Many illustrations. Bibliography, index.

TAMES, RICHARD. *Economy and Society in Nineteenth Century Britain.* London: Allen and Unwin, 1972. Relates the economy to population, standards of living, and so forth. Documentation, bibliography, index.

THOMIS, MALCOLM I. *Responses to Industrialism: The British Experience, 1780-1850.* Hamden, Conn.: Archon Books, 1977. Especially useful for the beginning student. Illustrations. Documentation, index.

CITIES

BRIGGS, ASA. *Victorian Cities.* New York: Harper and Row, 1963. Describes Manchester, Birmingham, and others as well as London. Illustrations. Documentation, bibliography, index.

DORÉ, GUSTAVE, AND BLANCHARD JERROLD. *London: A Pilgrimage.* New York: Dover Publications, 1970. Reprints edition of 1872. Dore did the illustrations, many of them unforgettable, and Jerrold, the text.

MAYHEW, HENRY. *London Labour and the London Poor.* 4 vols. New York: Dover Publications, 1968. Reprints edition of 1861-62. An astounding catalogue of London's lower stratae, with interviews and statistics. Illustrations.

TARN, JOHN NELSON. *Five Per Cent Philanthropy: An Account of Housing in Urban Areas, 1840-1914.* Cambridge, England: Cambridge Univeristy Press, 1973. Traces public awareness of need for slum clearance. Many illustrations. Documentation, bibliography, index.

OCCUPATIONS AND SOCIAL CLASSES

ANDERSON, GREGORY. *Victorian Clerks.* Manchester, England: Manchester University Press, 1976. Living conditions of these most threadbare members of the respectable classes. Illustrations. Documentation, bibliography, index.

DUNBABIN, J. P. D. *Rural Discontent in Nineteenth Century Britain.* New York: Holmes and Meier, 1975. The agricultural working classes. Documentation, index.

KEATING, P. J. *The Working Classes in Victorian Fiction.* New York: Barnes and Noble, 1971. Includes discussions of Gissing's working-class characters and Kipling's soldiers. Illustrations. Documentation, bibliography, index.

MELADA, IVAN. *The Captain of Industry in English Fiction, 1821-1871.* Albuquerque, N.M.: University of New Mexico Press, 1970. Deals with many conflicts, including that between new money and old gentility. Documentation, bibliography, index.

SAMUEL, RAPHAEL, ed. *Miners, Quarrymen and Saltworkers.* London: Routledge and Kegan Paul, 1977. Essays on these occupations as practiced in Victorian Britain. Illustrations. Documentation, index.

EDUCATION

HURT, JOHN. *Education in Evolution: Church, State, Society and Popular Education, 1800-1870.* London: Hart-Davis, 1971. Detailed, scholarly. Documentation, bibliography, index.

MURPHY, JAMES. *The Education Act 1870: Text and Commentary.* New York: Barnes and Noble, 1972. Very close focus; written for readers with previous grounding in the subject. Documentation, bibliography, index.

WEST, E. G. *Education and the Industrial Revolution.* New York: Barnes and Noble, 1975. Factual but not difficult for an American reader with little knowledge of British education to follow. Documentation, bibliography, index.

CRIME

ALTICK, RICHARD D. *Victorian Studies in Scarlet: Murders and Manners in the Age of Victoria.* New York: Norton, 1970. Extraordinary cases vividly described. Documentation, index.

HARTMAN, MARY S. *Victorian Murderesses: A True History of Thirteen Respectable French and English Women Accused of Unspeakable Crimes.* New York: Schocken Books, 1977. Special attention to the social background of the subjects. Illustrations. Documentation, bibliography, index.

RUMBELOW, DONALD. *The Complete Jack the Ripper.* Introd. Colin

Wilson. Boston: New York Graphic Society, 1977. Part of a large literature on these grisly and unsolved murders of London prostitutes. Illustrations. Bibliography, index.

TOBIAS, JOHN JACOB. *Urban Crime in Victorian England.* New York: Schocken Books, 1972 (1967). Factual yet lively; many associations with Dickens. Documentation, bibliography, index.

OTHER SPECIAL TOPICS

BUTT, JOHN, AND I. F. CLARKE, eds. *The Victorians and Social Protest: A Symposium.* Hamden, Conn.: Archon Books, 1973. Seven interdisciplinary essays. Documentation, index.

CURL, JAMES STEVENS. *The Victorian Celebration of Death: The Architecture and Planning of the Nineteenth Century Necropolis.* Detroit: Gale Research Co., 1972. Customs as well as cemeteries. Illustrations. Documentation, index.

IRVINE, WILLIAM. *Apes, Angels, and Victorians: The Story of Darwin, Huxley, and Evolution.* New York: McGraw Hill, 1955. Documentation, index.

KLINGBERG, FRANK J. *The Anti-Slavery Movement in England: A Study in English Humanitarianism.* Hamden, Conn.: Archon Books, 1968 (1926). Largely concerned with pre-Victorian era but deals with major events that set the stage. Documentation, index.

ROBERTS, DAVID. *Victorian Origins of the British Welfare State.* Hamden, Conn.: Archon Books, 1969 (1960). Relates years 1833-1854 to succeeding Victorian conditions and to those of the twentieth century.

SKULTANS, VIEDA, ed. *Madness and Morals: Ideas on Insanity in the Nineteenth Century.* London: Routledge and Kegan Paul, 1975. Extracts from the writings of nineteenth-century psychiatrists. Bibliography.

REFERENCE WORKS

Encyclopedia Britannica. Eleventh edition, 1911. Written for educated adults; authoritative and detailed on virtually all aspects of the Victorian period. Excellent indexes and cross-references.

Oxford English Dictionary. 13 vols. New York: Oxford University
      Press, 1961 (1933). Especially useful for the Victorian con-
      notations of words the meanings of which have shifted or of
      words Americans have traditionally used in different
      ways.
Victorian Studies. Indiana University. The leading scholarly jour-
      nal in the field. Interdisciplinary. Annual bibliography of
      great value.

Biographies of authors and other prominent Victorians often contain background material on the period, and some make a special
point of relating the figure under discussion to his or her cultural
environment. An example is Angus Wilson's *The World of Charles
Dickens.* New York: Viking Press, 1970.

Index